Profitable Seminars:

195 Tips
On Designing, Marketing
And Delivering The Goods

By Len Wood

 Training Shoppe, Rancho Palos Verdes, California

10 9 8 7 6 5 4 3 2 1

ISBN 0-9634374-8-8
Library of Congress Control Number 2001095697

**Publisher's Cataloging-in-Publication
(Provided by Quality Books, Inc.)**

Wood, Len.
   Profitable seminars : 195 tips on designing,
 marketing and delivering the goods / by Len Wood ;
 edited by Cheryl Duksta. -- 1 st ed.
   p. cm.
   Includes bibliagraphical references and index.
   LCCN: 2001095697
   ISBN: 0963437488

   1. Seminars--Planning--Handbooks, manuals, etc.
I. Duksta, Cheryl. II. Title.

AS6. W66 2002   658.4'56
                                    QB101-201255

Published by The Training Shoppe,
Rancho Palos Verdes, CA

Book and cover design by Casa Graphics, Inc.,
Burbank, CA

Dedicated to Florence Wood.
I fondly remember the wonderful
walking journeys to the Harbor Hills Library
and the life you put into the stories you read to us.
Thank you, Mom.

Acknowledgments

Several dozen people have contributed to this manuscript. Most are involved in the seminar business and have provided great stories and ideas from their own experiences. Special thanks to Paulette Ensign, Janet Groene, Carol Hansen, Jane Holcomb, Vicki Kieva, Dan Poynter, Suzanne Thomas, Kim Scutter and Joan Stewart for all their help.

Brigitte and Brian Charles provided continuing assistance on this manuscript. When I got stuck on some of the business items, Brian fired up his computer and solved them. Brigitte proofed the whole manuscript and made wonderful suggestions throughout.

Cheryl Duksta conducted the overall editing for spelling, grammar and usage and graciously answered all my questions regarding *The Chicago Manual of Style.*

The cartoons preceding each chapter set a humorous—albeit insightful—tone for the subject matter of each chapter. Humor is an important part of seminars, and cartoonist Jez Cuer captures that humor in his work.

Special thanks to Ernie and Patty Weckbaugh of Casa Graphics, Inc. Ernie used his creative talent to develop the book cover and internal design. Patty patiently typeset and formatted the manuscript through all the versions. Beyond this, their suggestions and encouragement were very important in moving the book along.

Working with all these talented people has truly been a pleasure. Thank you all.

About the Author

Whether it be the challenge of creating a new seminar, lining up a workshop site, or presenting a program, Len Wood has a passion for all aspects of seminars. Yet, Len was in his mid-forties before he conducted his first public seminar entirely on his own. Len developed the seminar, which was for public agency managers, from beginning to end, gathering all the material, designing the program, creating the brochure, lining up the meeting facility and

Len & June Wood

presentation equipment, marketing the seminar and then presenting it to a group of fifty eager participants.

Len spent most of his career as a professional manager in local government. In 1965, he started his career as an intern in the city of Santa Ana, California, while he was completing his bachelors degree in political science from California State College at Long Beach. From there, Len followed the typical local-government management progression path, moving on to the city of Burbank and then to Simi Valley, California, filling progressively responsible administrative positions. While in Burbank, he received his Master of Public Administration from the University of Southern California. In each of his cities, Len was privileged to have capable city managers who believed in coaching and mentoring young professionals.

In 1973, Len was appointed city manager of the newly incorporated city of Rancho Palos Verdes, California. He was responsible for putting an entire city government together from scratch. After successfully establishing the city, he moved on to become city manager of Claremont, California—home of the Claremont Colleges.

Len began experimenting with the right approach to management when he was awarded his first supervisory position. It didn't take long to learn that a strong directive approach only worked when he stood over people and watched them carry out orders. A participatory approach, on the other hand, gained buy-in and commitment from employees. Len incorporated the participatory style into his management methods and developed various techniques for involving people. He found that team building, goal setting and group-involvement techniques, when organized competently, produced positive results. He later found that these same techniques work in seminars.

In 1988, Len convinced his wife, June, to set up their own consulting business. With a lot of anxiety, they established Len Wood & Associates. As an adjunct to their consulting business, Len and June developed the Training Shoppe to provide training for local government professionals. They learned all the things to do and not do when designing, marketing and delivering seminars. During the same period, Len authored four books on local government: *Commissioner's Little Handbook, Elected Official's Little Handbook, Little Budget Book,* and *Local Government Dollars and Sense.* Much of the material for these books came from research for seminars or the information gathered during seminars. Len and June are now called on to present programs to city and county officials across the country. The 195 tips in *Profitable Seminars* summarize all the lessons Len and June have learned about seminars.

Introduction

It wasn't too long ago that a person entered the workforce with the expectation that they would find their niche in a chosen field and remain there for their entire career. While in college, I decided I wanted to be a city manager and that was where I set my sights. I never expected to do anything other than work in that noble profession. Little did I know at the time that I would leave city management in midcareer and become a consultant and author—nor did I know that I would be delivering seminars. Today, it is not unusual for people to have four or more careers during their lifetime.

From time to time, we all dream about doing something else. Whether you are at the beginning, middle or later stage of your career, seminars and workshops offer a great opportunity to try something new. They also provide a great way to transition into an active retirement. You can start building your own seminars before you leave your present job.

Seminars give you independence. You can operate your seminar business out of your home and at your own pace. You are in charge and you make the decisions when and where to present them. You get to travel to wonderful places and each seminar presents a new, exciting adventure. Perhaps the greatest reward is mentoring others—passing on important information and advice to willing learners.

The goal of this book is simple: to help you make money from seminars and workshops. Whether you are in the public or private sector, whether you work for a company, municipality, school district, or nonprofit, this book can help you develop your own seminars. This book takes you from thinking about doing it to delivering the final product: a topnotch seminar presented to an appreciative audience.

Think of *Profitable Seminars* as a guide to take you

along on your seminar-development journey. It covers the three distinct phases of developing your own seminars: creating, marketing and delivering.

The chapters are organized in the same sequence a person would naturally follow in developing their own programs. They discuss determining whether to conduct a seminar, identifying a seminar topic, finding and organizing information, compiling the program, selecting the presentation approach and equipment, picking a seminar location, developing a marketing approach, setting up for the seminar, delivering the seminar and evaluating the results. Although the book is organized sequentially, you can jump from chapter to chapter if you wish to skip certain topics.

Contents

Deciding to Create Your Own Seminar

If you can dream it, you can do it.
Walt Disney

Proudly, you stand facing several dozen people in the Plaza Room at the Hyatt Hotel in San Francisco. As you gaze out at the audience, your mind is at high alert. You feel the effects of an adrenaline rush. It is a little overwhelming that you are about to present a two-day seminar to over fifty people. Sure, you have done other seminars, but this one is different—it's all yours from beginning to end. You painstakingly designed it, tirelessly marketed it, and now you are about to deliver it. You have no one to fall back on—but that is exactly what you wanted.

You're relieved that all your efforts at promoting your first seminar have been a success. You are anxious. You ask yourself, will the participants like what you will be presenting? Will they find it valuable? Will they respond positively? But your slight nervousness is quickly consumed by your exhilaration. You're in the spotlight, and it's show time.

Things could have been very different. Your dear friend Ida Williams had the opposite experience with her first public seminar. She had twelve preregistrations and three on-site sign-ups. Promotion, equipment rental and room costs alone exceeded the meager registration fees she received. Because Ida wanted to gain valuable presentation experience, she decided to conduct the workshop anyway.

Your quest started nine months ago while you were attending a company-paid seminar on another subject. You drifted into a daydream and visualized yourself presenting a seminar to a packed audience that savored your every word. After that experience, you were never the same. You left the seminar with a dream to create one yourself. Since then you have spent all your free time planning, designing and marketing your own program. You found out that it was not easy, and there were several obstacles. No matter—success will erase all memory of the difficult times.

WHERE DO YOU BEGIN?

With the tremendous growth in information today, there is an insatiable thirst for specialized knowledge. The people who can fulfill this need are the ones who have gained insight and hands-on experience over the years from providing services or developing products. These people have invested countless hours in learning and mastering their specialty or skill.

If you are like most people who present their own seminar, you have developed an expertise in a specific area. Perhaps you are

- a real-estate broker who wants to offer a workshop to first-time home buyers;
- a stockbroker who wants to enlighten people about investing in stocks and bonds;
- a judge who wants to teach a session on winning and collecting a small claims judgment;
- a car salesperson who presents a workshop on buying a new car with confidence;
- a florist who wants to teach people how to make floral arrangements; or
- an author who wants to promote a book about using the pottery wheel.

No matter what your skill, expertise or talent, you can convert it into a seminar. Very simply, a seminar is the presentation of focused information in a particular field. The seminar provider brings together information from various sources and presents it in a coherent, understandable form. Anyone has access to the information, but most choose not to accumulate it. They may not have the time or desire to do so. The seminar creator determines the mixture of presented information, the organization of the information and how the information is interpreted. Thoroughness, relevance, timeliness and importance are the factors that will make your seminar valuable to people. To be successful in the public seminar business, you need to develop a quality seminar, sell it to your target market and present it in a convincing manner.

WHO PROVIDES SEMINARS?
Seminar providers come from all fields, trades and professions. Very few begin their seminar livelihood as public speakers. The majority of providers develop an expertise in their field or area of interest. Because of their knowledge, they are called upon to speak at meetings, conferences and training sessions. At some point, they decide to give their own seminars. Let's examine the profiles of some contemporary seminar providers.

Joe and Vicki Kieva
Joe and Vicki Kieva love traveling in their recreational vehicle (RV), and they have been doing it for over thirty-five years. Their passion for RVing has taken them to all fifty states, plus Canada and Mexico.

Since 1989 the Kievas have been on the road for seven to eight months each year, delivering seminars on RV-related topics. Many are provided at RV shows, where Joe and Vicki host two to three seminars per day. Their winter circuit is so busy that they book every weekend from the second week in January to the first week in April. They may go to Tampa, Florida, and then travel throughout the southeastern states to give their seminars. On occasion, they will park their RV in a campsite and fly to a distant show, if it is not practical to drive.

The Kievas drive a thirty-six-foot Country Coach with an office on board. It consists of two laptop computers, two small printers and a big file box that doubles as a console in their motor home. Seminar equipment includes a slide projector, easel and flip chart. They also carry seminar handouts and copies of their two books, *RVing Made Easy* and *Extended RV Travel,* which they sell copies of at their seminars.

One program, entitled Ten Tips for Choosing an RV, provides practical tips and helpful hints on shopping for an RV. The Kievas provide a fast-paced, lively, one-hour show, making alternate five- to ten-minute presentations. Their presentation approach is complementary, with Joe focusing on technical aspects, such as how to operate an RV, and Vicki providing interesting stories, such as the time they observed a herd of buffalo crossing a river in Yellowstone.

RV shows are not like typical seminars. A portion of the audience frequently consists of people who are tired of walking around and who want a place to sit down. A constant flow of people coming and going create traffic through the seminar. The adjoining booths inevitably have salespeople loudly proclaiming the attributes of their products. Joe likes to quip, "If you can handle an RV show, you can do a lounge act anywhere"(Kieva, personal communication, 1998).

Joe and Vicki are hired by show promoters, yet they must capture the participant's attention and keep them interested if they want to be invited back. Joe and Vicki's contagious enthusiasm for the RV lifestyle is what gets the majority of people to return for the second and even the third seminars given later in the day.

Although the Kievas do not market directly to their participants, they spend a considerable amount of time marketing to the various RV show promoters. Joe feels that this is the toughest part—making contact with, preparing proposals for and convincing show promoters to book the program. Their marketing efforts not only have resulted in bookings but also in two sponsors, the Good Sam Club and the Flying J travel business. Joe and Vicki also write two monthly RV advice columns. One, "RV Insight," has almost a million readers in the Good Sam Club's *Highways* magazine. The other column, "RVing Made Easy," is published in six regional magazines throughout the country. Joe and Vicki have a philosophy on life: Enjoy the journey.

Paulette Ensign

During her career, Paulette Ensign has served as a speaker, workshop facilitator, consultant, radio talk-show host and independent publisher. She founded and presided over Organizing Solutions and then became founder and chief executive officer (CEO) of Tips Products International. She self-published four books, a booklet, a videotape, and she produced an audiotape with Career Track Publications. Her most successful publication, however, is a sixteen-page booklet entitled, *110 Ideas for Organizing Your Business Life*. Published in 1991, the booklet has sold over a half-million copies in three languages.

Paulette's initial seminars were about organizing for business, and this led to the booklet. She has switched her emphasis and now tours the United States, providing a seminar dubbed How to Write and Market Booklets for Cash. She also delivers the seminar as a teleclass by telephone and is about to take the in-person class international to Europe. The seminar is based on the premise that everyone has an expertise that can make other people's lives easier, better or richer. All you have to do is identify your expertise and "the key to marketing those secrets is your own tips booklet" (Ensign, personal communication, 1999). The seminar investment is $99 to $198, depending on the length and format. Paulette provides basic, printed, handout materials as part of the seminar. Additional materials for sale include an eighty-page manual and a 2-1/2-hour video that contains the how-to's of writing, publishing and marketing a booklet. Her visual aids include overheads and a flip chart for the in-person classes. The most convincing visual aids are the booklets people have created after taking her workshop.

When asked about the payback she receives from seminars, Paulette says, "I love interacting with people, sharing the information that I've learned, prompting them to grow and benefiting themselves. The seminars always generate immediate and after-market revenues. I charge an entry fee for the seminars, plus I have related products and services to sell" (Ensign, personal communication, 1999). Paulette is very generous with her advice and material. "Take anything you want from the manual—ask me anything, copy anything do everything I've done. Everything except the mistakes—don't bother repeating even one of them. Please learn from mine."

Paulette promotes her seminars by a variety of methods, including direct mail, e-mail promotions, online announcement boards, radio and print interviews and calendar notices in local newspapers. She leverages her promotion efforts by engaging sponsors in her target market to promote and publicize her seminars.

The Tips seminar has led to a home-study course that includes a video, an eighty-page manual and the *110 Ideas for Organizing Your Business Life* booklet.

Joan Stewart

Joan Stewart's background as a reporter and editor of several newspapers, including the *Business Journal of Greater Milwaukee,* has given her the experience and contacts to establish her own seminar and media consulting business. She now helps businesses, nonprofit organizations and government agencies develop and maintain good relations with the print and broadcast media. Through customized seminars, workshops and one-on-one coaching, she explains how to convince editors and news directors to print or broadcast a story, how to be cool and confident while meeting with the media during a crisis and how to ace difficult interviews with reporters. She also creates publicity campaigns and offers a variety of writing and editing support services.

Joan publishes *The Publicity Hound,* a bimonthly subscription newsletter featuring "tips, tricks and tools for free (or really cheap) publicity" (Stewart, personal communication, 1999). She provides several half-day seminars with intriguing titles, such as

•   Hey Boss, Mike Wallace is on Line 2—A Workshop

on Survival Skills for Meeting the Media
- Savvy Media Relations: How to Get Free Print Space and Air Time
- "You Mean I Can't Tell 'Em to Buzz Off?"—How to Use Tact and Diplomacy with Customers and Co-Workers
- 101 Great Ideas for Marketing Your Business

The target market for Joan's seminars are corporate clients, small businesses, nonprofits, government agencies and trade associations. She creates what she calls a one sheet, which is a one-page flyer that includes a captivating title, a listing of seminar benefits (outcomes), a short description and at least one testimonial. The flyers also contain a short biography and a photo. Marketing consists of sending these one sheets with supplemental information to the various associations. She also posts information from the fliers at her Web site at www.publicityhound.com.

Through public speaking, Joan gets lots of free publicity for herself. "The local Chamber of Commerce asked me to do two workshops for them this year, which I did. I estimate that their excellent marketing resulted in at least sixteen thousand pieces of literature about the workshop being distributed through southeastern Wisconsin at no cost to me. This gives me credibility, establishes me as an expert in my field and provides tons of free advertising" (Stewart, personal communication, 1999). She also attracts many consulting clients from her audiences. Another important benefit is that she sells her newsletters from the back of the room at her workshops. She accepts credit cards, which helps to boost sales. In terms of visual aids, Joan uses overheads, flip charts and various newspapers and magazines.

Carol Hansen and Victor Grey

Approaching age fifty, Carol Hansen was hanging on to a high-stress corporate job. "I was overweight, unhealthy and generally unhappy with my life," she relates (Hansen, personal communication, 1999). She had a powerful desire to reverse this condition and start feeling good about herself.

On New Year's Eve of 1992, Carol attended a twenty-four-hour mediation that literally changed her whole life. The mediation inspired her to create a technique that would bring her body, mind and spirit into alignment—a process that would enable her to love herself just the way she was. The process took only five minutes a day and produced phenomenal results. Within thirty days of starting the process, her blood pressure and cholesterol levels normalized, and she lost seventeen pounds. Within ten months she was a whole new person—happy, energized, younger looking and ninety-two pounds lighter.

Heartened by her success, Carol and her husband Victor Grey began conducting seminars throughout the country and Canada. The two to three hour seminar is called Lighten Up, and it teaches people a process that helps them learn to love themselves, which in turn helps many to heal physical, emotional, mental and spiritual issues. Since then over four thousand people have attended their workshops.

Carol and Victor do not advertise their seminars directly. Instead, they book their seminars through Unity Churches and Churches of Religious Science. Once a church is scheduled, Carol sends a full-page master that the church uses to advertise the event. She also sends a press release for the local paper.

The seminar led to the development of several products that are sold at and after the event. The first product was the *Lighten Up* audiotape of the seminar, which sells for $15. This is their bestseller, with over six thousand copies sold. They now have three tapes, two books and some small items, including a booklet, prayer cards and postcards.

The cost of the seminar is minimal. "We make most of our money from the sale of our products. The seminar costs only $20, and we split those proceeds with the church. However, we keep all the profits from the sale of our books and tapes, and it is not unusual for us to make $1,000 to $1,500 in sales, even with a relatively small group of twenty to thirty people," says Carol (Hanson, personal communication, 1999). Carol and Victor provide participants with handouts and a class outline at the end of the seminar. They do not use visual aids. Carol describes their presentation approach as experiential. "We don't use any visuals, and we have never gotten any complaints from the 'visual' people in the group. We do use music, and we bring people through a couple of visualizations, so the seminar is experiential."

Wade Cook

Seminars are very big business to Wade Cook. In fact, they represent a multimillion-dollar enterprise for the self-made entrepreneur. He loves the seminar business, and he is good at leading seminars. He uses radio, television, direct mail and the Internet to advertise his seminars, including the free Wade Cook's Financial Clinic. This seminar has been masterfully choreographed and is used to influence participants to purchase his other seminars and products.

Wade is a captivating storyteller. During the Financial Clinic seminar, Wade tells the story about his job driving Yellow Cab no. 22 in Seattle. It didn't take him long to critically examine the taxicab business from the perspective of the driver. He found that virtually all of the drivers competed for the longer trips, such as the drive to Seattle-Tacoma International Airport, but it didn't make sense to Wade. He realized that when someone got into the cab and the driver dropped the meter, it was at that moment that the greatest profit was made. He earned $2 when the meter dropped. From then on, it was only ten cents per mile. Why not focus on shorter trips and drop the meter more often? It didn't take him long to outproduce the more experienced, but less savvy, drivers.

Wade then goes on to talk about his real estate career. While driving the taxi, he was able to plunk a portion of his profits into real estate. At first, he purchased and held real estate. He built up an impressive portfolio of nine rental properties and a net worth of $125,000. He notes that although it was great to brag about his net worth, there came a point when he didn't have enough cash to pay a $65 utility bill. Applying his meter-drop thinking to real estate, he switched his strategy from buying and holding to buying and selling.

"Not only was I accumulating wealth, I now had cash flow" (Cook, personal communication, 2000). It was at this time that Cook started giving seminars on his ideas and strategies.

Recognizing that stocks offered greater profit potential, Wade gravitated to Wall Street. He refined the lessons he learned in his previous endeavors and became successful doing a lot of little deals that produced big profits. These lessons became the basis for his Financial Clinic and Wall Street seminars.

Cook knows how to run seminars. He uses the free seminar to aggressively promote his other seminars and products. Right in the middle of the Financial Clinic, Cook acquaints participants with his two-day Wall Street Seminar costing $5,695, his Zero to Zillions home-study course at $1,295 and access to his Wealth Information Network (WIN) at $2,995 per year. He knows that people are less inclined to stay around after the seminar to sign up for his products and seminar, so he encourages participants to buy during the seminar. He stimulates them to act immediately by offering special reduced prices available just during the seminar. He offers a package of the Wall Street seminar, the Zero to Zillions home-study course and six months access to WIN at an approximate 65 percent discount.

Wade Cook has a large staff and continues his sales approach after the seminar. He follows up by mailing promotional material and a free audiotape, entitled *How to Make Money in a Sideways Market,* to all participants. The tape includes additional references to his books, seminars, home study course and Internet information service.

Janet Groene

Author Janet Groene loves working at the keyboard and can't foresee a time when seminars will replace her writing. Still, she sees seminars as a vital tributary in the nonfiction writer's income stream. "First, the money is good," she admits. "My fee is currently $1,000 per day plus expenses. Second, it's a way for me to meet my readers. They tell me a lot about what I need to include in future articles and books. It's a win-win situation because my books give me cachet and credibility, which in turn sells the seminar, which in turn promotes my books" (Groene, personal communication, 1999).

Groene's first book is for campers and sailors who have no ovens or refrigeration. A later book is about cooking in the RV galley, and another book is about boat camping. In her appearances at boat, travel, outdoor and RV shows she does a number of twenty-minute cooking seminars for each day of the shows, which can last three to ten days. The Groenes sometimes travel to seminars in their RV, and for ten years they had their own, twin-engine airplane for use in their travel writing business.

Janet's husband Gordon had been a professional pilot before the couple, when in their early thirties, decided to sell everything they owned and go to sea in a small sloop. In time, they added the RV, then the airplane, and evolved a new life as writers of thousands of newspaper and magazine articles and more than a dozen books.

In writing the first travel guides, the Groenes were swamped with presentations from hotels, restaurants and attractions that wanted to be listed. As the pounds of material piled higher, the Groenes became intrigued with how different people handled this appeal for free publicity. Most of the bigger companies had professional public relations counsel who knew how to follow through with writers, but many of the smaller places were novices. So Janet put together a four-hour seminar entitled Free Ink: How Small Business and Non-Profits Can Do Their Own Public Relations. Janet gives the seminar for groups such as convention and visitors bureaus and tourism promotion agencies.

Groene's newest book, *Successful Freelance Writing in the New Millennium,* opens the door for a new series of seminars aimed at hopeful freelance writers. "Unlike most authors, I don't sell my books at seminars," Janet reveals. "It's cumbersome when you have to make change and compute sales tax. It also can be humiliating, like passing the hat after your speech is finished. Plus, my cooking seminars are presented at shows where the show organizer pays me to be there as a personality and expert, not as a book peddler. I get a lot of interest from the media, which in turn helps publicize the show. I coordinate with my publishers, so they can tell their sales reps that my RV or boat books will be getting a lot of local publicity on those dates. They then work with bookstores to set up special displays or tie-ins throughout the host city. If I learn of a company that will have a booth at the show and wants to sell the books, I throw the business to them" (Groene, personal communication, 1999).

Janet adds, "Nor do I sell, promote and organize my own seminars. I find a group to do that. In the case of the convention and service bureaus that present Free Ink, it is a service to their constituents. I'm paid out of their general funds, and usually attendees pay nothing. My cooking seminars are presented at shows that pay out of their advertising budget; the freelance writing seminars will be offered to groups including bed-and-breakfast inns, which will offer writer weekends. I might earn more by selling my own seminars, but that would take time away from my first love, which is writing. All I want is my fee. If the organizers charge admission and clear $10,000, that is fine with me" (Groene, personal communication, 1999).

TIP NUMBER 1:
Identify Your Expectations

So, are seminars in your future? Early on, it is critical that you identify your reasons for wanting to do seminars. You probably have several reasons for your desire to do so. List and prioritize your reasons. These priorities will influence your decisions throughout the process. For example, if you are more interested in acquiring new customers, you may opt to spend more lavishly on facilities, food and beverages. If you are interested in creating a new profit center, you will be more inclined to look at the bottom line. Your reasons may be economic, personal or a combination of both. The following are some typical reasons:

- Open up another profit center for your business
- Increase your number of business clients
- Impart your knowledge and experience to others
- Mentor people within your field
- Find a business opportunity that supports your lifestyle
- Develop a backup career
- Promote your other products and services

TIP NUMBER 2:
Decide On Seminar Topics

Deciding on your seminar topic or topics is a pivotal step. Once you decide, you can begin devoting your efforts on seminar creation. One technique is to list five to ten topics you might like to develop into a seminar. You should select your seminar topics from your business or life experiences—something you really know and believe in. If you do not have a passion about your topic, it will be hard to enthrall an audience.

Once you have completed your list of possible seminar topics, develop a chart to compare and analyze the candidates you selected. When creating your chart, use as many categories as you think necessary. Although four categories are used in the chart below, Passion Level, Expertise, Information and Profit Potential, you may wish to add others, such as competition level and development cost. Weights for each category also can be adjusted to reflect your assessment of their importance. In this particular case, weights vary from one to five points, with high numbers reflecting strength and low numbers weakness. The critical factor is to be consistent and honest with yourself in your ratings.

Topic	Passion Level 1–5	Expertise 1–4	Information 1–3	Profit 1–4	Total
Collectibles	5	2	3	1	11
Supervision	2	4	2	3	11
Writing	5	1	2	1	9
Budgeting	2	4	3	3	12

1.   **Passion Level:** How much do you enjoy the topic? Do you spend your free time dabbling with the topic? Do you closely monitor events and activities happening in this area?
2.   **Expertise:** Do you have expertise and knowledge in this area? Do you have any credentials, such as certificates, books or awards?
3.   **Information:** How much information is available on this topic? Can you acquire it easily and inexpensively?
4.   **Profit Potential:** Are people interested in this topic? Is there a large enough potential market? Can you reach them without incurring too high of a cost?

The key to this exercise is to make an honest assessment of the possibilities. Be cautious, though; the highest number of points may not be the best determinant. In the example above, the Budgeting topic received the highest point total (12), yet Passion Level was rated relatively low. A high passion level or love for a topic is essential. If you are trying to inform or educate people, it is hard to influence them if you have little enthusiasm for the subject. If the presenter selected the budgeting topic, the program would most likely fail.

From your analysis, you may decide to work on multiple seminars. While creating my first seminar on management skills, I collected information on other topics and filed it in cardboard storage boxes. When I was ready to develop the next seminar, I had a running start with the information that had been accumulated.

TIP NUMBER 3:
Determine Your Seminar Approach

As a seminar provider, there are four different approaches you can use. Seminars are provided on a contract basis with organizations, by working for sponsors, as public seminars for a fee and as public seminars for free. Many seminar providers will use all four formats, as do several of the seminar providers profiled earlier in this chapter. The four formats are discussed here.

CONTRACT SEMINARS
Under the contract approach, you are hired by an organization to conduct a seminar for their employees. Businesses, government and nonprofit organizations will send out requests for proposals (RFP) or requests for qualifications (RFQ) to identified vendors. Interested vendors respond with a proposal. Your marketing time is spent on identifying and selling organizations that are in need of in-house training. A flat fee for each seminar or program is the most common financial arrangement. However, some seminar providers are paid by the hour or by the number of participants. Many seminar providers find that after they establish a reputation, organizations will seek them out and forego the RFP process.

Advantages
Contract training allows you to deal with one entity. You do not have to worry about mass marketing to get your registrants, so your economic risk is low, once you obtain the contract. The meeting room and audiovisual equipment

is usually provided by the contractor. If food and beverages are provided, they are usually provided by the contractor. You can customize the program for your audience.

Disadvantages
The type of program is determined by the contractor. The contractor also influences the content of your program. They do not want you saying things that are detrimental to the organization. You also can wind up with prisoners—people who do not wish to be at the seminar.

Some bid processes are long and tedious. They can consume great amounts of time and labor with no return on your investment. When applying for contract training, it is a good idea to check out the provider to make sure that they do indeed intend to award a contract to a provider. Although unethical, some organizations will go through a process just to get ideas from vendors on how to construct their own in-house program.

SPONSORED SEMINARS
Many organizations and associations sponsor seminars and workshops for members and interested participants. Sponsors include nonprofit organizations, universities, professional associations, trade groups, adult education programs, community colleges and religious groups. With this system you are hired to develop and conduct the seminar. The sponsor may use an RFP or RFQ process to find providers. More likely, it's accomplished through the marketing efforts of the seminar provider. The provider sends a letter and background material to the sponsor and suggests the program. The sponsor decides whether the program will produce registrations and compatibility with its overall goals. The seminar provider is paid a flat fee or an hourly stipend.

Advantages
As with contract training, the seminar provider deals with one entity: the sponsor. The sponsor provides for registrations, room, equipment and food and beverage arrangements. Many opportunities exist for sponsored seminars.

Many sponsors will permit the seminar provider to sell books, audiotapes, videos, pamphlets and other products to the participants. Some will want a portion of the proceeds; others will not. The provider usually controls program content, as long as it does not reflect negatively on the sponsoring organization. The people who attend these seminars are usually there because they want to be.

Disadvantages
The sponsor determines what programs will be provided. Pay is usually low for these types of seminars because many of these groups operate on a meager budget.

PUBLIC SEMINARS
The public seminar is the entrepreneur's forte. The entire package—design, marketing and delivery—is carried out by the seminar provider. Registrations are obtained by marketing directly to the participants by direct mail, e-mail, fax and print and broadcast media. The seminar provider makes the arrangements for the meeting facility, food, beverages and equipment. All of these activities are undertaken to produce enough registrations to generate a profit from the seminar. Fees are set to cover expenses and produce a profit.

Advantages
Because the providers are responsible for all aspects of the seminar, they receive all the rewards. When a seminar is successful in attracting participants, the provider reaps huge rewards, much more than contract or sponsored events. People who attend are usually there because they want to be and thus are more involved in the program.

The seminar provider determines the type of program offered and the content. Providers do not have to worry about someone vetoing a controversial topic or approach.

Disadvantages
Public seminars involve a great deal more risk than contract or sponsored seminars. If you do not get enough registrations, you lose the money you spent arranging for and

promoting the seminar. Public seminars require more work because you must make the food and beverage and equipment arrangements along, with the marketing efforts and processing of registrations. You are also required to deal with cancellations and no shows.

FREE AND LOW-FEE SEMINARS

Free seminars are provided at no fee (or at a very low fee) to participants for different reasons. A common use of free seminars is to entice participants to sign up for a fee-based seminar, other products, or both seminars and products. Acquiring consulting contracts is another purpose. The provider targets participants who are in need of or will require consulting assistance. The provider counts on impressing the participants and thus making it easier to solicit their business.

Advantages
Free seminars attract people who are interested in the topic. They have made the conscious decision to devote their time to attending, so they are receptive to your sales message. Free seminars are usually short—from one to three hours and usually do not provide food or beverages.

Disadvantages
Free seminars are risky. They generally cost more than other seminar formats, especially if promoters use costly print and broadcast media to reach large numbers of people. The seminar provider gambles that he or she will get sufficient sign-ups for the fee-based seminar or sell enough products to pay for all expenses and leave enough for an adequate profit.

Incidentally, not all seminars fall into these categories. Free seminars also are provided for philanthropic reasons. I provide free seminars on topics such as How to Run a Meeting or How to Work with City Hall for community groups. These are provided with no expectation of a fee or contract. The payback is a feeling that I am helping to promote good government. People also use free seminars to test ideas or to sharpen their speaking skills.

TIP NUMBER 4:
Think About Seminar By-Products

Once you begin providing seminars, you will find that people consider you an expert in your chosen area. This helps you obtain speaking engagements and requests to write articles. Also, you will find that the information you gather from your research and from the interchanges in your workshop provides the data for a book. Audiotapes, videos, software, assessments, case studies, and management instruments are some of the other spin-off products of your seminar efforts. These, of course, provide you additional profit centers while enhancing your reputation. So, when you begin your seminar career, don't limit yourself. Focus your thinking on products that can be developed from your efforts.

TIP NUMBER 5:
Don't Quit Your Day Job

If you are interested in developing your own public seminar, you don't have to make an irreversible decision. It is not likely that you will miss the boat if you take it slowly. Here are some questions to help you assess your readiness to begin providing seminars:

- Do you have special knowledge or expertise in the topic area?
- Do you have credentials on the topic, such as a published book, degree or professional reputation?
- Can you offer an improvement or variation over existing programs now offered?

- Will it take a significant investment to develop the program?
- Can you identify your target group relatively easily?
- Is your target group growing?
- Will your target audience benefit professionally, socially or economically?
- Does your seminar have repeat potential, or is it based on capitalizing on a fleeting trend or fad?
- Can you afford to lose your original marketing and development investment?
- Will you reap additional benefits in addition to potential profit?
- Do you have the time to put together a quality program?

If you have done an assessment and come up wanting, spend your time making yourself more competitive. You can begin working on the three components of a successful public seminar business while continuing your full-time job.

1. Collect information and ideas about your topic.
2. Immerse yourself in learning how to market your seminar.
3. Sharpen your presentation skills

Research your topic and broaden your knowledge in areas that need strengthening. Find opportunities to make public presentations, both paid and gratis. When you are ready, come out of the gates roaring. And finally, financial success may be your primary goal, but there are other rewards that you may reap while providing seminars, including the following:

- Sense of independence
- Meeting very interesting people
- Increased respect
- Helping people become successful
- Imparting your knowledge to willing learners
- Increased sense of accomplishment

- Recognition from your colleagues
- Becoming widely acknowledged as an expert in your field

These are the types of rewards that attract thousands of people to seminars throughout their careers and keep them active way beyond the normal retirement years. Once you become a seminar presenter, you can continue to present programs as long as you can inspire audiences and remain current on your topics. W. Edwards Deming, the father of the quality management movement, was still presenting his seminar to over 20,000 adoring participants at the age of 92.

2

Creating a Winning Seminar

To communicate, put your thoughts in order, give them a purpose; use them to persuade, to instruct, to discover, to seduce.

William Safire, *New York Times* **columnist**

Mark Twain once quipped that "it takes three weeks to prepare a good impromptu talk." Many of the things that you do during a seminar will appear spontaneous to your audience but in fact were anticipated and prepared for in advance. Designing your program is one of the most exciting and enjoyable tasks involved in developing your own seminar. This is your chance to show the world your organizing skills and your creativity.

Many people find starting the actual work of constructing a new seminar the most difficult task. Because of this they will procrastinate, waiting for a more convenient time. Of course, that time never seems to occur. This roadblock can be surmounted by using such techniques as the forty topics test, the question and answer method or mind mapping. When you think of your program, don't limit your efforts to just the presentation. You also should be thinking about creating a workshop notebook and handouts. These are necessary components of a successful seminar, and you will save considerable time if you create them at the same time as your presentation.

TIP NUMBER 6:
Take the Forty Topics Test

A good beginning to your presentation planning is the forty topics test. With this technique you think of all the topics you can for your proposed seminar and list them on the computer, index cards, or a piece of paper. Your ideas do not need to be refined and can be listed in abbreviated bullet form. Don't evaluate or criticize them at this time—just list them. The process of recording topics will suggest additional ideas to you. After you get all your ideas and concepts recorded, you can categorize and refine them. If you are able to compile a list of at least forty different topics, it indicates that you have a considerable amount of knowledge in your subject area. It also signifies that you are indeed ready to develop a seminar. You also may wish to share your list with other people and get their reaction. This list not only demonstrates your readiness but also forms the basis for your new seminar.

TIP NUMBER 7:
Use the Partner Question
and Answer Method

The partner question and answer method is another approach you can use to begin creating your seminar. This technique involves using a partner who stimulates your thinking by asking questions such as

1.   What is important about your subject area?
2.   What do people need to know about the topic?
3.   Why do you want to do a seminar on this subject?

4.   What pitfalls do people need to avoid?
5.   What lessons do people learn the hard way?
6.   What benefits will you offer to participants?
7.   What do you intend to offer that others do not?
8.   What do you want your participants to remember
      from the session?

The partner continues to prompt the seminar developer with follow-up questions such as "What else?" and "What other ideas are related to that idea?" The question and answer method stimulates you to identify the important issues and concepts. Vocalizing them helps you to organize and focus your thoughts. Saying them out loud also allows you to gauge their significance. All ideas should be recorded or written down as they are discussed. Simultaneously recording them on a flip chart and visually displaying them inevitably leads to additional thoughts.

TIP NUMBER 8:
Mind Map Your Seminar

Mind mapping is a system for collecting random thoughts as they occur. Tony Buzan is attributed with the origination of mind mapping and has written several books on the subject including the *The Mind Map Book.* Joyce Wycoff also wrote an excellent book on the subject, entitled *Mindmapping: Your Personal Guide to Exploring Creativity and Problem-Solving.*

Proponents of mind mapping say that it maximizes your brain's untapped potential. It is a pattern of organizing thoughts that relies on both the right and left side of the brain. The idea is to take a blank sheet of paper, start in the exact middle with your theme or topic and then start jotting down associated ideas. For simplicity, try to use key words or symbols instead of phrases. Then, you draw lines from the central theme and write associated thoughts at the end of the lines. You then draw lines from these thoughts to other thoughts. The lines can be long or short, straight, curved or wriggly. You can also use basic graphic designs, including boxes, stars and arrows.

The result, according to theorists is full exposure of your idea. Mind mapping is a favored technique of composition teachers who use the problem approach to writing. It is also a good technique for people who are not sequential organizers—those who learn or plan best with a more global picture, a random approach.

To make a mind map, look at your idea and make free-flowing associations. Use whatever you can think of: location, function, size, shape, problems, benefits, opportunities or threats. The cartoon at the beginning of this chapter is an example of a mind map for a coin collecting seminar.

Mind mapping is a powerful way to generate new ideas because it taps into one's right-brain creativity. The prerequisite of mind mapping is rapid-fire thinking—don't labor too much on any one idea. Record the first thoughts that come into your mind. This spontaneity is what makes mind mapping so useful.

People develop mind maps on 3 x 5 index cards, on letter-size paper or on a flip chart. They also can be created with Post-It notes. David Straker's book, *Rapid Problem Solving with Post-It Notes,* suggests six techniques like mind mapping, using 3M's revolutionary product. The mind maps can be created alone or with a group. One of my first experiences with mind mapping involved using mind mapping to develop a new business marketing plan. Butcher paper was taped in one continuous stream around three walls. Talk about excitement, energy and creativity—we were all disappointed when we had to move on to the next subject.

There also are computer programs that help you develop mind maps. Computer-based mind maps allow you to easily change or restructure the mind map by effortlessly moving words or trees of words around. You can also highlight different parts of the map by using bold, brilliant colors and even different fonts.

TIP NUMBER 9:
Use an Outline Approach

Some people find it helpful to use outlines to plan their seminars. By writing down the main points in summary fashion, they can put the program together more quickly. It also helps them avoid wasting time on irrelevant or marginal topics. A typical outline approach appears as follows for a short workshop on road rage:

A. Main Topic	A. Managing Road Rage
1. Subordinate Topic	1. Causes of Road Rage
a. Supporting information	a. Cutting people off
b. Supporting information	b. Driving too slowly in left lane
c. Supporting information	c. Tailgating
2. Subordinate Topic	2. Defusing Road Rage
a. Supporting information	a. Avoid eye contact
b. Supporting information	b. Give space
B. Main Topic	B. Adjusting Your Attitude
1. Subordinate Topic	1. Get Yourself Help
a. Supporting information	a. Do not go home
b. Supporting information	b. Go to a public place

The main ideas project the broad topics of the module. Subordinate topics are the various components that expand upon and help support the main ideas. Supporting information consists of explanations, examples, opinions and definitions, which support and define the subtopics and main idea. Most presentation software programs such as Microsoft PowerPoint have an easy to use outline feature. Once created, your outline can be converted to slides with a click of the mouse.

TIP NUMBER 10:
Develop a Tentative Seminar Title

Early on in the process you should begin thinking about your seminar title. The single most important advertisement of your seminar is its title, so spend time developing and refining it. You want to make sure it will appeal to and attract your desired audience. People use different techniques for creating titles. Some of the different styles include the following:

1. Titles that frame a question: How Secure Are Your Computer Files?
2. Titles that solve a problem: How to Handle Angry and Emotional People
3. Quantitative titles: Nine Deadly Enemies of Excellent Communication
4. Simple and descriptive titles: Professional Telephone Skills
5. Interactive titles: Everything You Should Know about Budgeting
6. Personal titles: Charting Your Career Success

Another approach is to use a two-part title, the first being provocative and the second informative, such as Get Rich: How to Invest in Bonds.

The title is critical and should be open to change as you complete your seminar. Create five to ten titles and test them with friends. You can do this by giving them your list and asking them to rank them in order. After they have done so, make sure you follow up and ask their reasoning for the order. These seven titles were tested for a basic supervision course for government employees:

1. The First Time Supervisor
2. How to Be an Effective Supervisor
3. Honing Your Supervisory Skills
4. The Public Sector Supervisor
5. The Successful Supervisor's Seminar
6. The Step-by-Step Guide to Supervising Employees
7. Management Skills for First-Time Supervisors

The clear choice of prospective participants and their managers, was The Public Sector Supervisor. As a follow-up, we questioned the responders. Most thought that the phrase *Public Sector* was important. Its seems that many of the private sector seminars that they had attended did not cover many of the special issues government employees encounter. The Public Sector Supervisor conveyed the idea that this workshop was targeted to their special issues and problems.

Don't forget about a subtitle. You can supplement the main title by adding a complementary subtitle. Here are some examples:

Title	Subtitle
The Public Sector Supervisor	How to Grow Great Employees
Presentations for Cowards	Ten Things to Reduce Stress
Top Delegators Are Top Achievers	Now You Can Master This Crucial Skill
Conflict Management	Controlling Highly Charged Situations
Essentials of Direct Mail	Five New Ways of Marketing Today

TIP NUMBER 11:
Develop Learning Outcomes

You are now ready to develop your learning outcomes. Learning outcomes are the things you want your participants to be able to do as a result of attending your seminar. For a supervisor's workshop the participants might learn how to

- improve subordinate performance and satisfaction;
- reduce employee turnover;
- receive fewer grievances;
- lower employee absenteeism;
- receive fewer customer complaints; and
- improve the supervisor's chance for promotion.

Learning outcomes establish the benefits people will receive if they attend your seminar. View them as your personal promises to them. Participants evaluate the success of the seminar based on your delivery of these promised outcomes.

Your learning outcomes should be precise and should clearly communicate the specific benefits the participant can expect. A good way to do this is to use verbs that suggest action, such as in the following titles:

1. Win Your Small Claims Court Case!
2. Solve 95 Percent of Your Macintosh Computer Problems
3. Conduct Effective Spot Audits within Five Minutes
4. Rid Your Workplace of Sexual Harassment Claims

As you examine other seminar provider's brochures, you'll notice weak verbs, such as *understand, appreciate,* and *comprehend.* Try to avoid them; they weaken your offer. Here are some weak learning outcomes:

1. Better Understand the Small-Claims Court Process
2. Appreciate the Features of Your Computer
3. Learn to Identify Macintosh Computer Problems
4. Become More Aware of Sexual Harassment Issues

TIP NUMBER 12:
Decide on the Length of Your Seminar

As you put together your program, you will begin to get an idea of how long the seminar should be. The typical public seminar used to be one day. It started around 9:00 A.M. and finished around 4:00 P.M. Although a great many public seminars are still one-day seminars, some seminars use several other approaches, including the following formats:

- One to two hours
- Half day (three to four hours)
- One day (six hours)

- One and one-half day (ten hours)
- Two days (twelve hours)
- Three or more days (eighteen or more hours)

As a general rule, you want to make your seminar as short as you can but still do justice to your topic. Obviously, if you are offering a seminar entitled The Five Critical Steps to Stock Market Success, you want to schedule enough time to cover all five. You also must take into account the amount of time your participants have. Some, such as dentists, only can afford to be absent from the office for a short period. A one- to three-hour seminar is preferable to them and to similar groups that have tight schedules. Although other workers are able to be gone for one day, two days may be too long. I have found that there is a 40 to 70 percent drop in attendance between a one-day and a two-day seminar on the same topic. Cost is another important consideration. The longer the seminar, the higher your labor, equipment, facility, food and beverage costs. Although you have the option of increasing the seminar price to offset the additional expenses, expect to lose participants because of the increased cost. Even though you may lose participation with a longer session, this does not mean that you will make less profit on your seminar.

TIP NUMBER 13:
Determine the Appropriate Audience Level

In some cases, a mixed audience can result in a more dynamic event. The experienced people help the neophytes learn at a faster rate. But generally, the opposite is true. The experienced people dominate the session. Knowing your audience's familiarity with the topic gives you an idea as to how much basic information—and in what detail—to include in your seminar. Your approach with novices will be very different from that of experienced people.

I once held a seminar on public budgeting and failed to clearly specify the audience level of the program. As a result, I wound up with a blend of beginning, intermediate and advanced participants. Although the majority of the audience was composed of beginners, the advanced participants used their familiarity and confidence with the topic to hijack the session. They kept diverting me to topics and subjects that required intimate knowledge of budgeting. It didn't take long for the beginners to become confused and agitated. The postseminar evaluation forms said it all—the advanced budgeters indicated that the session was too basic, and the beginners felt that the session was too technical. I had set myself up for failure by not adequately indicating the level beforehand. I solved this problem with a banner on the promotional brochure indicating: For Beginning and Midlevel Budgeters.

Here are some questions to help you identify the appropriate level for your audience:

- What do they already know about the topic?
- What things do they not know about the topic?
- How much should they know?
- What is their experience and background in the area?
- What myths and misconceptions do they carry about the topic?
- What mistakes do they make?
- What topics do they not need information on?

How do you get this information? Group surveys, individual interviews and observations of your target audience can provide such data.

TIP NUMBER 14:
Create Your Slides

You are now ready to create your slides. Go through your lists, outlines or mind-map diagrams and identify the main topics or subjects. Begin your slides by converting the main topics into slide titles. These titles can be recorded on word processing or presentation software. You can also write these titles at the top of index cards or blank sheets of paper.

Once you have recorded all of the topics, you can begin developing bullets for each of the slides. Short, crisp statements should be used. Don't use complete sentences because you will wind up reading them when you present them to a group. Most slides should have no more than three to five bullets that explain or amplify the main point. The bullets need not be completed all at once. Many will require additional research. The next step is to arrange them in a logical presentation sequence.

At this point you should also identify the topics you will not cover in your seminar. Determine the reason for doing so. Is the information too advanced? Is it too elementary? Or is it of limited value? For example, at a seminar on giving presentations, one should not spend too much time, if any, talking about view graphs or opaque projectors because they are virtually obsolete.

TIP NUMBER 15:
Select a Presentation Software
Program

Computer presentation software programs have literally revolutionized the seminar development process. Aldus Persuasion is one of the early software programs that was developed specifically for presenters. It enabled presenters to develop a professional presentation on a personal computer. Microsoft's PowerPoint is now considered the premier software program for developing workshops and seminars. Other presentation software includes Harvard Graphics, Corel's Presentations, Freelance Graphics and Astound.

Electronic presentation software is revolutionary; it allows novices to incorporate graphics, charts, photos, cartoons, sounds and video into their presentations. These programs make everyone a presentation design expert by allowing them to plan, organize, revise and present a first-class electronic presentation. Alternatively, professional looking 35 mm slides or overhead transparencies can be made from this software.

PowerPoint is provided in the Microsoft Office Suite for both Macintosh and PC. This business strategy has enabled PowerPoint to become the dominant presentation software.

Selecting a presentation software package is one of the most important buying decisions you will make. Because PowerPoint is the benchmark, the capabilities of this program are covered here. Before making a decision you will want to compare other programs to the industry standard.

POWERPOINT'S MAIN FEATURES

PowerPoint provides the Slide Content Wizard that prompts you through a multistep process to create an actual presentation. To start the process you type your title and bullet information in a preset outline or right onto a slide. The slide is the basic component of the PowerPoint program. Once the outline or slides (comparable to storyboards) are developed, the seminar designer can do the following:

1. Choose from over one hundred templates that have been created by professional artists. Templates can be changed by simply selecting another format. Template choices are offered in both black and white and color.

2. Select slide colors from several hundred predetermined color schemes that have been produced
   by graphics experts. You can also customize the
   color scheme by mixing and matching your own
   preferences.
3. Use it as a word processing program by creating
   bulleted lists, using different font types and sizes,
   finding and changing text and checking spelling.
4. Insert clip art. Although PowerPoint includes a
   clip art library, you can also import clip art.
5. Import photographs, pictures, graphs and drawings.
   You can size the imported item to make it larger
   or smaller.
6. Create line graphs, pie charts, bar graphs and
   tables within the program by selecting the charting feature, selecting the type of chart and typing
   in the information on a worksheet. Although not
   as sophisticated as some of the advanced charting programs, the PowerPoint charting component
   meets most presentations needs. More sophisticated charts can be developed in other programs
   and then imported into PowerPoint.
7. Design organization charts and flowcharts. These
   charts contain basic building blocks that can be
   built upon and modified.
8. Create diagrams and freehand drawings. The program has several already established shapes (tri-
   angle, rectangle, circle, etc.) that can be sized,
   shaded and colored. A free-form tool allows for
   creative additions.
9. Print the presentation as an outline, notes page,
   audience handout or individual slides. The Handout Master provides an option of listing two,
   three, six or nine slides on each page. These handouts can be titled, formatted and numbered to
   make handouts or insertions in a seminar
   notebook.

POWERPOINT'S OTHER FEATURES

A separate feature called the PowerPoint Viewer permits people who do not have the PowerPoint software to view your presentation on another computer. A copy of the Viewer disk is sent along with a copy of your presentation. There are several alternatives to PowerPoint, but most have a significantly steep learning curve and a far smaller user base. Besides the learning curve, a problem with all of the non-PowerPoint programs is that you can't count on people having a reader to view the presentation if they want to. That makes the option of putting the slide file on a Web site for downloading or putting it on disk more complicated.

The Slide Sorter is a very useful organizing feature. You can display all of your slides in reduced form on the computer screen or the wall. These miniature slides can then be repositioned by dragging them from one spot to another. It beats the old method of laying overheads on the floor and manually arranging them.

It is a good idea to check out the Web sites of the companies that provide presentation software. These sites offer useful tips, downloads and software patches along with keeping you up to date on the latest versions.

PowerPoint: www.microsoft.com/PowerPoint
Astound: www.astoundinc.com
Freelance Graphics: www.lotus.com/freelance
Presentations: www.corel.com
Harvard Graphics: www.harvardgraphics.com

TIP NUMBER 16:
Take Classes on Your Presentation Software

A very important issue when using presentation software is training, specifically the amount and availability of training.

Check with the computer stores that sell the presentation software to see what training and support is available. Basic PowerPoint techniques are very easy to learn alone, but it makes sense to take a short class on PowerPoint to learn all of its capabilities. A class also will give you a chance to see all of PowerPoint's possibilities. I have seen presenters who have invested a considerable amount of money in hardware and software and yet failed to understand most of the features of their software.

Presentation graphics programs permit you to explore and be creative but likewise, one can get carried away with adding bells and whistles to presentations. Keep your program simple, especially in the beginning.

TIP NUMBER 17:
Use Supplemental Activities to Energize Your Seminar

"This was the best seminar we've ever had. By involving us in real life exercises, Len Wood made it meaningful and enjoyable," exclaimed Mary Wirtes, President of the Southern California City Clerks Association, as she adjourned the meeting. Ms. Wirtes' enthusiasm is partly because of the three supplemental activities I used during this short two-hour seminar.

Supplemental activities are used for several reasons. One purpose is to break the monotony of the presentation. Put yourself in your participant's shoes; there is nothing worse than listening to a presenter drone on and on. The charisma that wins over participants can make the presenter delusional; the presenter thinks, "They want me to keep going." Don't fool yourself. It can blind the presenter to the fact that participants get antsy. Even if you are a great presenter, supplemental activities help to change the pace and let people experience other things. The longer the seminar, the more important that variety be injected into your seminar.

Another reason supplemental activities are used is to provide participants hands-on experience by having them perform a task or explore an idea. If you want people to learn a task, have them do it. Another purpose of supplemental activities is to get people involved. Some participants are reluctant to participate in a large group but feel comfortable interacting in a small group. Smaller groups of three to eight people (breakout groups) are used to gain the benefit of the interaction that comes from the more intimate setting.

Any supplemental activities you decide to use must be carefully prepared; instructions should be easy to follow and you need to know the approximate time the audience will take to complete the activities. Your audience should be able to relate to them easily; the best supplemental activities are reflective of real-world situations. Supplemental activities that can be used to add pizazz to your program include the following:

1. *CASE STUDIES*

The Harvard University Graduate School of Management popularized the case study method. A scenario is developed (or recounted) to demonstrate a specific business topic such as a marketing, operations or customer service problem. Participants are asked to read the case and then respond to questions, such as, How would you deal with this problem? Cases can be reviewed individually or in a group setting. The most effective method is to use small groups of three to eight participants to examine the case. I usually have them record their findings on a flip chart and have a spokesperson report to the entire group when the session is over.

Although it is possible to purchase case studies, you may find that few directly apply to your subject matter. Alternatively, you can create your own case studies. Think of interesting or difficult situations you have had to deal with and convert them into case studies. Your cases can be real, embellished or even fabricated, just make them realistic so that the participants can integrate newly learned information to real-life situations.

A common criticism of case studies is that they take

longer to read than to discuss. You can avoid this problem if you eliminate unnecessary details and limit the case study description to one page. A typical case study will take from fifteen to thirty minutes to read and discuss. Appendix A includes a simple case study on decision making that I created for a supervision seminar.

2. *DISCUSSION GROUPS*
Discussion groups are one of the most popular supplemental activities. Participants sit in a circle or around a table and discuss a topic or problem assigned by the seminar leader. People feel more comfortable in these smaller groups and are more apt to ask questions and share their experiences with other members. Group members are usually given a set period of time to discuss the issue and to record their findings on a flip chart. A spokesperson (or the entire group) reports his or her group's findings to the entire seminar group. Specific questions or problems that relate to a seminar issue should be used.

3. *BRAINSTORMING*
Brainstorming is a good discussion group technique. In 1941, Dr. Alex Osborn invented the process we now call brainstorming. Dr. Osborn termed it *organized ideation,* and he described it as a process by which we can use our brains to storm creative problems in a way that keeps judgment from inhibiting imagination. Brainstorming, to be most effective, requires a member of the group to act as a facilitator. The person who performs this role focuses on the process rather than the issue and helps participants express and summarize their thoughts. The atmosphere is one of free-flow thinking consisting of suggesting, listening and building on ideas. Most important, the facilitator must avoid judging or filtering ideas. All ideas should be recorded in a manner that does not stiffle the group The ground rules for brainstorming are as follows:

- Everyone participates in the discussion.
- Ideas must be recorded and displayed on a black-

board or flip chart for everyone to see. Visual display leads to additional ideas.

- The group generates as many ideas as possible. The quality of the idea is not important in the early stages of brainstorming.
- No criticism or judgment should be allowed while ideas are being generated. Brainstorming does not work when this rule is forgotten.
- The generation phase continues until all ideas are exhausted or when a predetermined time limit occurs.
- The group then discusses and evaluates the listed items.
- Priorities are then established.
- An action plan is developed.

4. *REVERSE RAINSTORMING*

Another good group problem-solving method is reverse brainstorming. This technique is used to discover flaws in a proposed solution. You use the same approach as used for brainstorming, but in this case, participants are encouraged to do the following:

- Make a rapid-fire listing of all the things that are possibly wrong with the proposed solution, process or system.
- Prioritize the weaknesses in order of their significance for the proposed course of action.
- Take each of the major flaws and brainstorm ways of overcoming them.

If brainstorming or reverse brainstorming is used in your seminar, make sure that you select topics that expand and challenge participants' knowledge about a relevant topic.

5. *TESTS AND QUIZZES*

An important component of my budgeting seminar is the module on budgeting techniques such as averaging, rounding, indexing and trend analysis. In the past, participants simply hated hearing me pontificate on such mundane subjects.

I used to dread the module on basic budget techniques and considered dropping it. After observing a lot of folded arms and receiving several negative evaluation comments, I knew that I had to try something different. In desperation, I created a budget techniques quiz form that has twelve questions on the budget techniques. Participants are put into groups of two and asked to compute the answers. After about thirty minutes, I provide participants with the correct answers and instructions on how to compute them. The reaction continues to amaze me. People love the exercise and will not put it down until they complete it. They even work into their lunch hour if they have not completed all the answers.

Another supplementary activity is tests. Tests can be created in various formats—multiple choice, true-false, matching, or fill in the blanks. Be careful when constructing these type of activities. Make them challenging, but not too difficult. If they are complex, include written guidelines on how to solve the problem. When administering the exercise, make it fun, more of a game and not the dreaded pop quiz that we all faced as students.

6. *DOCUMENT OR PRODUCT ANALYSIS.*

If your seminar involves a document, you can develop a checklist that helps participants evaluate it. Reviewing annual reports can be boring. Give participants a copy of the document and ask them to use your already created checklist to evaluate it. They love it. An abbreviated example of such a checklist is shown in Figure 2.1.

Annual Report Assessment (Figure 2.1)

_____ Does the CEO's message address significant issues and trends?
(0–4 points)
_____ Are graphics used effectively?
(0–2 points)
_____ Is the document effectively organized?
(0–2 points)

_____ Does it include overall challenges and threats?
      (0–3 points)
_____ Are the prospects on winning lawsuits discussed?
      (0–2 points)
_____ Would stockholders feel this is a user friendly report?
      (0–4 points)
_____ Total Points

Compiling total points allows you to compare different documents. This same approach can be used with virtually any item or object. For example, a presenter of a writing seminar can provide participants a poorly written memorandum and ask them to critique and then rewrite it.

7. ROLE PLAYING.

Role playing is one the oldest group techniques. It usually involves an unrehearsed enactment of a contrived situation. Role plays take different forms. Here are some of the more common approaches:

Modeling.

Two people demonstrate a situation in front of the entire group. The group takes notes and offers suggestions after the session has been completed. An example might be how to work through a tough one-on-one negotiation. Another example is one person giving a partner a performance evaluation. They then switch roles. A variation is to have an observer watch the interaction and then provide constructive criticism to the two participants.

Specified roles.

From two to seven people are given specific roles which they are asked to play while interacting to deal with an issue. These exercises usually involve several people involved in a conflict such as a contentious court battle.

General roles.

Participants are asked to perform as a member of a group. They are not given specific roles but they are asked to

behave as a group member. An example might be a dys-
functional staff meeting.

Role playing takes more involvement and energy than any
of the other exercises. Role playing permits participants to
shed their persona and adopt another which can result in
very powerful learning experiences. However, presenters
should be careful with role playing. Some people find role
plays threatening and do not like to perform in front of others.

8. DEMONSTRATIONS
The demonstration is an effective training technique. The
seminar leader uses it to show how a function, task or job is
carried out. The demonstration also is used to emphasize an
important point. If you use demonstrations, make sure
you practice them thoroughly. There is nothing more hor-
rifying than to start a demonstration and then forget the
concluding steps.

9. HANDS-ON ACTIVITIES
Hands-on activities are very effective for teaching people how
to perform tasks. I once took a workshop on rebuilding car-
buretors. It involved a lecture and demonstration. After-
wards, I decided to rebuild the carburetor on the family car.
The dismantling process went fine, and although I was able
to put the carburetor back together, I wound up with six extra parts—three screws, two gaskets and a small spring. Of
course, the carburetor didn't work too well, and it confirmed
my wife's judgment regarding my mechanical skills. What
went wrong? Although I had observed the workshop presenter demonstrate the entire process, I had not experienced
it myself. The workshop would have been much more effective if the participants actually had followed along with their
own carburetor, taking it apart and putting it back together.

10. THE HOT SEAT.
The *hot seat* is an increasingly popular technique. The concept involves offering individual participants the opportunity to get in front of the group and present a vexing prob-

lem or challenge. The workshop leader and participants then offer suggested solutions. Hot seats work best with small groups of experienced participants. The hot seat can energize a group near the end of the session or right after lunch.

TIP NUMBER 18:
Create a Workbook
for Every Course

As you create your basic program, you also should be planning and compiling your course notebook. Most seminar participants expect a workbook or notebook and will be disappointed if they don't get one. Although seminar providers take different approaches to the workbook design and contents, almost all believe that some sort of document is necessary. With that in mind, what do you include in your notebook? One of the first questions is whether you include copies of your slides. Presenters have different opinions regarding this. Some believe that participants should be given a copy of every slide shown. This makes it easier for them to take notes. Another view holds that slides are proprietary and should not be provided to participants. The problem with this position is that many participants who pay for a seminar believe that they are entitled to copies of the material used in the seminar. My own view is that it is best to provide copies. Following are some other information items that can be included in the workshop notebook:

- Seminar agenda
- Table of contents
- A bibliography and list of resources
- Related items—letters to the editor, research papers and speeches you have written
- Feature articles about you and your activities
- Reviews of books you have written

- Relevant articles
- List of relevant Web sites and e-mail addresses
- Glossary

I like to include a list of participants so that people can network after the session. If you include a list, you might get the participants permission before doing so. Also, be sure to get permission from other authors to reprint their material. Many printers will not print copyrighted articles if permission has not been obtained.

TIP NUMBER 19:
Create Handouts

Handouts are used for supplemental activities and new or late-breaking information. For example, I conduct surveys in early workshops and provide the results to participants in subsequent workshops. Handouts also are used to correct erroneous information contained in the seminar notebook.

You may wish to develop a nifty format for your handouts with a smart logo and border. Copyright information should be included at the bottom of each page such as ©Len Wood & Associates. Many seminar presenters also include a photo and brief biography on all their handouts. Because handouts get passed around, this affords the presenter additional exposure.

If you intend to provide your seminars several times, resist the temptation to print all your notebooks and handouts at once—it will save you money. You will find that you will want to improve the material after your first session. If you print a few at one time, you won't be out the cost of the materials you don't use.

TIP NUMBER 20:
Test Your Seminar

After you have completed the design of your seminar, it is a good idea to conduct dry runs. Feedback from these practice sessions will help improve your program by identifying awkward and unclear sections. Dry runs also help you identify and expand interesting sections. I go through several dry runs for new programs. I begin by giving the seminar alone and recording myself. I then review my performance and make changes. I follow this by inviting colleagues, relatives and friends to listen to the presentation and to critique it. Dry runs are of most value when reviewers are honest and note things that need to be improved or changed. Make sure, however, that they note the strong parts of your presentation as well.

Adult education classes offer a wonderful place to road test and perfect your seminars. One of the largest adult education organizations is the Learning Annex (www.learningannex.com). This organization offers short, inexpensive courses in Los Angeles, New York, San Francisco, Toronto and San Diego in such topics as personal growth; business and career opportunities; showbiz and media; health and healing; sports and fitness; spirituality and relationships. Most of their classes are from three to six hours. The Learning Annex proclaims that they send out a monthly publication that reaches over 2.5 million people.

The Learning Annex is constantly looking for new presenters. You can obtain a copy of the course proposal requirements through their Web site or by calling 310-478-6677. There also are adult education offerings in every area. Most high schools, community colleges and universities offer adult education opportunities.

Know Your Competition

*If you don't have a competitive advantage,
don't compete.*

Jack Welsh, General Electric CEO

After you select your subject area, you want to find out everything you can about your competition. Competitive analysis is the process of evaluating your competition's program, finding opportunities and turning them to your benefit. It involves identifying your competitors and assessing what they are doing—including determining their strengths and weaknesses. You want to find where they are most vulnerable to determine if they have left you a market niche. Fred Gleeck, who refers to himself as an information marketer of seminars, books and tapes, counsels, "If I find a seminar I really like, I don't try to replicate it. I don't want to redo Tony Robbins seminar. It's great. I'm looking for other little niches. I like to do what is called caulking work. I look for the gaps and fill them with specific niche materials within the markets that I deal with. Ask the questions; where are the gaps? Where am I going to caulk? What is missing?" (Gleeck, personal communication, 2001).

TIP NUMBER 21:
Collect Seminar Brochures

Some of the competitive information you need can be gleaned from Web sites. Other information can be obtained from seminar brochures. Be sure to get yourself on the mailing list of all the seminar and workshop companies you can identify that provide programs similar to yours. You will find their addresses and phone numbers at a local library or on the Internet. You can get on their mailing lists by contacting them and asking to be included. The following table includes a list of some of the national providers of business seminars:

Provider	Address	Phone	URL
American Management Association	PO Box 169 Saranac Lake, NY 12983	800-262-9699	www.amanet.org
CareerTrack	9757 Metcalf Ave. Overland Park KS 66212	800-488-0935	www.careertrack.com
Dun & Bradstreet	PO Box 71186 Chicago IL 60694	212-692-6600	www.dnb.com
Fred Pryor Seminars	PO Box 2951 Shawnee Mission KS 66201	800-255-6139	www.pryor.com
Langevin Learning Services	P.O. Box 1221 Ogdensburg NY 13669	800-223-2209	www.langevin.com
LERN	P.O. Box 9 River Falls WI 54022	800-678-5376	www.lern.org
National Businesswomen's Leadership Association	6901 West 63rd St. Shawnee Mission KS 66201	800-258-7246	www.natsem.com

National Seminars Group	6901 West 63rd St. Shawnee Mission KS 66201	800-258-7246	www.natsem.com
Padgett Thompson	11221 Roe Avenue Leawood KS 66211	913-451-2700	www.ptseminars.com
Skill Path Inc.	6900 Squibb Road Mission KS 66201-2768	913-362-3900	www.skillpath.com
Keye Productivity Center	11221 Roe Avenue Leawood KS 66211	800-821-3919	www.ptseminars.com

Adult education, parks and recreation, community college and university extension programs are also good sources for competitive information. These groups regularly mail out brochures and catalogues on their offerings.

TIP NUMBER 22:
Attend Your Competitor's Seminars

Another way to evaluate a competitor's seminar is to attend one of their sessions. On-site inspection will provide you with a treasure trove of information, such as the topics covered, equipment used, participant characteristics and training methods used.

Talk to as many participants as you can when you are scoping out a competitor's seminar. It is best to use open-ended questions to get a participant's true feelings. Here are some questions to ask to engage participants in helpful conversation:

- Why did you select this seminar?
- What do you expect to get out of the session?
- Who is paying for the session?
- What do you like about the session?

- What do you think of the presenter?
- What could be improved?
- Would you recommend that other people attend?

In addition to querying participants you also should assess the seminar. Here again, you can ask several questions:

- Does the program deliver on the promised objectives?
- Does it focus on the important issues?
- Can you do it better?
- What was your overall reaction after the session?
- What did you learn?
- What was not covered?

TIP NUMBER 23:
Complete the Seminar Competition Evaluation Worksheet

As you evaluate your competition, their strengths and weaknesses will become apparent. Following is a worksheet to help you evaluate a competitor's seminars.

SEMINAR COMPETITION EVALUATION WORKSHEET

1. Company or Organization Providing Seminar

The Training Shoppe

2. Seminar Name and Description:

This seminar teaches local elected officials how to oversee, analyze and control municipal budgets.

---

3. Seminar Locations
Seattle, Boise, Miami, Chicago, Atlanta and Denver

4. Seminar Length and Times
One day, 9:00 A.M. to 4:00 P.M.

5. Cost
$195 for one person, $165 for two or more from the same organization

6. Seminar Leader's Credentials
Former city manager and finance director; author of four local-government books

7. Promised Benefits
- *Identify financial-crisis warning signs*
- *Avoid being victimized by adverse financial actions*
- *Ask penetrating budget and financial questions*
- *Improve public confidence in financial oversight abilities*

8. Target Audience
- *Mayors, city council members, board of supervisor members, city managers, finance directors and budget officers*
- *Most recently elected with little background in public finance and budgets*
- *Age grouping 35—60; gender: 40 percent male, 60 percent female*

9. Food and Beverages Provided
- *Coffee, decaf and tea in morning*
- *Hot lunch selection excellent*
- *Soft drinks for afternoon break*

10. Materials Provided
- *Forty page course workbook and eight handouts*
- *Copy of book, entitled* Local Government Dollars & Sense

---

11. Equipment and Visual Aids Used
- *LCD projector*
- *Two flip charts*
- *Large screen (12 ft)*

12. Seminar Strong Points
- *Seminar leader had extensive experience in local government*
- *Session moved fast with good interaction*

13. Seminar Weak Points
- *Not enough time to consider all aspects of some topics*
- *Session is basic—need a follow-up for more experienced participants*
- *Some topics are boring and could be dropped*

14. Participant Comments
- *Would like more detailed information on budgeting*
- *Spent too much time on accounting aspects and not enough on management's role*
- *Would like to know more about downsizing*

(A blank copy of the Seminar Competition Evaluation Worksheet appears in Appendix B.)

The information from your evaluation should help you identify areas where other seminar providers have left voids. According to William Draves, "More and more marketers are looking at the competition to find out what gaps exist in the marketplace, and then to develop programs around what the competition is not doing, instead of what the competition is doing."(Draves, personal communication, 1999).

As a local government manager, I sought out seminars to improve my leadership and management skills. However, most of the seminars offered were designed for private companies. The seminar firms presenting these seminars had made a marketing decision to focus on private enterprise issues. Since there are so many more private companies than public organizations, this made good business sense.

While I was able to glean valuable information from these sessions, there were several topics that were unique to local governments that were not covered. Information on public budgets, elected officials, taxes and public hearings were some of the subjects that I wanted covered. However, this information was of little value to private sector managers. Talk about a market gap! Once I began developing my own seminars, I designed a seminar specifically for local government managers. I had discovered a marketing gap and filled it.

4

Where to Get Your Material

Whomever you are presenting to probably has access to the data. The presentation is not about presenting data. It is about what value you are adding to the information.

Richard Atkinson, Chief Communications Technologist for Northrop Grumann Corporation

As you design your seminar, you will be spending a portion of your time collecting and categorizing information. This material is needed to enrich your program. During the gathering stage, you want to accumulate all the information you can pertaining to your subject area. Sources include books, magazines, newspapers, television programs, audiotapes and videotapes, professional journals, interviews and Web sites. Look for stories, analogies, comparisons, figures, charts and facts that can be used to embellish and strengthen your presentation.

TIP NUMBER 24:
Collect and Store Relevant Information

Make copies of important items. I accumulate information in a standard storage box. Most of my seminars average one storage box for each day of a presentation. When you accumulate information, remember to collect

1. information and ideas to strengthen your seminar presentation;
2. content for your course notebook and handouts;
3. information and ideas for related seminars you may decide to create; and
4. ideas for your future book and other products on your selected topic.

Yes, *book*. Most seminar providers eventually write a book on their topic. After presenting your program several times, you will discover that you have developed specialized knowledge that very few people possess. You have become an expert, and people are willing to pay you for your written, as well as spoken, words. Even if you are not interested in writing a book now, collect and store information with the idea that you may be writing a book someday.

TIP NUMBER 25:
Consider Using Clipping Services

You also can use a clipping service to accumulate seminar information. Companies, called clipping services, are set up to monitor newspapers, wire services, journals and magazines from around the world and provide clients with articles on specified topics. Bacon's, Burrelle's and Luce are the largest clipping services. Their coverage is nationwide and they also monitor radio, television and the Internet. Local coverage is provided by state and regional clipping services such as Minnesota Clipping Service. The company provides complete coverage within the state: 31 daily newspapers, 384 non-daily newspapers and 148 magazines.

Most services require a flat monthly fee such as $100 to $400 plus a nominal charge ($1.00) for each clipping provided. If you use a clipping service, ask if they require a minimum term. Some services have a three- or four-month minimum. Internet clipping services are generally less expensive, but the value of clippings may be less since there are no quality standards on what is posted on the Internet. Excite Newstracker provides a free clipping service at www.excite.com/info/newstracker/quickstart.

TIP NUMBER 26:
Search for Books on Your Topic

Visit several book stores and check to see if there are any recent books on your topic. Supplement your search at your local library and on the Internet. Several Internet bookstores exist, including the following:

- Amazon.com—www.amazon.com
- Barnes and Noble—www.barnesandnoble.com
- Borders—www.borders.com
- Books a Million—www.booksamillion.com

Search for books using all the words that relate to your topic. You'll find different but related titles by doing this. For example, I found different lists of books by using the keywords *seminars, conferences, workshops, speeches, marketing, presentation equipment, speaking* and *presentations.* Many of the books listed on these Internet sites include professional reviews and customer comments. These comments can be especially useful in determining what items are important to people. As you discover these books, keep track of them so you can list them in your seminar bibliography. If you find that someone has just published a book in your subject area, interpret it as a favorable sign. It means that the topic is important enough for someone to spend money and time writing, marketing and publishing a book to cover it. On the other hand, if there are no recent books on your topic, don't be dismayed. It may signal an opportunity to fill a market gap.

TIP NUMBER 27:
Use Seminar Resource Internet Sites

There are several seminar and training resource sites available to presenters. Some Web sites you may wish to investigate include the following:

American Seminar Leaders Association (ASLA). The ASLA is composed of seminar and workshop leaders who seek to enhance their professional skills and market their products and services more effectively. ASLA provides a variety of resources for developing and improving presentation skills, including a discussion board, newsletter, referral program and a Presenters University.

American Seminar Leaders Association
2405 E. Washington Boulevard
Pasadena, CA 91104
Phone: (800) 735-0511/Fax: (626) 798-0701
E-Mail: info@asla.com
Web site: www.asla.com

The American Society for Training and Development (ASTD). ASTD is a professional organization dedicated to promoting workplace learning and performance. ASTD represents 70,000 professionals from 150 countries. ASTD offers a wide collection of periodicals, books, newsletters, research reports and videotapes. This site has a chat room, discussion forum and links to other training sites. ASTD permits trainers to post seminars to a list of over 250,000 training programs. Many chapters also provide train-the-trainer programs.

American Society for Training and Development (ASTD)
1640 King Street, Box 1443
Alexandria, Virginia, 22313-2043, USA
Phone: (703) 683-8100/Fax: (703) 683-8103
E-mail: customercare@astd.org
Web site: www.astd.org

The Learning Resources Network (LERN). LERN is an international association devoted to lifelong learning and offers information and resources to providers of lifelong learning programs. LERN members come from all areas of training and are engaged in conducting business classes, leisure learning, community education, online courses, staff training, contract training, public seminars and conferences. The association provides information on such topics as marketing, brochure creation, program pricing and promotion. LERN maintains a message board and several online events for trainers including seminars, discussion groups and training programs.

Learning Resources Network (LERN)
1550 Hayes Drive, Manhattan, Kansas, 66502.
Phone: (800) 678-5376
E-mail: info@lern.org
Web site: www.lern.org

The National Speakers Association (NSA). NSA is an alliance of 3,800 professional trainers, educators, humorists, motivators, consultants and authors. Publications include *Professional Speaker* magazine and *Who's Who in Professional*

Speaking: The Meeting Planner's Guide. NSA has a program to certify professional speakers—The Certified Speaking Professional Program. NSA provides several local training seminars and workshops each year. An annual national convention also is held each year. There are thirty-seven state and regional chapters of NSA.

National Speakers Association (NSA)
1500 South Priest Drive
Tempe, Arizona 85281.
Phone: (602) 968-2552
E-mail: Information@nsaspeaker.org
Web site: www.nsaspeaker.org

Toastmasters International. Toastmasters is an international not-for-profit educational organization devoted to helping people sharpen their public speaking skills. Some 180,000 members belong to over 8,000 local clubs. The clubs have regular meetings to give members the opportunity to learn and to practice making presentations.

Toastmasters International
23182 Arroyo Vista
Rancho Santa Margarita, CA, 92688
Phone: (949) 858-8255
Fax (949) 858-1207
E-mail: stills@toastmasters.org
Web site: www.toastmasters.org

Training Forum. Training Forum™, a division of Interactive Training, offers trainers a comprehensive resource of training products and services. The Training Forum Web site provides a Speakers Database, which lists high-powered speakers; an Events Database listing over 400,000 seminars, conferences and training events, which are updated weekly; and an Association Directory of 10,000 business organizations in the United States. Presenters can submit their seminar for listing in the Events Database and can interact with authors of monthly training articles.

Training Forum
A Division of Interactive Training, Inc.
100 Cummings Center
Suite 457J
Beverly, MA 01915
Phone: 978-921-1755
Fax: 978-921-1490
E-mail: info@trainingforum.com
Web site: www.trainingforum.com

Training SuperSite. This multipurpose site includes a library of hundreds of training and presentation articles. The database lists over thirty-five thousand seminars and conferences. This site also includes access to *Presentations Magazine,* which includes insightful tips and techniques on speaking and presenting. You can also sign up for a free subscription to *Presentations Magazine.* The Training Supersite also rates over 250 training resource sites.

Training SuperSite
Lakewood Publications
50 South 9th Street
Lakewood, Colorado
Phone: 1-800-328-4329
E-mail: info@lakewoodpub.com
Web site: www.trainingsupersite.com

TIP NUMBER 28:
Interview Experts

Some of your best information will come from interviewing experts in your subject area. People like to be interviewed; in fact, most are flattered when asked for an interview. Sending questions beforehand gives people a chance to think about their answers, thus making the interview more efficient. Tony Snow, the TV commentator, says the key to interviewing is to "ask crisp short questions." Do not put too many thoughts into each one or you risk having them answer just part of the question, or the least relevant part. "Long, multiple part questions give the responder the opening to duck the hard parts," says Snow (Snow, personal communication, 2000).

I get permission to use a recorder for the interview because I sometimes get caught up in the conversation and fail to write down important points. Most people do not mind the recorder and appear to forget about it once they get into the interview. When interviewing experts, I ask questions, such as the following, to elicit information that can be passed on to seminar participants:

- What lessons have you learned?
- What mistakes did you make?
- What obstacles did you encounter?
- What advice were you given that did not work?
- What are your favorite stories?
- What topics would you include in a seminar?
- What errors do beginners make?
- What topics should be deemphasized?

TIP NUMBER 29:
Use E-mail and Listservs
for Interviews

One very good way to interview busy people is to do so by e-mail because so many people now have e-mail addresses. You can send out questions in the morning and get responses before noon. Moreover, you are not limited to local sources—you are able to obtain quotes and information from all over the world.

Unsolicited e-mail interviews, however, do not receive a high return rate. I received returns of 2%, 2%, 3% and

5% from four different e-mail interviews sent to highly targeted groups. An important lesson I learned was to limit the number of questions asked. The fewer the questions, the higher the return rate. Another technique is to invite people to skip the questions they do not wish to answer. Even though the return rate is low, you can get very excellent information through e-mail interviews.

Another approach is to find listservs or message boards used by people who are members of your target audience. Post individual questions on the selected sites or invite people to participate in an interview.

TIP NUMBER 30:
Use the Internet for Research

The Internet has opened up a vast new area for research. Be on the look out for good research sites. You can get some of the latest information by monitoring Web sites, listservs, chat rooms and message boards that apply to your seminar topic area. When you see something that is relevant, e-mail the originator for additional information. It is a good idea to identify yourself to people on the list and ask them if you can use the information they provide in your seminar. Most people are happy to help. An excellent Internet site that lists several thousand listservs and discussion groups is at www.topica.com.

What if you're trying to locate a research site and you cannot remember the domain name? You can still take a guess at www.amnesi.com. This site lets you put in a partial domain name and get a list of registered domain names that closely match your guess.

When researching on the Internet, you should avoid these pitfalls

1. *Trivia pursuit.* Don't get caught up in pursuing interesting but irrelevant information. The Internet is vast, and it is easy to get carried away. Keep yourself focused on your topic. This should not stifle your creative juices, just look to the relevance of items.

2. *Fail to pursue.* The opposite of trivia pursuit is failing to pursue. If a topic looks promising, spend the time to pursue all the leads. You need to make the judgment as to how relevant the information is.

3. *Accept trash as gospel.* Anybody can post items on the Internet. Verify the information before you use it.

4. *Forget to bookmark.* Make sure you bookmark the home page of important sites, so you can go to them again. Bookmarking also is valuable, in case your computer freezes or crashes. For really important sites, I record the Web address along with a short description in a log. If you do not wish to bookmark in your computer, record it the old fashion way with pen and paper.

5. *Channeled to dead ends.* As you get into a topic and follow it down a path, don't get so channeled that you forget about the other main branches. Internet research is like following a river. If you go down a tributary, don't forget to go back to the main channel and take some of the other tributaries.

6. *Give up too soon.* If you cannot find information, look for other search engines. Attack the problem from another angle by using different search words. Look for other related topics.

7. *Overload your main e-mail mailbox.* As you search sites, you will come across several that offer free newsletters and reports. It does not take too many to overload yourself with a multitude of items that you do not have the time to read. One approach is to use a different screen name that is devoted entirely to these items.

8. *Conduct research at the wrong times.* When is a good time to research? Just as you try to avoid a library at peak usage times, you should avoid the Internet at peak times. The Internet Traffic Report, (www.internettrafficreport.com) can tell you if the Internet is congested. This site uses a scale from one to one hundred to rate how busy sites are around the world.

9. *Fail to create a failure file.* Always remember to create a file with instructions on how to remove yourself from listservs and newsletters. When you first sign up for an enticing new listserv, product or newsletter, you may not think about discontinuing the item. At some point the information may become irrelevant or outdated. Some providers start off with high quality information and then let it degrade. When this occurs, you don't want junk cluttering your computer.

10. *Acquire stale information.* How do you know if you have old information? Look to see when the information was posted. Many sites and pages have a "last changed" date.

11. *Fail to recognize case sensitivity.* You need to determine whether the search engine you are using is case sensitive. For example, Altavista is case insensitive until you use uppercase words. That means that *employee grapevine* will produce *Employee Grapevine*, *Employee grapevine* and *employee grapevine,* and even *eMployee Grapevine*. Once you use capitals, it becomes case sensitive and *Employee Grapevine* will not locate lowercase words.

 Tip Number 31:
Collect Germane Stories

We all love stories. We enjoy hearing them, and we enjoy telling them. Your audience will be more receptive to you if you share something personal. David Armstrong, author of

Storying Around, is the President of Armstrong International. He uses personal stories to promote company policies and values. "Stories are an excellent way to train people. They are simple, they are timeless, and they capture people's attention and imagination" (Armstrong 1992, 8).

Collect as many stories as you can that relate to your topic area. Think of critical incidents and defining moments in your life. The best stories for your seminar come from your own life experiences. Find those that tell about the problems you faced, how you learned an important lesson, or how you overcame a tremendous hurdle. Use humility—some of the best stories are those in which we poke fun at ourselves, but be careful about bragging about yourself. Audiences are not particularly enamored by these types of stories.

Record the story details and incorporate them into your seminar. Nancy Miller, seminar provider and author, suggests that a good story can be used to illustrate many different points. "Identify your stories, write them down and then think of the lessons that apply" (Miller, personal communication, 2000). After you have identified your stories, examine each one and make a list of the points or lessons that can be used to illustrate your point. However, only use stories that are relevant to the subject at hand. Here are some questions to ask yourself to bring out the relevance of a story:

- Why do you remember the story?
- What makes it different?
- What things could not be controlled?
- What was surprising?
- What incorrect assumptions were made?
- What went right?
- What went wrong?
- What would you do differently?
- What did you learn?
- Will other people find the story interesting?

You can tell your stories over and over and not be afraid that someone has heard them before. I once gave a workshop at a conference on how to conduct meetings. During the seminar I told a story about a meeting that had gone bad. The next day I was giving the same workshop in another location. To my surprise, three of the people in the workshop had attended the previous day's workshop. To minimize what I thought might be boredom, I skipped the story about the meeting that went bad. As I completed the topic, one of the participants, in a very disappointed tone, yelled out, "Aren't you going to tell everyone the story about the bad meeting?" He had told his colleagues about the story and was anxiously waiting for me to retell it.

The National Storytelling Association, at (800-525-4514), 116 West Main Street, Jonesborough, Tennessee, 37659-0309, is a wonderful source for information on storytelling. The Web site, www.storynet.org has several references, including a section on how to become a storyteller.

TIP NUMBER 32:
Build a Clip Art Library

I like to use clip art in my presentation slides to capture people's attention. For some of my early seminars, I retained a professional artist to develop cartoons for slides. They were colorful, professional looking and obviously drawn for the seminar subject. People loved them. However, they were expensive. If a tight budget rules out the use of an artist, ready-made clip art can be obtained through several sources. Art and stationary stores, printing and graphic arts publications, clip art software and the Internet are great sources for all types of clip art.

When using clip art, make sure that it imparts the image you are trying to convey. I have seen slides that contained unrelated images that served no purpose—other than to cloud the message. Don't use clip art if it does not add anything. Also, when combining clip art figures, make sure they are compatible. Presentation software allows you to enlarge, reduce, blacken, screen and modify clip art to make the right fit for your slide.

Tip Number 33:
Collect Pertinent Quotes

Quotes from famous—and infamous—people can emphasize the points you make in your presentation. Your local library will have books devoted entirely to quotations. There are also several Internet sources that provide listings of quotations by category.

Don't confine your search to published quotes. Solicit quotations from experts in your field and also look for their public comments at seminars, press conferences and television interviews. If you intend to use one of these quotes, it is a good idea to get permission from the person you are quoting. Here are three sites that provide quotations:

*   **The Quotations Home Page:**
    www.geocities.com/~spanoudi/quote.html
*   **The Quotations Page:**
    www.quotationspage.com
*   **Bartleby Quotations:**
    www.bartleby.com

Tip Number 34:
Examine Canned Programs

For some topics you may be able to purchase canned programs from training suppliers. Programs can be purchased for topics such as supervision, presentation skills, time management, conflict management, sexual harassment and customer service. Purchasing already developed training programs saves you research and development time. It also permits you to determine what other experts consider to be the most important topics in a particular area. Questions to ask when purchasing a training program include the following:

1. What is the cost? Is it reasonable and affordable?
2. Is there a trainer's guide? How easy is it to follow? Does it include trainer's notes, suggested questions and answers?
3. Is there a course book for participants? Is it easy to follow? Is it informative?
4. What is the quality of the course content?
5. What visuals are provided? Are overhead transparencies, handouts, flip chart templates and case studies provided?
6. What restrictions are on the usage? What are rights in terms of modifications? HRD Press in Amherst, Massachusetts has the following policy regarding customization:

> The materials that appear in this book, other than those quoted from prior sources, may be reproduced for educational/training activities. There is no requirement to obtain special permission for such uses. We do, however, ask that the following statement appear on all reproductions.
>
> Reproduced from *20 Training Workshops for Customer Service,* by Terry Gillen. Amherst, Mass.: HRD Press

7. Check to see if the program is returnable. If the program is not adequate for your purposes, you want to be able to return it.

Tip Number 35:
Use Charts, Tables and Graphs
to Present Material

Well-constructed charts, tables and graphs can add interest
and credibility to your seminar. Translate information into
tables and graphs when appropriate. The most enduring
book on statistics and charting is Darrell Huff's *How to Lie
with Statistics.* Huff first published the book in 1954, and since
then it has been republished in six editions and 39 printings.
The book is a clear and humorous look at how statistics are
manipulated and puts to rest the myth that numbers never
lie. The examples are from the 1940s and 1950s, but the concepts they illustrate are still relevant today.

The real genius of *How to Lie with Statistics* is Huff's
presentation of statistical information in an understandable
form. While his purpose was to show how people manipu-
late data, the value to seminar designers is how to present
information so people can quickly grasp the point being
made. Instead of using standard line or bar charts, Huff used
figures and cartoon examples to show relationships. For example, to show the demise of the rhinoceros population, he
presents a large half-page rhinoceros cartoon to show its
population in the year 1515 and a tiny rhinoceros that was at
least 50 times smaller for the year 1936.

Tip Number 36:
Be Sensitive to Copyright Laws

No doubt you have thought about reproducing copies of
magazine, journal or newspaper articles for inclusion in the
course notebook. In doing this, you may run afoul of the copy-

right laws. Copyright infringement results even if you reproduce just one page of a copyrighted document without the author's permission. In fact, Kinkos is so sensitive about this issue they will not duplicate any material without written permission from the author or proof from you that it is your original material.

Deciding on Your Presentation Approach

For the first time during the trial, the paper evidence was easy to follow, as the defense attorney used an over head projector to illustrate his closing argument to the jury.

Seattle Times **account of a high-profile criminal trial**

How will you present your seminar? Some workshops are presented as straight lecture with the seminar leader relying on personality, voice and gestures. Today, it is harder to keep an audience's attention with straight lecture, especially if the seminar is longer than one hour. People are visually oriented. The pervasive influence of movies, television and video has prompted people to expect visual aids to be used in seminars and meetings. Most of what we learn is learned visually. Experts feel that when the spoken word is not buttressed by visuals, as much as 70 percent of what is said is misunderstood or forgotten within minutes.

There are several presentation tools that can help stimulate interest, increase learning and enrich your presentation. Modern technology has provided new options for conveying information and concepts at your seminars. Computer-based presentations can dazzle audiences with brilliant color, animation, sound and video. But you also have

some of the tried and tested methods that do more than an
adequate job.

TIP NUMBER 37:
Select Your Presentation Media

No single approach works best for all seminars and in many
cases several types of media are desirable. Your budget is
one of the most important determining factors of what media you select. Although you may desire to use some of the
latest electronic devices, they are expensive to purchase
or rent.

PRESENTATION FACTORS TO CONSIDER
Along with your budget, the following factors will influence
your selection of a media presentation package:

Number of participants. The media selected must be appropriate for the size of your group. As an audience
grows in size and diversity, it becomes harder to keep
the group's attention. I recently attended a free sales
seminar in which the presenter was using a single
whiteboard for a crowd of over two hundred people.
As he scribbled some important information on the
board, he apologized, saying, "I know you can't see
this in the back of the room but bear with me." Several participants left the room as soon as they could
gracefully exit. An overhead projector would have
worked much better for this size group.

Room size and room layout. The meeting room must be compatible with the media used. Rooms with too many
windows that cannot be covered adequately may not
be compatible with projection equipment. Flip charts

or handouts are the preferred options in these cases.

Degree of interaction desired. In general, projection equipment tends to discourage interaction especially if the lights are dimmed. If you want to encourage a high degree of interaction, you may wish to minimize the usage of liquid crystal displays (LCDs), video and slide projectors.

Complexity of the information being presented. Overheads, slide projectors and LCDs may be preferable if you are presenting complex charts, graphs or tables. With all of these, you can progressively reveal parts of the entire table or chart, thus helping participants to focus on the pieces. Color, when used effectively, can also enhance understanding.

Length of seminar. The longer the seminar, the greater the need for different types of media. For a two-day or longer program it is not unusual to see the presenter using an overhead projector, LCD, video player and flipcharts. On the other hand, with a one- or two-hour seminar, the presenter may not rely on any equipment.

Familiarity with the equipment. Ability to use the equipment is also a factor. I have seen presenters attempt to use LCDs without the foggiest notion of how to perform routine tasks associated with LCDs, such as backing up to a previous slide or putting the machine on standby. Presenters should be careful about using new media without a thorough road testing. It is hard to figure out a new procedure with faces staring expectantly at you. One of these experiences can make shambles of your workshop.

Portability. If your sessions are held out of town, you will want to consider the portablilty of your equipment. How heavy and bulky is it? Does it pack compactly?

Is it easy to carry? Will it fit in an airplane storage compartment? When you carry your LCD projector and personal computer, some airport security stations require you to open them up and turn them on to check for explosives. You also have to be especially careful to guard against theft while traveling.

PRESENTATION EQUIPMENT CHOICES

As a presenter you have several equipment choices to enhance your programs. Each type has its own characteristics, benefits and limitations. Presentation equipment should be used to supplement your program by increasing interest, reinforcing your verbal message and illustrating concepts that are hard to visualize. You should not use equipment just to impress the audience with your technical skill or artistic ability. This detracts from your message. The six most common presentation tools include the following:

1.   Flip charts
2.   Whiteboards and chalkboards
3.   Overhead projectors
4.   Slide projectors
5.   Video and film projectors
6.   Computer-based presentation equipment

TIP NUMBER 38:
Master the Use of Flip Charts

Flip charts are seminar presenter's number one presentation tool. They are universally available, and it is hard to imagine a meeting room without a flip chart. I liken them to the seminar provider's Swiss Army Knife because they serve multiple purposes.

ADVANTAGES OF FLIP CHARTS

They can be used for welcoming seminar participants, presenting material, recording information and recording evaluation comments at the session. They are inexpensive, easy to prepare and convenient to use. Lenny Laskowski, professional speaker and author considers flip charts invaluable: "While everyone seems to be interested in creating high-tech computer generated presentations, the flip chart still continues to be the most effective presentation media of all" (Laskowski, personal communication, 2000).

Preparation

Flip charts can be prepared prior to the seminar so you can check to make sure that the important issues are included and words are spelled right. Charts can be presented simply or can be given a professional look. You can use stencils and projected images to letter and draw on the charts. You also can introduce simple cartoons, charts and tables. Using different colors, underlines and borders adds interest to the flip chart pages. Objects can also spice up a presentation. I have pasted items such as large leaves to signify autumn and large play dollars for a budget seminar.

Use

Flip charts are easy to use. You can elect to use or not use prepared material. Pages can be easily turned back to review previously presented information or to summarize the entire presentation. If the material lends itself to reuse, the flip chart is a good medium. Once created, you can use the presentation over again. I also use selected pages from one flip chart presentation for other presentations. This is accomplished by tearing out the page and taping it in the new presentation pad.

Lighting

Flip charts can be used with the lights on so you can connect with your audience. You are the focus, not the media. You can see people's faces and their reactions. When you really want to command a situation, the flip chart is an excellent presentation tool.

Spontaneity
An added benefit of flip charts is their spontaneity. You can capture the essence of the seminar by recording what is going on for all to see. They are a great tool for recording audience input, capturing brainstorming ideas and recording ideas gathered in small discussion groups.

Portability
The flip charts made for traveling are quite portable. The easel and flip chart are carried in a compact carrying case. They are not heavy and can be carried and set up with relative ease. They also can be checked as baggage. An alternative is to carry your prepared flip chart pages and rent an easel.

DISADVANTAGES OF FLIP CHARTS
Flip charts have some disadvantages—as one presenter said, "Don't let your flip chart turn into a flop chart."

Readability
You cannot use standard flip charts in a large room. Flip charts lose their effectiveness as the number of participants increase. The breaking point, when you should not use a flip chart, is when attendance is somewhere between thirty-five and forty participants.

Informal
Unless prepared professionally, most flip charts are informal. Depending on your seminar, this can be viewed as a benefit or a detriment.

Condition of Equipment
Easels can be a problem. Older ones may have lost their fasteners so that the pads cannot be secured. Poorly constructed easels may become wobbly and not stand straight, or may even collapse during a presentation. Even new easels have their problems. New sturdy-looking easels that were set up

for a presentation to New York City Managers could not hold the flip chart pad. It kept falling down. No matter what I or the hotel staff tried, nothing could hold the pads up. The problem was only solved by a hotel staff member acting as an easel.

Audience Acceptance

Hastily prepared flip charts that are poorly drawn, messy or incomplete can lower your audience's impression of your workshop's quality. I have found that audiences accept just about any type of markings on a flip chart drawn in action during a presentation but they do not have the same tolerance for charts that were prepared so hastily beforehand.

Eye Contact

When presenting information from your flip charts try to maintain eye contact with the audience. This is difficult and takes practice. When constructing flip charts, stop speaking and write out your comments coolly. Then turn, face your audience, and speak. Do not talk to your flip chart. Your audience will not hear what you are saying and will get frustrated.

Select the Appropriate Pad

Flip chart pads come in lined, grid and unlined versions. The unlined version is great for freeflow illustrations and processes. Lined and grid flipchart tablets have faint blue horizontal or checkerboard lines that are invaluable for lining up letters and objects.

Skip a Page

Leave a blank page between each page of prepared text. This keeps the underlying page from showing through and distracting from the current chart.

Markers

Continue to purge your set of markers and get rid of semidry and dried out markers. Most marker sets include yellow and light pink markers. Get rid of them; they do not show up well on flip charts. When using markers, use the thick side of the marker. The wider line looks better. Many people do not like the lacquerbase markers. Although they may be necessary for whiteboards, they should not be used on flip charts because they tend to bleed through the paper. The Sanford Company manufactures Mr. Sketch scented markers. These fragrant markers, which were originally created for children, have become very popular with seminar presenters and participants.

Prompters
You can make light pencil notes on your flip charts to remind yourself of key points. Put the notes in a recognizable place to enable you to glance quickly and determine right away whether there is a note on the page. One of my early mistakes was to scatter pencil notes at different places on the flip charts. They proved worthless because during the session, I could not find them easily.

Amount of Information
Do not try to put too much information on flip charts. Too much becomes too hard to follow. Flip chart paper is inexpensive, so go ahead and use different pages. If you want people to see a series of charts at once, you can tape them to the wall. Masking tape works well for this purpose. The 3M company has created a flip chart pad that has self-stick adhesive sheets. These can be posted to most wall surfaces such as vinyl, paneling, wallpaper and even concrete. The size is 25 by 30 inches which is a bit smaller than the standard-sized pad of 27 by 34 inches.

Write Legibly and Use Large Lettering
Your lettering should be two to five inches tall. On a blue lined flip chart each line is one inch. You should also use new marker pens whenever available.

OTHER TIPS

- When purchasing flip chart pads make sure they are perforated at the top to make tearing pages off easier.

- Keep the original box that the flip chart pads came in. It helps to keep pads neat looking.
- My wife June finds that a more evenly balanced chart can be created if she designs the page on paper before drawing it on the flip chart sheet.
- Don't dump an elaborately designed flip chart for a small mistake. Use correction fluid to cover up a mistake.
- Use a border or borders to frame text. It looks good and increases interest.
- Use frames, bullets, symbols, circles and boxes to enhance the look of the chart.
- Use bright, bold colors that complement each other.
- Use combinations of colors. Experiment to decide which combinations work best.
- Put different color Post-it notes to mark pages that you will be jumping ahead or back to.
- If you are addressing a small group you can use a tabletop flip chart. This portable flip chart converts to a sturdy tabletop stand thus eliminating the need for an easel stand.

TIP NUMBER 39:
Learn to Use Chalkboards and Whiteboards

The traditional blackboard is a wonderful presentation aid. Most hotels and conference centers provide chalkboards for meeting rooms. The whiteboard evolved from the old chalkboard. Whiteboards are usually white in color, magnetic and coated with a porcelain finish. They are less messy and allow the use of marking pens, which adds a variety of colors. However, you must use the right type of marker so that it can be erased easily.

Whiteboards are low cost and simple to use. There are no bulbs to burn out. The act of writing on the board creates the impression of spontaneity. Information once it has been recorded and displayed can be erased easily. Mistakes can be corrected quickly. Whiteboards are best for spontaneous idea development and brainstorming sessions. Whiteboards are meant for a small audience. After about the fifth row of tables, whiteboards are too difficult to read.

Electronic whiteboards are the latest step in the evolution of the chalkboard. Technology has been added to increase its functionality. Some are stand-alone whiteboards that come with their own printers. Notes written on the board's surface can be printed out on a 8-1/2 by 11-inch copy to hand out to your audience. More sophisticated boards connect to a computer allowing you to save whiteboard notes to a computer file. Some can be combined to projection systems to transform the whiteboard into an interactive computer screen. However, the more sophisticated the more expensive. In addition, many hotels and meeting facilities do not have electronic whiteboards for use.

TIP NUMBER 40:
Don't Overlook Overhead Projectors

The overhead projector is one of the oldest projection methods. It achieved prominence during World War II, when it was used for military briefings and training on various topics. Its popularity grew because of its flexibility and ease of use, and it is now the mainstay of business, education, government and the military.

ADVANTAGES OF OVERHEAD PROJECTORS

Overhead projectors are the presentation medium of choice by seminar providers. They are universally available at all meeting facilities. This allows you to travel light, having to carry only your transparencies. Technological advances in lighting have made them brighter and they are much quieter than in the past. They remain popular with seminar providers because of their affordability. A good overhead projector can be purchased for about one-tenth the price of the least expensive laptop and LCD projector combination. The following sections discuss some other advantages of overhead projectors.

Size of Group
The overhead projector works with small as well as large groups. I have successfully used overheads for a group of three and for a group of over five hundred. If the group gets too large, it becomes difficult for the back-row participants to clearly see the transparencies. If you have a large group, get the biggest screen available and project the image as high as possible on the screen. This will help the participants in the back see over the participants seated in the front rows.

Preparation
Overhead projector transparencies are easy to create. They can be prepared quickly and inexpensively. This permits you to easily update your presentation by discarding outdated transparencies. Advances in computer software permit seminar providers to inexpensively add color to their overhead transparencies. Cartoons, graphics and tables also can be easily added.

Reliability and Use
Overhead projectors stand up well even to the occasional abuse meted out by users. They do not have moving parts, so they are not prone to mechanical failure.

Overhead projectors are easy to set up and focus. They also are easy to use. You do not need an operator to use the projector, but with a large audience you may find it advantageous to have someone change the transparencies for you while you concentrate on the audience.

Transparencies offer you flexibility in your presentation. You can elect to skip or reorder your transparencies if the situation warrants. You can revisit previously shown transparencies. You also can reveal information point by point thus preventing your participants from reading ahead and coming to premature judgments or conclusions. This technique is known as revelation. If you wish to refocus attention on yourself for a major point, you can turn off the projector and all eyes revert to you, the presenter.

Reuse
Transparencies hold up well, especially if a frame is used. Once you create your presentation, you can easily add or delete transparencies to keep your presentation up to date and reflective of current events. If you use a standardized template, you can use transparencies in other presentations.

Lighting
With most modern overhead projectors, you don't have to turn down the lights when using the overhead projector. This allows you to clearly see the audience and respond to questions, concerns and even gestures.

Spontaneity
Special marking pens allow you to write on the transparencies during your presentation. If you carry marking pens and formatted transparencies, you can have participants fill in information on a transparency and show the results to the entire group. In one of my seminars, I have small groups of participants prepare goals for their business units, write them on preformatted overheads and then show them to the other audience members. Each group then receives constructive feedback on the relevance and importance of the goals.

Portablity
Several companies have developed portable overhead projectors that are lightweight and compact. This allows you to easily carry them to distant meeting sites. However, many of the portable overheads project a lesser-quality image than the standard projectors.

DISADVANTAGES OF OVERHEAD PROJECTORS

Overhead projectors have their disadvantages including burned out bulbs, low quality overheads and poor techniques for use.

Bulbs

Burned out bulbs are the most common malady of the overhead projector. Many overhead projectors have a lever that allows you to switch to a back-up bulb. Make sure that you check the back-up bulb before the session begins. You don't want to find out during your presentation that it has burned out and has not been replaced.

Quality of Overheads

Although the computer has made it easier to create professional-quality overhead transparencies, some presenters refuse to take the time to make them presentable. Some make overheads from a memorandum page or chart. There is nothing worse than viewing a detailed letter or memorandum that has been put on an overhead. Photos don't reproduce well on overheads. The quality of the projected image is not as good as that of a slide projector.

Use

Unless they have help, presenters must stay near the projector to change transparencies. Some presenters tend to rely too heavily on their transparencies. They put them on the screen and then read them word for word to the audience. This tends to irritate and bore participants. Some speakers will leave the projector on continuously instead of turning it off after they are done with it. Some of the older projectors are noisy. This makes it especially important to turn it off when people are done viewing a transparency.

TIPS ON USING OVERHEADS

Here are some tips on maximizing the use of overheads.

Designing Transparencies

Keep your transparencies simple. The purpose is to illustrate key points. Use bullets and limit the number to five or less. Make sure text is large enough to be read. Letters should be no smaller than thirty-point type. For larger groups increase the size of lettering. Your transparencies can be either horizontal (landscape) or vertical (portrait). Once you select an orientation, stick to it. It can be distracting to switch back and forth between vertical and horizontal.

Delivery Techniques

Don't stand in front of the projector. Some presenters get so involved in their presentation, they forget that their body can block the image. If a flip chart is being used in conjunction with the overhead, make sure the flip chart is positioned so that it is not necessary to move in front of the screen to get at it.

   Some experts tell you to turn the projector off when you're not using it. They say that it is distracting to your participants. Perhaps, but if you forget, don't worry. The power of your presentation wins over an overhead or slide.

Revelation and Masking

Revelation is a technique of uncovering or revealing points as you discuss them. A piece of paper is placed between the glass and transparency making it less likely to fall off as you slide it toward you. Masking is a process of showing the entire transparency and then covering everything else as you discuss individual points. Masking works best with tables of numbers or diagrams. Some people get offended by the use of revelation which is odd since LCDs use revelation very effectively. I use revelation sparingly, when I want people to focus on individual points and not jump to the bottom line.

Don't Read

Beginning presenters have a tendency to read from their transparencies. Before your session, practice paraphrasing all the points listed on your slides. Then explain why each is important and provide support by using examples. This will help keep you from reading the bullets. As a general rule, you should discuss, no matter how briefly, every bullet point you put on a slide.

Transparency Film
Make sure that the film you select stands up. Lettering on some transparencies flakes and falls off after being displayed a few times. Colored transparency film should be used sparingly because it is harder to read, especially in a lighted room.

Frames
The 3M company provides frames for transparencies. Frames help center the transparency on the glass and prevent light glare around the edges. Mounting transparencies in frames helps protect them and extend their life. You also can make pencil notes on the frames to remind yourself of important points. Post-it notes also can be used to accomplish the same purpose.

TIP NUMBER 41:
Don't Discount Slide Projectors
Prior to the introduction of the LCD projector, the slide projector reigned supreme. It was the medium of choice for presenting color slides, photographs and clip art.

ADVANTAGES OF SLIDE PROJECTORS
Before computer-generated visuals, the slide projector was the premier tool for presenting highquality, colorful, three-dimensional still pictures. Given its relatively affordable price, reliability and availability, it is still one of the most important meeting presentation tools. The following section discusses some of the advantages that make slide projectors so effective.

Size of Group

The slide projector works with small as well as large groups. With a zoom lens, a slide projector can be positioned at the back of a ballroom-size meeting room and project a brilliant image to a screen in the front. The slide projector works just as well in a small board room for five or six participants.

Preparation

Full-color slides can be produced very easily with presentation programs such as PowerPoint, Corel or Harvard Graphics, and an ink jet printer. Photographs, graphs, tables and charts can be imported and made part of the slide. Once slides are designed and a print made, they can be taken to a slide production service, which can create slides for approximately $10 each. It is also possible to create the slides in-house if you have a film recorder. Another nice feature of slides is that they can be duplicated very inexpensively. Slides can be mounted in cardboard, plastic or glass. Cardboard is the cheapest but should be avoided because the cardboard can jam the projector if it is bent or warped. Glass slides are heavy and will not jam a projector. The glass also helps create a sharper image. Plastic mounts are the most common and rarely jam the projector. They also are affordable.

Use

Slide projectors are easy to operate. Once the focus is set, you only need to push the remote button. New slides appear on the screen, and there is no need to line them up as is required with an overhead transparency. You do not need an aide to help with the projector, and the remote allows you to move around the room freely. Although most slide projectors are similar, some have different features including an automatic timer that advances slides after a set period of time. As with all presentation equipment, practice operating the slide projector before the session starts. I have seen presenters mistakenly activate the advance button and not be able to turn it off.

Reuse

Plastic or glass-mounted slides last a long time if stored in a dark place. Once you create your presentation, you can easily add or delete slides. If you use a standardized template, you can use slides in other presentations.

Portablilty
Slide projectors are relatively light and compact and are easily transported. Sturdy carrying cases are available that protect the projector, lenses and accessories. Most slide carousels are interchangeable, so you can carry the carousel and rent a slide projector.

DISADVANTAGES OF SLIDE PROJECTORS
While slide projectors can project brilliant colors on a screen, they have several disadvantages that have convinced me to quit using them for fee based seminars.

Reliability
Besides using projection bulbs, slide projectors have moving parts, making them more subject to possible malfunctions than overhead projectors. The three most common problems are carousel jamming, the remote control breaking and the bulb burning out. Presenters must also be careful about inadvertently dumping the slides when trying to loosen a jammed slide or when inserting a new one.

Lighting
You need to dim the lights (unless you use a rear projector) when using the slide projector. This makes it difficult for you to see participants' faces and connect with them. It also makes it difficult for participants to take notes.

Operation
If you are using a room that is hard to darken because of windows, skylights or direct sunlight, the visibility and effect of the slides is greatly reduced. You must also watch constantly for slides that have been inserted upside down or backwards.

Usage

Participants who are asked to view slides in a darkened room for more than thirty minutes tend to get drowsy. Some actually fall asleep! Slide presentations should be limited to a maximum of twenty to twenty-five minutes and broken up with other presentation approaches to avoid this problem.

TIPS ON USING SLIDE PROJECTORS

- Number your slides so that if they are mixed up you can put them in order quickly.
- A technique to check to see if slides are in order and right side up is to put them in a slide box right side up and draw a diagonal line with a marking pen from beginning to end. A break in the line enables you to quickly see if a slide is out of order or upside down.
- Standard slide carousels hold either 80 or 160 slides. The large-capacity slide carousels are great for slide storage but have a greater tendency to jam.
- You can add new text to existing slides by typing out descriptions and having the slide producer rephotograph them.
- When creating slides, decide whether your slides will be horizontal or vertical and use that format throughout the presentation. A presentation that switches back and forth is distracting to the audience. The most common slide format is (horizontal) landscape.
- Before the workshop, set up the projector and go through every slide to make sure they are focused, in order, and large enough to fill up the screen.
- Find out where the projection bulb is and how to replace it. Make sure that the replacement bulb works.
- Pace your slides so your audience will not get bored. When showing a slide make sure participants have enough time to grasp its meaning and understand it. My wife June gave me great advice concerning their use. "Don't click too slowly you'll bore them. And don't overreact and click too quickly. You know your slides, so it does not take you as long to comprehend

the message. Observe the audience and pace yourself based on their reactions."

Tip Number 42:
Use Video as a Supplement

Video is rarely used as the primary visual aid in a seminar. It works well as a supplemental method to emphasize an important point or change the presentation approach. Video should be used sparingly, and only if it accomplishes something that could not be done with another medium.

Videotapes are good options for seminar modules that don't need—or benefit from—interaction. Video is expensive—expect to spend several hundred dollars to several thousand dollars, depending on complexity and quality. Try to limit these types of presentations to twenty minutes or less. After that point, viewers may lose interest and get fidgety.

ADVANTAGES OF VIDEO

1. Video is colorful and can easily capture an audience's attention.
2. Video is relatively easy to use.
3. The room does not need to be darkened for video.
4. Video can be used with both large and small groups.

DISADVANTAGES OF VIDEO

1. Video tends to date quickly, especially if real people and objects are used. Outdated dress, hair styles and automobiles can divert audiences. Cartoons and illustrations tend to last longer.

2. It can be difficult to find a video that fits your program. The video may have some items that do not fit or are counter to the points you are attempting to emphasize.
3. The presenter has the limited role of turning the equipment on and off.
4. Video players are subject to malfunctions.
5. Video is expensive to produce.
6. Equipment is bulky and awkward to transport. Tapes, however, are easy to transport.

TIPS ON USING VIDEO

Video is best used by integrating it with course material. An effective use of video can be made by turning it off at critical points and discussing an issue or topic raised during the presentation. Another approach is to present questions to participants before the video is shown and then have them work on the questions after the showing. The following list details specific tips for using video.

- When using video, dim the lights rather than turn them off.
- Review the video prior to your presentation for focus, clarity and volume.
- Fast forward the videotape to the starting point prior to your presentation. You don't want to be fumbling after you've started—it will only add to your anxiety level.
- If you use video in an interactive mode, make sure you have access to a remote control so you can move around the room.
- For large groups it is best to project the video on a screen rather than a monitor.

Tip Number 43:
Learn to Use Computer-Assisted Presentation Products

The personal computer has revolutionized presentations. You can create a first-class presentation within hours using a personal computer, a presentation that used to take professional artists several days to design. For the seminar presenter, the payoff from computer-based presentations results from their magnificent on-screen slide show capabilities. You can present your seminar on your computer monitor or television screen. Another option is to link your computer to an LCD projector and display your slides on a screen or wall. To reap the full benefits of a computer-based system, you need a laptop computer, presentation software and an LCD projector.

ADVANTAGES OF COMPUTER-ASSISTED PRESENTATIONS

Computer-assisted presentation equipment has revolutionized the seminar business. If you can afford an LCD or similar machine, get it.

Size of Group

You can use computer-based presentations with both large and small groups. For very large audiences, you can use multiple screens or monitors. A zoom lens permits you to fill the screen with the image from wherever the projector is located.

Preparation

Computer-based presentations project beautiful, professional looking slides with colorful graphics. Unlike slides or overheads, if you don't count your time, production costs are nonexistent. There is no need to purchase supplies, such as overheads and frames, or send slides to a lab for processing.

Presentations can be prepared in advance or created in real time. The latest information can be instantaneously typed into the computer and shown on the screen. For example, near the end of a break, I can type some of the questions and comments I received during the break into the computer and project them on the screen. This technique adds a realtime element to the seminar and stimulates discussion-especially when you include participants names. Talk about customization!

Use

Computer-assisted presentations allow you to increase interest by using powerful special effects. You can

- Access the Internet during a seminar to showcase your Web site. You can also pull up other sites.
- Draw on your slides while you are giving your presentation. It is possible to switch to this mode while actually running your presentation.
- Interject videos, movies and sound clips during your presentation.
- Build slides. You can create slides that highlight the current bulleted item, dim previous bullets and not show upcoming bullets.
- Make last minute changes and create a new slide within seconds.
- Carry hidden slides that can be accessed only if you need them.

Reuse

Once a computer-assisted seminar presentation is created, you can rearrange, delete, or add slides with no additional cost and very little effort. Although computer-assisted systems cost more, you do not have to pay for new transparencies or slides.

Portability

With the development of the ultralight LCD projectors (five pounds or less), it is much easier to transport this equipment to distant meeting sites.

DISADVANTAGES OF COMPUTER-ASSISTED PRESENTATIONS

Computer-assisted presentations do have their disadvantages.

Use

Because you are working with a computer, software program and projection device, you have more possibilities of things not working right—or more often, not working together. This is especially true if you are renting some of the components. When your system goes down, it is not like replacing a burned out bulb. The biggest problems I encounter deal with compatibility. There are numerous LCD projection devices, and each one seems to require different hookups. This problem is compounded for presenters who use Macintosh equipment because most connections are PC based.

Because computer-based presentation programs provide so many options, it is easy to get carried away. Be careful about creating more interest in the software than the material you're presenting. You want to deliver your information in a smooth, natural way where the electronics and special effects are not too dominating.

Computer-based projectors have the same sleep-inducing qualities as slide machines. Try to break up your presentation with other activities.

Bulbs

LCD bulbs are much more expensive than slide and overhead projector bulbs. They also tend to dim over time as they are used.

Lighting

A darkened room used to be required for computer-assisted presentations. This made it difficult to interact with the audience. The newer projectors have such stong illumination, that the lights can be kept on.

Cost
Although prices continue to drop, the setup for computer-based presentations still requires a sizable investment as compared to overhead or slide projectors.

TIPS ON USING COMPUTER-BASED PRESENTATIONS

1. Use a remote control to advance or reverse your visuals. Without this device, you must stand by your computer to change visuals. An alternative is to have a helper change the slides.
2. Make sure your presentation is copied to the computer's hard drive and back it up on a disk and the Internet. A back-up disk should be carried with you just in case your computer crashes.
3. Don't overuse the progressive disclosure feature—building the text on slides by unveiling one line at a time helps when you want to emphasize a slide. If you do it with every slide, you are going to bore your audience to death.
4. Blank the screen when people have had time to review the slide and you have moved on to another item.
5. Learn to use the hidden slide feature in your presentation program. Having slides in the backup mode permits you to expand and contract your seminar depending upon how much time is available.
6. Don't be reluctant to use the draw feature on slides during a presentation. Some presentation programs allow you to use a tool to make notes and designs on your slides while you are giving a presentation.

7. If you are using an LCD projection panel, use a high-intensity overhead projector. Otherwise, the image will look bland and washed out.

8. If you are using a monitor, make sure it is large enough for the size of your audience. In some cases, you may need more than one monitor.

9. Don't get carried away with special effects. Use the same transition for your slides. As an alternative, switch the transition type when you begin a new module or topic.

10. Remember accessories, including a remote, mouse, batteries (if a laptop will be used without AC power), a back-up modem and extra disks.

11. Do several practice runs on your presentation. You can see how the slides look, how the transitions work and how the whole thing looks when put together.

Tip Number 44:
Have a Back-Up Presentation Mode Available

A word of caution: Always have a back-up presentation mode if you use electrical or mechanical equipment. No matter how comfortable you are with the technology, you don't want to be surprised with equipment that is incompatible, is not available or does not work. The best way to prepare yourself is to think of a terrible scenario such as getting off an airplane in New Orleans and all your equipment, slides and notes decide to fly on to Spain. No matter—you must still give an interesting and informative seminar to expectant participants or lose your entire up-front seminar investment.

6

Finding the Right Place to Present Your Seminar

The room droned on more than I did.

Trainer William Stone,
frustrated about the noisy air conditioner

Before you can initiate an earnest marketing approach, you must select and confirm the place where you intend to hold your seminar. You don't want to be in the position of having enough registrations for a profitable seminar with no place to host it.

This chapter deals with selecting a satisfactory workshop location and making sure the meeting room setup complements your seminar approach. There are several factors that must be considered when selecting a site for your seminar. Among them are the date, location, meeting size, available facilities and cost. There also are several different venues you can use—hotels, public and private meeting facilities, recreational settings, cruise ships and even your own home.

TIP NUMBER 45:
Select Your Seminar Date

Obviously, you cannot schedule the seminar until you secure a place to conduct it. As a general rule, you should start looking for your seminar location six to eight months before the event. You can shorten this time, but you may find the room choices are limited. Reservation personnel can advise you on low-usage dates and about other organizations that are holding meetings at the times you are considering. Major organizations select their conference locations at least two years in advance. Some are so large that they reserve most of the available meeting rooms in the city where they are holding the event.

You will want to determine the weather at the time of year you are considering the seminar. Seminar providers avoid the northwest and northeast during winter and the southeast during the high-humidity season. Many will schedule events in San Diego and Miami during the winter to provide a sunny incentive for snowbound participants. Likewise, it would be a shame to schedule a cruise seminar to Alaska during late season—only to be denied a view at Glacier Bay because of too much ice.

Before selecting the date for your seminar, it is a good idea to check the Internet for other things that are happening on the chosen days. The *Daily Globe* site (http:// dailyglobe.com/day2day.html) provides an extensive archive of special weeks, famous people's birthdays, holidays and events for each day of the year. For example, if you are considering January 22 for your seminar, here are some of the events and activities listed as occurring on that day:

Birthdays	Holidays	Events
Joseph Wambaugh	St. Vincent's Day Published	Ist American Novel
Linda Blair	Saints Day	Atom 1st Split
Ivan III (the Great)	Ukrainian Day	Laugh-In Debut
Lord Byron	Dance of the 7 Veils Day	Battle of Anzio
Sam Cooke	Answer Your Cat's Question Day	*Roe v. Wade* Decision Reached

In addition, during this week people celebrate International Printing Week, Jaycee Week, Worldwide Kiwanis Week and National Thrift Week. With this information, you can make decisions as to whether any of these holidays and events will conflict with your seminar. If your event theme or purpose fits in with a holiday, try to schedule it just before, during or after the holiday. On the other hand, if it does not fit in, don't schedule around it. The general rule is to avoid scheduling seminars around holidays and vacation periods.

Consider what days of the week are best for your audience. For a management group, Monday may not be a good day. They need to get to work and take care of their in-basket. On the other hand, barbers and hair stylists may prefer Monday for a workshop because that is their traditional off day.

After you select the seminar date, you then need to know the starting and ending hours of your program. If you are putting on a half-day or shorter seminar, the hotel may fit you in, even though they also have booked the room before or after your session. If you are putting on a one-day seminar, they may book the room for early evening. In these cases, the hotel enforces the time lines very rigidly. I have had banquet set-up workers come in and begin dismantling tables when my seminar ran over a wee bit. When setting seminar starting times, try to help participants avoid peak traffic hours, especially in the larger more congested cities, by setting start times, such as 9:00 or 10:00 A.M., or even 7:00 A.M.

TIP NUMBER 46:
Select the Type of Facility

There are several different types of facility choices available to the seminar entrepreneur. The most common include the following:

> Hotels and motels
> Convention and conference centers
> University and college sites
> Library meeting rooms
> Public buildings
> Public schools
> Community centers
> Mountain retreats
> Spas and resorts
> Cruise ships
> Your home

The Guide to Unique Meeting and Event Facilities, Web site address www.theguide.com provides a listing of over 4,000 meeting facilities in North America. The site permits you to search for unusual sites by indicating criteria such as location, meeting space required, date of meeting and number of rooms required. Information is provided on the following types of facilities:

1. College and university campuses
2. Conference centers
3. Retreat centers
4. Camps and lodges
5. Cultural, historical and event venues

TIP NUMBER 47:
Select the Seminar Region and City

The next step is to begin a search for a place to hold your seminar. Whether you are planning one seminar or a series of seminars, a typical search begins with selecting a region of the country, that is, southwest or east coast, and then selecting several candidate cities. Appendix C contains a listing of cities that are frequently used by the national seminar companies for their programs. If a city is used for a seminar by a national organization, it usually means that the city has met their criteria. Although the criteria for each organization varies, there are some things that help qualify a city, including the following:

1. Located near a major airport
2. Has a large population base from which to draw
3. Has convenient freeway access
4. Has an ample supply of meeting and sleeping rooms
5. Has a strong business draw
6. Has large state or federal government presence
7. Located near a college or university
8. Is close to or is the state capital
9. Has a strong cultural and entertainment base
10. Has a convention center
11. Has strong media activity—newspaper, radio and television
12. Has a good image

A good site selection technique is to narrow your possible cities to three and then apply your own criteria that match the type of seminar you are presenting.

Don't forget to match your program to the site. One year I thought it might be nice to include Las Vegas as a site for a series of budgeting workshops. Wanting to tie together business with pleasure, we booked the Hilton Hotel on the Vegas Strip. Unfortunately, I did not think through the issue. People do not come to Las Vegas to think about budgeting. In fact, they are preoccupied about making risky money decisions—how to beat the blackjack dealer or the slot machines.

The Las Vegas budgeting program produced the lowest registration of all the seminars in the series; in fact, it drew 60 percent fewer participants than any of the others. Because we received a minimum number of registrations, we went ahead and put the seminar on. Unfortunately, my minivacation turned out to be very costly—the faulty business decision soured the pleasure part.

A technique to increase attendance is to hold your program at the same location as a major conference that attracts the same participants as yours. For several years, I held a preconference, budgeting workshop for local elected officials one day before the Annual League of California Cities Conference. Many participants liked the idea of getting to the conference early, especially if it was held in a tourist-friendly city, such as San Francisco or San Diego. I found that the preconference format worked better than a postconference session because most people did not wish to stay around after the conference.

TIP NUMBER 48:
Select the Specific Seminar Site

Once you have selected the city or cities where you will be presenting your seminar, you need to select a hotel or meeting facility. Appendix D contains a list of national hotel chains, along with their toll-free phone numbers and URLs. Most of these Web sites have a wealth of helpful information, such as maps, room rates, meeting room configurations and sizes. The Embassy Suites site includes steps on planning a meeting online, along with meeting space available at each location. The Hilton site offers software that can be used to plan and communicate meeting room setups.

The hotel and meeting facility business is very competitive. Expect the personnel to be responsive and concerned about landing and keeping your business. If they are not responsive, go elsewhere. Find the person in charge of booking meeting rooms and develop a working rapport. Hotels differ in their staffing approach, so this person may be in the sales, catering or banquet department.

Something that is overlooked is the importance of selling your seminar to the hotel and meeting people. Make them think that your seminar is the most important event in the world and that they are a part of it. They book numerous meetings, so you want to stand out to them. Be up front; indicate to them that you are shopping facilities and give the criteria you will use to make the decision. If you are nearby, they may invite you for a site inspection. Sometimes, they offer lunch. Take them up on the offer; it will give you an idea of the food quality.

Many facilities maintain a book of letters from satisfied customers. Ask to see this book. It will give you an idea of which companies use the facility. It also will give you an idea of the type and quality of service to expect.

TIP NUMBER 49:
Use the Facility Selection Checklist

Here is a checklist of items that can help you select a facility for your seminar:

FACILITY SELECTION CHECKLIST

Hotel _____

Address _____

Contact person _____

Title _____

Phone number _____ Fax _____

E-mail _____ Web site _____

1. Access

- Is there a major airport within one-half hour driving time to the site?   Yes ☐   No ☐
- Does the airport provide free shuttle service to the airport?   Yes ☐   No ☐
- What other public transportation is nearby (i.e., train, bus)? _____
- Which major freeways are close to the facility? _____
- How close are the freeway on-ramps and off-ramps in miles? _____
- Is there a rush hour traffic problem   Yes ☐   No ☐
- Will road construction around the site be occurring at the time of the seminar?   Yes ☐   No ☐

2. Parking

- Is adequate free on-site parking available?
  Yes ☐   No ☐
- If there is a parking fee, will the facility validate?
  Yes ☐   No ☐
- If there is a charge for parking, what is it?
  Parking Fee _____
- What is the valet parking fee?
  Valet Fee _____

3. Accommodations

- What is the price range for sleeping rooms?
  From _____ to _____
- Will the facility offer room discounts to seminar
  participants?   Yes ☐   No ☐
- Is the facility clean and neat looking?   Yes ☐   No ☐
- Are adjacent hotels within walking distance that can
  accommodate participants?   Yes ☐   No ☐
- Is the site equipped to accommodate the needs of
  handicapped people?   Yes ☐   No ☐
- Will the hotel work with you on a late checkout?
                                           Yes ☐   No ☐
- Rate the cleanliness of the facility on a scale of 1 to 5
  (5 being *excellent*) 1 2 3 4 5

4. Food Service

- Does the hotel have a coffee shop or coffee service in the
  early morning?   Yes ☐   No ☐
- Is food service available in meeting rooms?
                                           Yes ☐   No ☐
- Will the facility provide (at no charge) a separate
  location for meals?   Yes ☐   No ☐

5. Surrounding Areas

- Are restaurant and shopping areas within
  walking distance?   Yes ☐   No ☐
- Are there local entertainment options for
  participants (i.e., theater, sports)?   Yes ☐   No ☐
- Is it safe to walk around the area at
  night?   Yes ☐   No ☐
- What are the major entertainment
  options_____

The following sections include issues to consider when completing the Facility Selection Checklist.

ACCESS TO THE FACILITY

Convenient access is an important consideration to your seminar participants. Look for a facility that is served by different transportation modes. How far must the participants travel? If they must travel more than one hundred miles, make sure that an airport is close to the site. If they are flying, low-cost or free airport shuttles are important. If they are driving, closeness to major freeway off- and on-ramps is crucial. Investigate the traffic patterns surrounding the facility. Does the area get congested at peak periods? Also, determine whether the site has easy ingress and egress. Some sites appear great on maps, but they are nightmares to drive to and from during peak traffic hours.

PARKING AVAILABILITY

Adequate parking is important to your participants. I once conducted a seminar at a hotel in Orange County, California, next to the Knotts Berry Farm amusement park. A national firm was providing a free seminar with a huge draw at the same hotel. It didn't take long for the hotel parking lot to fill up. My participants began arriving one hour later and found no parking available at the hotel. The only parking was in an adjacent lot run by Knotts, and they charged vehicles $9.00 to park. All thirty-five of my participants wound up in the amusement parking lot. Many were late to the session, and several were furious about the unannounced charge. To restore civility, I offered to reimburse participants, which they dutifully accepted. This obviously impacted my bottom line and taught me several lessons about parking, including the following:

- People must be warned about parking charges beforehand.
- If there is a parking charge, negotiate a validation process with the hotel for a portion or all of the fee.
- Get assurances (or a guarantee) from the hotel beforehand that there will be parking available for your seminar.

ACCOMMODATIONS

Overnight room accommodations are important if your participants require a room before or during the seminar. If you have several participants who want to stay overnight, you should attempt to negotiate a reduced rate for them. Although you should make it easier to rent rooms, avoid getting involved in directly renting rooms for participants. You may wind up footing the bill for no shows. With cruises and resort facilities, however, you may be required to make arrangements, provide deposits and guarantee all the rooms you reserve.

You will want to examine sleeping rooms to determine their cleanliness and quality. Also check their support facilities—exercise rooms, health clubs and eating and dining facilities. Safety and handicapped provisions are important factors to consider. Remember, if you get involved in arranging for accommodations, even if it is limited to negotiating group rates, people will hold you accountable for the quality of the experience.

For yourself, if you are staying overnight, you may wish to arrange for a late checkout. If you are flying out, it is convenient to have a private place to change and freshen up after the seminar. Recognize, however, that many facilities want you out at the stated checkout time and will resist any requests to extend. I have found that I have more success with a late checkout arrangement when I request it at the time of contracting for the meeting room. If you do this, make sure that the late checkout is specified in the agreement or a side letter.

FOOD SERVICE

Whether you provide food or leave meal arrangements to participants, you want to make sure that food options are available and that the food is of satisfactory quality. If possible, eat at the establishment prior to your seminar. If you are considering serving dinner, lunch or breakfast at your seminar, get a copy of the menu and check selections and prices. Also, having food served in the same room as your seminar is very distracting during setup and cleanup. Check to see if the facility can provide a separate location such as a patio, large hall area or adjacent room for the meal. Many will provide this eating location without an additional charge.

SURROUNDING AREAS
The proximity of the facility to other attractions becomes more important if participants are going to spend the night. The ideal facility is one that is located in a safe neighborhood that has restaurants, shopping and entertainment establishments close by. A real plus is if it is safe for participants to walk around at night.

TIP NUMBER 50:
Use the Meeting Room Assessment Checklist

The meeting room location and layout have a significant impact on the success or failure of your seminar. Think of the meeting room as your personal office for the length of the seminar. Is it built and set up to enhance presentations, or does it have features that distract you or your participants? A bad location or an inadequate room can get you off to a bad start or even ruin an otherwise brilliant workshop.

As mentioned above, there is nothing like an on-site inspection of the meeting room you will be using before you book it. However, that may be difficult if the meeting room is being used during your visit. You may be shown a comparable room that turns out to be very different from the room you wind up with. Here is a checklist for selecting the meeting room.

MEETING ROOM ASSESSMENT CHECKLIST

Facility _____

Address _____

Contact person _____

Title _____

Phone number _____ Fax _____

E-mail _____ Web site _____

1. Meeting Room Cost and Deposit

Cost   _____

Deposit   _____

2. Meeting Room Size and Configuration

Total square footage   _____

Room shape (i.e., rectangle, round)   _____

Capacity   _____

Dimensions   ____ by ____

Are breakout areas for smaller groups
available at no cost?   Yes____ No ____

3. Meeting Room Characteristics

Room colors   _____

Does the room have posts or lights that
block participants' views to the front? Yes____ No ____

Are windows a distraction?   Yes____ No ____

Is the room located at the end or in
between other meeting rooms?   Yes____ No ____

Can flip chart paper be taped to the
walls?   Yes ____ No ____

Are the dividers between rooms
soundproof?   Yes____ No ____

Is the ceiling fourteen feet high?   Yes____ No ____

4. Lighting and Utilities

Can the lighting be controlled within
the room?   Yes____ No ____
Are lights shining over or
on the screen?   Yes____ No ____
Are there sufficient electrical outlets?   Yes____ No ____
Can the air conditioning be controlled
within the room?   Yes____ No ____
Is there is a phone line for Internet
access?   Yes____ No ____

5. Meeting Room Furnishings and Fixtures

Does the room have distracting mirrors
on the walls?   Yes____ No ____
Do the drapes adequately close to
prevent light from shining in?   Yes____ No ____
Is the door at the rear of the meeting
room?   Yes____ No ____
Do chairs have cushions that are
comfortable?   Yes____ No ____

6. Equipment

Does the facility provide any free audiovisual
equipment? _____
Who rents equipment and what are their rates?
(name and phone) _____
- Overhead projector _____
- Screen_____Size: _____
- Overhead projector _____
- Flip chart holders _____
- Full flip chart pads_____
- Slide projector_____
- LCD or other projector_____
- Podium_____
- Microphone _____

- PC _____
- Monitor _____
- Video player_____
- Tables _____
- Other equipment _____
- Other items _____

The following sections discuss the issues to consider when using the meeting room assessment checklist.

MEETING ROOM COST AND DEPOSIT

Should you attempt to negotiate the price of the meeting room? Yes. You want to get the best price you can. Some people will secure a satisfactory meeting room and then shop around for a better price. I do not use this approach because of the time and effort it requires. I prefer to do a spot phone or Internet check of the prevailing meeting room prices within the area and then attempt to negotiate a fair price with my preferred meeting facility. If they are competitive, I go with them. I like to translate the difference in room rates to the number of participants that it will take to close the gap. Very rarely does the higher rate exceed the cost of the lower rate by more than the registration fee of one to three participants. Why not go for the better room and put your energy into getting more participants?

The price of meeting rooms varies widely and is influenced by several factors, such as the location of the facility, the season, occupancy rate, day of the week, room size and demand for the room. You are in a much better position to bargain for a meeting room if there are no major events being held and if there are rooms available. You also are in a better position to negotiate if your group will need sleeping rooms and meals. The negotiation approach I find most successful is to get an idea of the price ranges for meeting rooms within the area, select a lower figure, and indicate that I have a limited budget that cannot exceed the specified price. I am always more successful when I include lunch for the participants. Facilities will usually reduce the meeting room cost from 50 to 100 percent if you serve a meal during the seminar. I was also able to use the City of Sacramento training facility for a management skills workshop by providing three free enrollments to the city's employees.

Should cost be the major factor in your decision? No. Although you should keep your costs as low as possible, meeting room characteristics are more important. You may get a great deal on a meeting room only to find that it has physical flaws that hurt the image or the presentation of your seminar. You first want to secure a room that has a good layout, satisfactory ambiance, adequate lighting and functioning utilities.

A facility may put a meeting room on tentative hold while you firm up your plans. Within a few weeks (or when they get another query about the room), you will be asked to make a definite booking. At that time, they will send you a contract and ask for a nonrefundable deposit. In many cases, the request for deposit comes before you have received any registrations. This is up-front risk money, and you should be prepared to lose it. One thing you can do to minimize the risk is to negotiate the amount downward as much as possible.

Read the contract carefully and determine what the provisions are. A cancellation provision that has crept into some contracts provides that if the event is canceled, the renter forfeits the deposit, as well as an amount equivalent to the total meals ordered. Don't accept this provision. As with all contracts, ask for an explanation of all the items that are unclear. Although it is tedious, have the contractor take you through the contract and explain every provision. I also ask them to cross out items I do not agree with.

Even though the phone numbers and Web site addresses (Appendix D) are provided for the national hotel chains, don't use them to set up your meetings. Use them to get in touch with the specific site you are considering. You will have a better chance of getting a negotiated rate at the local level.

You may also be asked to fill out a credit statement or leave an open credit card. This is especially true in highly competitive areas, such as San Francisco, New York, Chicago and Houston.

MEETING ROOM SIZE AND CONFIGURATION

Determining the right meeting-room size is difficult, at best, and almost impossible for your first seminar. In most cases, this decision must be made before you receive any registrations. If the participant estimate is too high, you will incur an additional expense for an unnecessarily large room. You will also find yourself in a room too large for your group. More difficult, if your estimate is too low, participants will be crammed into a small room. Or worse yet, you may not be able to accommodate your entire group.

Level with the hotel about your quandary. Give them your best estimate of the minimum and maximum number of participants. Ask them if it is possible to change if there are larger or smaller rooms available when the number of participants becomes known. If your participant count changes, notify the facility immediately. In most cases, they will attempt to accommodate your group if they have other rooms available.

The type of session you hold and the amount and type of equipment you use will influence your decision on the size of room needed. If you are going to use interaction exercises, participants are going to need more space than if they remain passive and merely watch. Likewise, the more audiovisual and training aids you use, the more space you will need to function properly. Recognize that in many cases, hotels and facilities do not take these factors into account when estimating needed room space.

An otherwise adequate room can be deemed useless if it is poorly designed. Bob Pike, editor of *Creative Training Techniques* newsletter, says the ideal seminar meeting room has a width to length ratio of 1:1.2, such as 100 feet wide by 120 feet long. "Asking for rooms with close length to width ratios keeps you out of long, narrow rooms that feel more like boxcars than a flexible learning environment," says Pike (Pike, personal communication, 2000). Actually, I have found that a room configuration of 1 to 1.4 is satisfactory for most seminars.

When estimating the room capacity, make sure that the facility uses the type of room setup you intend to use. Round tables take considerably more space than classroom seating.

MEETING ROOM CHARACTERISTICS

Every meeting room has its own personality. Some are old, dark, cramped and generally depressing. Many older hotels with beautiful and charming outside exteriors have depressing meeting rooms. In contrast, some of the newer ones are beautifully decorated, gracefully furnished and open and inviting. Most fall somewhere in between.

When selecting your meeting room, check the colors. Room color can affect the general attitude of the participants. Are they compatible with the theme of your seminar? As a rule, the best colors for informational seminars are soft, low-key colors, such as beige and earth tones.

Determine how high the meeting room ceiling is. A low ceiling creates a claustrophobic feeling. It also makes viewing of the screen difficult for the participants seated in the back of the room. I prefer a ceiling at least fourteen feet high.

Does the room have posts that block participant viewing of audiovisual materials? What about lighting fixtures hanging from the ceiling? Many meeting rooms are not only used for seminars; they are also used for service club meetings, wedding receptions and banquets. Ornate chandeliers may be great for weddings and other social events, but you want to make sure that these fixtures do not obscure participants' views of AV screens and flip charts. Windows also can be a distraction if there is a great view outside. Are there screens or drapes that can be closed?

I use flip charts in my seminars and like to tape them to the walls during the session. If you have this need, make sure that there is sufficient space to tape your charts at eye level or higher. In some meeting rooms, this is not possible because the walls are full of mirrors, pictures, windows and fixtures. You want to make sure that the facility will let you tape or pin charts to the walls.

How satisfactory are the barriers between rooms. Are they soundproof? A good test is to take a portable radio with you when you check the room. Place the radio behind the barriers next to your room and turn up the volume. How much noise can be heard? Is it tolerable?˙

Unfortunately, many of the physical factors of the meeting room are fixed and cannot be changed. But some things can be done to enliven the room. Can distracting pictures be removed? Try posting colorful flip charts on the wall as soon as possible. Ask the hotel to decorate the room. If it is a particular season or day, have them decorate to the theme. This is where the *Daily Globe* Web site can be helpful. Is it near Halloween or Christmas? What about St. Patrick's Day? One year in an old hotel in downtown Sacramento (the hotel was the *in* place but very drab), we enlivened the room with green and white crepe paper, gold pots and leprechauns. The room was a hit to the envy of other seminar leaders.

UTILITIES AND LIGHTING

Seminar providers find out very quickly how important participant comfort is. If people are not comfortable, you are not going to have a successful seminar. The five most common participant complaints, in frequency order, are as follows:

1. Too cold
2. Distracted by outside noise
3. Too warm
4. Can't see
5. Can't hear

Most of these complaints arise from the room infrastructure—heating, cooling, electrical and lighting systems. Fortunately, most thermostats are now locked in a box and cannot be changed without a special key. This has ended the battle over the thermostat, which arises when people fight over their preferred temperature setting.

In many older meeting rooms, the air conditioning is turned on in the morning to make sure the room is sufficiently cool in the afternoon. As a result, the room becomes very cold in the morning. It remains cold until the room fills with people, and the outside air warms up. In the seminar confirmation letter, suggest that participants wear layered clothing. This will prepare them for the changing temperature. When someone complains about the coldness, check to see if they are sitting below a vent. If so, move them away from the vent. In addition, get participants moving around with group activities. When you have complaints, keep pressure on the front desk, manager and engineer to solve the problem.

Find out how to operate the meeting room lighting. If you use a mixture of slide projection, flip charts and group activities, you need to know how to operate the lighting system. Check to make sure spotlights do not shine on the screen. I have had cases where ceiling spotlights shined directly on the screen, and the only remedy was to unscrew the bulb.

Meeting room phones also should be checked. Find out where they are so you can contact hotel personnel when needed. If you intend to access the Internet, make sure the lines are capable of handling Internet hookups.

MEETING ROOM EQUIPMENT, FURNISHINGS AND FIXTURES

Many seminar providers accumulate their own presentation equipment, such as easels, overhead projectors, slide projectors and projection screens. For seminars that are held within driving distance, they save money by using their own equipment. For seminars out of town, they must decide whether to attempt to carry equipment with them or rent it. If your seminar is being sponsored by an organization, always insist that they provide the necessary equipment.

When I first began using an LCD projector, I trundled all over with it and my laptop computer. After several trips, however, I decided it was not very practical. The equipment was heavy and bulky. Airport screeners not only wanted me to turn on my computer, I had to hook up and turn on the

LCD. I also had to worry about theft at the airport and hotel room. I decided the hassle was such that it would be more practical to rent the equipment or revert to the old trusty overhead projector when traveling.

If you are doing contract training, always check to see if the contractor has an LCD available. Make sure your computer is compatible with their LCD. I use Macintosh equipment and have found that most providers do not have the necessary hookups for Macintosh. They say they have Macintosh hookups—and at one time they did have them. But, due to lack of use, they have been set aside or lost.

If the room has window drapes or shades, make sure they close properly. You do not want outside slivers of light blazing through when you are showing slides. Some rooms have large drapes that can only be closed by a motor operated by site personnel. Make sure that you can open or close them before the session. Mirrors can also present a problem. I presented a workshop in a recreation center dance room that doubled as a meeting room. Every wall was adorned with mirrors. A four foot band of mirror proved to be very distracting to participants as every time they looked up they saw themselves. The problem was solved by taping flip chart paper over all the mirrors.

If there is only one door, make sure it is at the back of the room to minimize disruptions and make it more comfortable for participants.

Here are some other things to check:

- Are the chairs comfortable? Are they cushioned? Don't overlook participants' comfort.
- Do the tables have skirts? People are uncomfortable sitting at tables that do not have skirts.
- Is there a portable stage or bandstand that needs to be moved?
- Are microphones available? Do they work?
- Is the meeting room sufficiently buffered from kitchen, convenience area, elevator and restroom noise?
- Will the facility provide breakout rooms or tables for small group discussions and activities?

Find out who provides audiovisual equipment and get a copy of their price list. Most hotels and meeting facilities use a contract service to provide seminar equipment. Prices can vary considerably. You also might check to see if the hotel provides free equipment such as chalkboards and flip charts. You also should check to see what amenities the facility provides. Common amenities include candy, mints, note pads, pens and pencils.

TIP NUMBER 51:
Determine the Participant Seating Setup

The room setup is another important function that needs careful thought. The setup you select will be influenced by the amount of audience participation you want and the size of the room. If your seminar simply involves providing information, you can use a theater-type arrangement, with chairs lined up in rows. If, however, you intend to use small group discussions or demonstrations, more room is required. There are four basic room setups (with variations) that you can use for your seminar—theater, U shaped, classroom and cafe. Each has its advantages and disadvantages.

Theater.
The theater setup focuses the entire group toward the speaker and the visuals that are being used. Theater setups provide a chair for each participant lined up in rows, without tables. This setup does not encourage interaction as most of the participants see the backs of other participants' heads. Theater setting is the most efficient in terms of seating capacity—it allows more people into a room than the other configurations. If you use theater-style seating, try to set up one or more aisles so that you can get closer to the audience. Allow from ten to twelve square feet per

participant for this type of seating. However, with all seating arrangements, remember to leave front space for the speaker and AV equipment.

If you use the theater setup, it can be made more interactive during your session by having, for example, the first, third and fifth rows of participants turn around and face the participants behind them. This assumes that the chairs can be moved.

Classroom.

With this setup each person faces forward and has a table surface in front of them for note taking and reading. The classroom setup works best when the goal is to impart information. The seminar presenter is in a position to see all the participants. The focus of the participants is toward the front. Similar to the theater arrangement, interaction is not one of the benefits of this setup as participants see the back of someone's head. If you are using eight-foot tables that are eighteen inches wide, allow from seventeen to nineteen square feet per participant for this type of setup.

U Shape.

The U-shaped arrangement is a preferred setup for a group of six to twenty-four participants when interaction is desired. With this setup, tables and chairs are arranged in a U shape, with the seminar leader and AV equipment situated at the open end. The presenter can make close contact with all participants by entering the U. Although I have seen groups of sixty arranged around a U, I would not recommend it. The primary benefit of the U is to let people look at and talk to each other. As you extend the size of the U, people lose the ability to see and hear each other. As it expands outward, it pushes participants against the walls. Also, very few rooms can handle a large U shape setup. This setup is the least efficient in terms of seating capacity. To form the U, tables are pushed outward toward the walls. This leaves a large void in the middle of the room. Some presenters will use a double U configuration to take up some of this space. If you are using eight-foot tables that are eighteen inches wide, allow from thirty-six to forty square feet per participant for the U-shaped layout.

Cafe.
The cafe (also referred to as banquet) setup involves a cluster of round tables. From three to ten people are seated at each table. The cafe setup is good for stimulating interaction between small groups of people. With this setup, the presenter works from the front of the room. If the seminar leader is alternating between presentations and group activity, it is a good idea to use half-round seating. With this setup, participants face forward, using only half of the table. Assuming four-foot rounds with six chairs, allow fourteen to sixteen square feet per participant.

The following table shows the seating capacity for the four configurations for three different size rooms.

Setup	Required Square Feet Per Person	Seating for a 625 Square Foot Room	Seating for a 952 Square Foot Room	Seating for a 1,800 Square Foot Room
Theater	10 to 12	52	80	150
Classroom	17 to 19	32	50	94
Cafe	14 to16	39	60	112
U Shaped	36 to 40	15	25	45

It is a good idea to submit the room setup requirements in writing, accompanied by a sketch showing the location of tables, chairs and equipment to the banquet manager before the session. Keep a copy and bring it to the session.

TIP NUMBER 52:
Determine Whether You Will Serve Beverages and Meals

Most seminars that are provided for a fee customarily include beverages as part of the program. For morning seminars, coffee, decaf and tea are usually served. For afternoon seminars, soft drinks are the preferred beverage. A full-day seminar may include coffee in the morning and soft drinks in the afternoon. Most hotels and meeting facilities will not let you bring in beverages or food for participants, so you are at their mercy. When obtaining the price of beverages and meals, find out the service charge and sales tax. These two items can raise the cost for beverages and meals from 20 to 30 percent.

For seminars less than four hours, meals usually are not provided to participants. For a one-day or longer seminar, you must decide whether to include meals as part of the program. Although there are relatively few studies on the impact of meals on participants' decisions to attend, those conducted seem to support the notion that lunches are not a major inducement to register for seminars. Howard Shenson, in his book *How to Develop & Promote Successful Seminars & Workshops,* cites one study that showed that lunches were not important in obtaining registrations. The promoter divided in half a mailing list of forty thousand names for a strategic planning seminar, with half the brochures offering a lunch and the other half not mentioning lunch. The mailing that included lunch produced thirty-six registrations, whereas the no-lunch mailing produced thirty-eight registrations (Shenson 1990, 168). Other studies seem to support this conclusion: that meals in themselves do not influence participants' decisions to register.

Meals, however, can be used as a trademark. The Western Governmental Research Association (WGRA) offered thousands of seminars to public officials for over twenty years, with lunches being provided as part of the program. People knew if they attended a WGRA seminar, lunch was included. The practice was so ingrained, that competitors knew that they would have to provide lunch to successfully compete with WGRA.

If you are not going to serve lunch, check to see if there are enough restaurants in the area to accommodate participants during the lunch break. Some areas have enough eating establishments, but they are so busy during the lunch hour that participants cannot get in and out in a reasonable period of time. This may induce you to provide lunch or, as an alternative, schedule the lunch break before the peak usage period.

If you are presenting a seminar that extends beyond one day, you may want to include meals. These meals can be used as opportunities for guest speakers and for participants to get to know each other on a more personal level. Another approach is to hold a networking breakfast prior to the seminar. This also gives you and the participants an opportunity to get to know each other.

Many hotels will reduce or even waive the meeting-room price if a meal is served. The practice varies and is dependent on the number of participants, the cost of the meal and the availability of meeting rooms. Don't expect much of a break if all the meeting rooms are booked.

If you decide to provide a meal, make sure that the facility is capable of delivering the meal when you want it. You don't want to be served after a large group is served. Large groups inevitably take longer than planned and sap the energy of the servers. You also should avoid having lunch served in your meeting room. Setup is intrusive and disrupts your seminar. Seminar start-up may be delayed if servers do not return to clean up at the scheduled time.

Another consideration is the menu. You need to match the menu to your participant's customary expectations. You obviously wouldn't serve hot dogs to a management group, or quiche to construction workers. A heavy lunch will make your participants sleepy and lethargic—so go on the light side. In every group you will find some who prefer a vegetarian dish. Most hotels will provide an alternate menu if you notify them beforehand.

Seminar providers use two other meal options. One is to give participants a meal coupon that can be exchanged at the hotel coffee shops and restaurants. A limit is usually placed on the coupon, such as "This coupon can be used for a lunch priced up to $15 at the Jolly Roger Coffee Shop or Striker Restaurant." A second approach is to provide lunch but offer a discount to participants who do not wish to attend the sit-down lunch. If you use this approach, make sure that participants specify their preference sufficiently in advance so that you can make arrangements with the hotel.

TIP NUMBER 53:
Monitor Advanced Shipments of Seminar Materials

If you cannot carry notebooks and handouts with you, shipping will be necessary. Unfortunately, when you ship material, you increase the risk of it getting lost. Or your packages may arrive at the specified designation, but it may be too late to use them in your seminar.

Determine how facility personnel handle materials. Find out how many days before the seminar your packages should be sent to the facility. If material is sent too early, it may be moved to an obscure location that people forget about. You should find out where the material is stored and who is responsible for overseeing it. Ask what happens if material gets lost. I ask for the home phone number of the person responsible for custodianship over seminar shipments. Even if they do not provide the number, this request usually produces more attention to the safekeeping of my material.

TIP NUMBER 54:
Consider Home-Based Seminars

A sometimes overlooked place to hold seminars is one's own home. Dan Poynter, author of over eighty books and revisions, including his highly successful book *The Self-Publishing Manual,* has been hosting workshops at his beautiful Santa Barbara mountain home for the last sixteen years. Each year, Dan conducts four book promotion workshops in his house for eighteen participants, who come from all over the country. Dan believes that a home-based workshop is very special, "People appreciate it because it is personal. A special bond is created. They relate to you when they see where you live and work. It allows me to show my business approach" (Poynter, personal communication, 2000).

According to Dan, a seminar conducted at home costs less than a hotel-based seminar, but you need to consider indirect costs, such as wear and tear on your furniture, fixtures and carpeting. The constant usage, trafficking and spillage will require more frequent cleaning and replacement. You also should expect much higher utility bills because you must maintain a comfortable environment, using heating and air conditioning, for your participants. Although your systems may work well for a four-member family, they may become stressed and inefficient when called upon to provide comfort to a group four to five times as large. Functioning bathrooms are extremely important and need constant attention and maintenance. A plumbing stoppage can ruin an otherwise successful seminar and require you to have a reliable plumber standing by to respond immediately. Then, too, participants need access to phones, and if there is no convenient way to call out, you will wind up providing and underwriting phone service for your participants. Although cellular phones are helping to lessen this problem, you must still expect to incur a cost for phone calls.

If there are no eating establishments nearby, you must provide meals. "When you get into the food business, you want to make sure the menu is compatible with the expectations of your participants," says Dan. "The majority of the people who attend my workshops are in the 40 to 60 age range and they desire quality food" (Poynter, personal communication, 2000). Dan has adapted the menu to his participants liking and has made meals an important part of the program. At the end the first day's session, Dan provides a barbecue dinner for attendees and any accompanying spouses who are not attending the seminar. "The barbecue provides a relaxed atmosphere for people to mingle, to get to know each other on an informal basis and to develop business contacts."

In-home seminars allow Dan immediate access to data, material and equipment. "If someone needs information, I have access to all my files. I can query computer databases and make sufficient copies very quickly. I could never carry all this information and equipment to a distant hotel meeting room"(Poynter, personal communication, 2000).

If you are considering offering seminars out of your home, check with neighbors to make sure that they do not have any problems with it. Home-based seminars have little impact on neighbors, other than parking, traffic flow and perhaps noise. Check with your local government before you send out a brochure advertising your home as a seminar site. There may be zoning codes that regulate home business activities. The following checklist contains issues to consider before using your home for seminars:

HOME-SEMINAR CHECKLIST

1.   Do you have an adequate meeting room for participants? Most homes are not designed for group activities.
Make sure that you have at least one room that can accommodate all your participants. This room needs comfortable
seating and adequate space so participants are not too
cramped.

2.   Can you control the sunlight? Many homes are built
to take advantage of sunlight. In the case of seminars, you
want to block it out so that it is not a distraction, especially if
you are using projection equipment.

3.   Do you have sufficient parking? Some of your participants will be arriving by their own vehicle and you will
need to have sufficient parking available. You also need to
be prepared for those who bring small and large motor
homes.

4.   Do you have the infrastructure to support seminars?
Your air conditioning and heating system must also be able
to handle the additional load. What could be a very pleasant
experience can turn into a nightmare if the room climate is
not maintained at a comfortable level.

5.   Do you have a sufficient number of bathrooms? You
need sufficient bathrooms to accommodate all of your participants. You don't want participants standing in lines waiting to use a bathroom. I tried using my mountain cabin for
seminars. It had a great view and plenty of sleeping rooms
but inadequate bathroom facilities. This simple fact ruined
an otherwise wonderful mountain experience.

6.   Have you checked with your neighbors? Meet with
your neighbors before you decide to hold a seminar in your
home. Typical concerns are parking, traffic flow and noise.
You'll find that most appreciate being told before the

session, rather than during. Very rarely will you find any objectors, unless they are mad about something else.

7.	Does your local government allow home occupations? Many local governments require a permit to operate a business out of one's home. They also may apply conditions, such as limiting the number of seminars or the number of participants for each seminar.

8.	How will you handle meals? Do you have a restaurant nearby that can accommodate your seminar participants? Can you make arrangements for them to sit together and eat at a specific time? Do you intend to provide some of the meals yourself?

9.	If you intend to handle meals, do you have the facilities? Will you cater meals or cook them on site? If you cook them onsite, do you have the kitchen facilities that can handle a large group?

TIP NUMBER 55:
Consider a Cruise Seminar

Attending a seminar while leisurely cruising on an ocean or river appeals to many people. There is nothing quite like standing on the deck, leaning out over the rail and observing the tantalizing waves while contemplating an intriguing topic that was discussed moments earlier at the onboard seminar.

Cruise ships now visit close to two thousand ports located all over the world. You can sail any sea and all the major navigable rivers. You can select a small intimate ship with fewer than fifty passengers or a large, MEGA ship with over three thousand passengers. Cruises range in length from two days to six months and longer. Cruise ships no longer have different ticket classes. Although people pay different prices for cabins based on deck, size of room and view, everyone has total access to every area on the ship. Each person enjoys the same service, activities, food and entertainment as everyone else on board.

When properly planned, cruise seminars offer better value than land-based seminars. Food does not cost extra, and cruise ships will arrange for private parties for no or minimal cost. Most ships have meeting rooms that can be used for seminars. Many also provide audiovisual equipment, including slide projectors, overhead projectors, screens, white boards, easels and flip charts. Some are even providing LCD and other advanced projectors. Both the meeting room and standard equipment are usually provided at no additional cost.

When Tim and Kim Scutter of the Personal Strengths Publishing Company decided to establish an annual conference, they wanted to provide a meaningful and memorable experience for participants. "We wanted participants to network and enjoy the full experience of a seminar without intruding phone calls. Confinement on a ship increases the opportunity for people to sit down and chat with each other," says cruise coordinator Kim Scutter. "Getting people away from their offices and out on the ocean relaxes them. They can bring their spouses and make it a family outing. It is like taking a mini-vacation while working" (Scutter, personal communication, 1999).

Personal Strengths Publishing decided on a four-day, three-night cruise. People boarded the ship on Friday afternoon and disembarked Monday morning. "We selected a weekend cruise because it is easier for consultants and trainers to take off Friday through Monday. A week-long trip is a bit much. A weekend is easier on their schedules," advises Scutter. Participants boarded in Los Angeles, cruised to Ensenada, Mexico, and returned to Los Angeles.

TIP NUMBER 56:
Plan in Advance for a
Cruise Seminar

A cruise seminar requires a great deal of advanced planning and more coordination than a land-based seminar. You should begin your planning no later than eighteen to twenty-four months before the projected seminar date. A good starting point is to select a destination. Do you want to cruise the Caribbean, Panama, the Mississippi River or the Mediterranean? Once you decide on where you are going, you can determine which cruise lines provide cruises to the destination. Several Web sites are available that will help you select a cruise ship and destination. They also provide cruise planning, cruise line selectors, message boards and chat rooms, shore excursions, customer satisfaction polls, floor plans and sample menus. Here are five such sites:

1.   CruiseMates: www.cruisemates.com
2.   The Travel Company: www.mytravelco.com
3.   Cruise Ship Center & Cabin Exchange:
      www.cruise2.com
4.   TravelPage.com: www.cruisepage.com
5.   Get Cruising! www.getcruising.com

When working with a travel agency, see if they have a cruise specialist on staff who has a Master Cruise Counselor's Certification from the Cruise Lines International Association, which means he or she has undergone training and visited at least fifty ships. The cruise specialist should be able to give you general information about the ship you are considering. When using a travel agent, be cautious of those who promote a single cruise line.

Mary Long, President of Travel Resource Center, has arranged and presented hundreds of seminars aboard ships.

She has also written a book, *The Complete Guide to Conducting Seminars at Sea.*

TIP NUMBER 57:
Critically Evaluate the Cruise Ship Before Booking

Once your seminar participants step aboard the cruise ship, they are literally captives for the entire journey. Unlike a land-based seminar, they cannot change their venue. For this reason, cruise seminar participants closely link the quality of the cruise ship and its amenities with the success or failure of your seminar. You do not want to select the wrong ship for your seminar.

Cruise Reviews at www.crusiereviews.com provides a wealth of information on the major cruise ships. You want to visit this site before making a final selection on a cruise ship. Passengers who have experienced the cruise beforehand post reviews on this site. Personal information for each reviewer is provided, such as name, occupation, number of cruises taken, sailing date and itinerary. Some reviewers also will list their e-mail address for further information. Here are some review excerpts from different travelers to give you a sample of the valuable information provided:

FOOD AND SERVICE

> *The food was much better than we anticipated. In fact it was excellent. (I am a retired owner of an award winning restaurant on Long Island which was noted for service).*

> *I was overall disappointed with the restaurant service. The waiter himself never said two words to my husband and I. Ditto for the Maitre'D and Head Waiter. I believe the ship needs to concentrate more on the quality of their food rather than the quantity.*

SHIP ACTIVITIES

Ships activities while underway—too few. More fun please.

We saw some of the greatest shows I think we have ever seen. A Beatles Look-alike Band (sounded like them too). The 5th Dimension was on board to entertain one evening. Great!

CABINS

I would strongly advise anyone considering this ship to look very carefully at where their room will be before booking on this ship. Under no circumstances would I accept a room in the back half of the ship. It's too noise.[sic]

Once on board we were directed to our cabin and our luggage was waiting for us. Our cabin was great and we had enough room for five of us.

OVERALL COMMENTS

After cruising with the line three times, I feel terribly let down in the way that my problems were handled. As I write this review, some three weeks later, the ship has yet to respond to my cruise agent about the matter. In addition, my Fed Ex letter to the Ship Line President has gone unanswered.

Reviews will not only give you an insight to the quality of the ship but also will identify the things that are most important to passengers.

TIP NUMBER 58:
Make a Deposit to Reserve Cabins

Deposits are required to hold cabins for group events. You need to estimate the number of participants, book the cabins and then advertise the seminar. It is critical that you leave enough time in between the booking time and the registration cutoff period. For the Personal Strengths Publishing Seminar, the cruise line requested a $50 per person deposit at the time of booking to hold eighty cabins. Another $50 was then required within two weeks of booking. Final payment was due approximately forty-five days before the cruise. "Our company put up the entire deposit to block the space and I was not too worried because they promised to refund our entire deposit if we canceled within a certain time frame," says Scutter (Scutter, personal communication, 1999).

For the first conference, Scutter booked some of the least expensive cabins. "We were looking for a reasonable price for participants. We didn't want really expensive cabins that would make it impossible for some people to attend. So we picked lower-priced cabins, which were located in the bottom decks. Some people had a hard time with the ship movement. The second year, I found that there was not that much difference in the group price for cabins on the higher decks. People were more comfortable and much happier with the higher level cabins" (Scutter, personal communication, 1999).

TIP NUMBER 59:
Insist on an Onboard Inspection

Many of the tips in this book suggested for land-based seminars apply to cruise seminars. However, cruise seminars are more complicated and a bit more risky. If possible, arrange for an onboard site inspection of the ship before booking. Pay special attention to the meeting rooms, cabins and dining areas. Prior to Personal Strength's first cruise seminar, Kim Scutter did not visit the ship beforehand. This was a mistake she says. "The formal meeting rooms were in the bowels of the ship. There were no windows and people felt confined," relates Scutter (Scutter, personal communication, 1999). Ships have lounges and private areas on virtually every deck. Convince the ship's activities coordinator to reserve these spaces for your meetings. People enjoy the changes in location.

Here are some other issues to consider when planning your cruise seminar:

Find out the name of the meeting coordinator for your selected ship. Don't settle for the name of a person in the corporate offices. You want the onboard coordinator.

Determine your equipment needs and find out whether the cruise ship has enough equipment available. If they only have two overhead projectors, yet four scheduled seminars, you may have a problem. If possible, reserve the equipment.

Leave time for participants to visit each of the ports of call the ship visits. The longer the cruise the more important this is. You can schedule items that are less important during these times, or duplicate sessions—for example, one session when people are allowed to get off the ship and another session when they get back. Most shore visits last from four to eight hours.

Determine meal times. Most ships have set times for meals. There is usually a first and second seating for lunch and dinner. Determine these times and schedule your sessions around these times. You also may be able to have private dining set up for your seminar group.

Get a list of ship events and determine which ones you will coordinate with your program. Each ship offers a variety of activities, ranging from the captain's cocktail party, the formal dinner, shore excursions and briefings.

Consider using guest speakers for parts of your program. Guest speakers not only add value to your program but also present items you may not be as strong in. Many ships provide free cabins for every fifteen (or more) fully paid passengers (excluding third and fourth cabin passengers). Consider using a free cruise to entice guest speakers. Most will jump at the opportunity.

Schedule early morning breakfast sessions. These can be some of your more productive sessions.

Find out if there are other seminars being given at the same time. Find out how the ship coordinates these programs. I have seen a smaller group bumped by a much bigger group thirty minutes before the smaller group's session was to begin.

Prepare a participant information letter. This sheet should provide information on the frequently asked questions regarding seminar topics and times along with key ship information.

Make disembarking arrangements beforehand. Joan Austin had just completed her first seminar at sea. The ship entered the harbor around 6:30 A.M. and docked around 7:00 A.M. Joan was scheduled to present another seminar in a hotel that was only twenty minutes away. There seemed to be sufficient time to get off the ship and arrive for her next seminar which was scheduled to begin at 9:00 A.M. Once docked, the ship just sat there for over ninety minutes while Joan became anxious and agitated. Finally, an announcement was made that passengers would disembark by decks, with the lowest ones leaving first. Joan was on one of the upper decks and her deck was not called until 8:50 A.M. Not only was she late to her seminar, several people had already left. If you are on a tight schedule, be sure to make arrangements with the cruise director to disembark with the first group of passengers.

Provide the ship's website to participants. Once you decide upon a ship for your seminar, include the ship's website in your advertising brochure. Most ships have extensive websites that provide passengers information on the ship and its itinerary. Passengers can view photographs of the ship including state rooms, dining facilities, recreation activities, children and teen programs and entertainment areas. Some cruise lines such as Princess (www.princess.com) even provide a bridge cam that transmits live pictures every few minutes. These website features will help you market your program.

Consider a group photograph. A seminar cruise is a memorable event and photographs will help people remember it. A group photograph of all seminar participants is a nice memento to provide participants when closing the seminar. You can arrange for a group photo with the ship's photographer.

Dr. Ava Cadell, sex therapist and author of *Love Around the House,* was taking a leisurely five-day cruise vacation. She mentioned to one of the ship's officers that she did seminars on ways to stimulate romance in a marriage. This got her an invite to the captain's table and a request to do a two-hour seminar for the passengers. She had about fifty participants show up for the session, and they all wanted a copy of her book. "I learned two lessons, says Cadell. "First, never miss a marketing opportunity and second, bring enough books" (Cadell, personal communication, 2000).

7

Marketing
Your Seminar

Question: Is your advertising getting results?
Answer: It sure is. Last week we advertised for a night
watchman. The next night we were robbed.

Phil Harwitz in *The Wall Street Journal*

Some businesses use seminars as a tool to educate and acquire new customers. Businesses develop single-page flyers
that advertise seminars and display them on the front counter
for customers to pick up as they pay for merchandise. This
simple process may attract enough participants to justify putting on a workshop. If not, the workshop is not held. This is
just what John Jelson does. People who come into his camera store, asking questions about cameras or photography,
are provided a flyer announcing a two-hour, modestly priced
Introduction to Photography workshop. Another flyer offers
advanced workshops, such as Shoot Like the Magazine Pros
and Portrait Photography. This passive marketing approach
works well for his purposes. Several of the people who attend his seminars wind up buying a new camera, telephoto
lenses or other specialized equipment. More important, he
acquires long-term customers by establishing a rapport with
them at his workshops.

Jelson's approach is one of several ways to announce

seminars and workshops. Besides referrals and in-person marketing, you can use several different marketing mediums. Here are the most popular marketing methods:

DIRECT MAIL
Letters
Brochures or flyers
Catalogues
Postcards and Web cards

PRINT
Newspaper ads and articles
Magazine and journal ads

ELECTRONIC
E-mail and listservs
Web pages
Internet newsletters
Bulletin and message boards
Seminar Web listing services
Faxes

AUDIO
Radio ads or news stories
Audiotapes and CDs

VIDEO
Videotapes and clips
Infomercials

Many of these marketing approaches are used in conjunction with each other. For example, a seminar promoter may use a direct mail brochure along with faxes and e-mails. The promoter may even follow up with a video clip of a seminar in progress.

With so many choices, how does one determine which marketing mediums to use? Before deciding, you should develop a seminar marketing plan.

TIP NUMBER 60:
Develop a Seminar Marketing Plan

Getting people to attend your seminar is dependent on the effectiveness of your marketing efforts. You can design and produce the best seminar in the world, but no one will know about it if you do not market it. As a seminar provider, you must get information about your seminar into the hands of potential participants. Marketing is expensive, and you do not want to squander your efforts on people who have no interest in attending your program or buying your products.

Your seminar has a special market. It consists of all the people who want to know about and can benefit from your topic. If you are putting on a fraud detection seminar for governmental auditors, your potential market includes all the auditors working for public agencies. It also includes private auditors who consult with government agencies and university professors who teach the subject. But not every auditor is interested in your program; their area of interest may not include fraud, or they may be well versed in the topic and do not need your seminar. If you can narrow this group down to a more specific group, such as newly appointed forensic auditors, you can target your market segment, thus conserving money and effort. You can also redouble your marketing efforts by just focusing on your target group. For example, you may be able to afford one mailing to your target group. With a smaller, more focused target group, you can make three or four mailings. Likewise, by narrowing your target market, you can focus your publication advertising. In the auditor example, you would ignore the general auditing magazines and advertise in magazines for forensic auditors.

As you develop your marketing plan, you will wind up gathering the information to help focus your advertising and promotional efforts. The plan identifies your target audience and the type of advertising needed to reach it. A good marketing plan should be written. It does not have to be formal, tedious and detailed—the number of words is not important. Just make sure the plan contains the essential information. The test of a good plan is whether you use it as an actual guide. Following is a sample marketing plan for a seminar entitled Guarding the Public Checkbook.

SEMINAR MARKETING PLAN

1. **Seminar title:**
   Guarding the Public Checkbook
2. **Seminar description:**
   This seminar will teach local elected officials how to oversee, analyze and control municipal budgets. It will also increase their competence and comfort level when dealing with complex financial issues.
3. **Potential participants:**
   - City council members
   - School board of trustees
   - County board of supervisors
   - Candidates for elected office
   - City managers
   - Finance directors
   - Budget officers
   - Community activists
4. **Participants' places of residence:**
   Throughout the United States
   States with the most potential participants: Illinois, California, Florida, Texas, Michigan and Washington
5. **Projected size of participant market:**
   Total of 87,000 local governments in the United States
   - Cities: 36,000
   - Counties: 3,000
   - Special Districts: 33,000
   - School Districts: 15,000
   - Over 500,000 elected officials serving on local governing bodies
6. **Assumptions about this market:**
   Participants will attend a quality program.
   They want a workshop leader with practical experience who knows about the financial and budgeting issues with which they must deal.
   Participants will not drive more than three hours or fly more than one thousand miles.

Most elected officials have never attended a public
finance class.
7. **Participant benefits:**
Win praise from colleagues and increase constituent
confidence in their financial abilities by:
  • Saving taxpayers money
  • Avoiding typical governing body blunders
  • Finding hidden money in the budget
  • Analyzing complex financial reports
  • Dissecting and understanding investment reports
8. **How to reach participants:**
First class mail—Brochure and letter
  (five thousand letters)
Bulk mail follow-up letter and brochure
  (five thousand letters)
E-mail to two thousand potential participants
E-zine—Two ads in *Nations City Weekly*
Radio interviews in target city (no cost)
9. **Competitors:**
City and county management associations
State associations of cities
County supervisors associations
Universities and colleges
10. **Advertising approaches of competitors:**
Nations City Weekly
Public Management magazine
Direct mail brochures
Referrals
E-mail notifications
11. **Other advertising approaches to reach target market:**
Web site
News articles
Direct fax
Referrals
12. **Competitors' charges:**
For a one-day program, prices range from $200 to $400.
For a two-day program, prices range from $350 to $695.
All provide a discount for the second and third
  participant from the same organization.

13. Strengths of competitors:
High target market visibility
Maintain excellent, up-to-date mailing list
Credibility
Provide current government information
Captive audiences with certificate program

14. Weaknesses of competitors:
Make sessions more interactive to increase participant
    interest
Feature workshop leaders who are experienced trainers
Provide more relevant source material
Vary activities from straight lecture to reduce boredom
    and make workshops more interesting

15. Strengths of my seminar:
Len Wood is a professional trainer with practitioner
    experience
I make sessions more interactive with actual case studies
    and real-life examples
I provide comprehensive course workbook with
    up-to-date material

16. My seminar's exclusive features:
Each participant will receive a copy of Len Wood's book
    Local Government Dollars & Sense: 225 Financial Tips for
    Guarding the Public Checkbook
Participants will receive the Budgeting Effectiveness
    Inventory, a one hundred-question survey that
    measures budgeting effectiveness

17. Seminar leader qualifications:
Professional trainer
Author of four books on topic
Extensive experience as finance officer and city manager

18. Test market:
The seminar will be test marketed in two regional
    markets, Seattle and Chicago
Two mailings will be sent to every potential participant

19. Test market objectives:
Receive one registration for every twenty-five brochures
    mailed

> Receive one registration for every fifty follow-up
> brochures mailed
> Achieve an enrollment of thirty to fifty participants per
> workshop
> **20. Seminar goals:**
> My main goal is to make a profit from seminars. Each
> seminar should result in a net profit of $3,000
> A second goal is to sell my other products. Each seminar
> should result in a minimum sale of fifty books and
> tapes
> A third goal is to get local officials excited about local
> government budgeting

This sample marketing plan has twenty items. You will note that it includes information about competitors. This information can be gleaned from the Seminar Competition Evaluation Worksheet described in Chapter 3. You can add or delete items depending on your needs and the availability of the information. Even if you don't have precise information, an educated guess is usually better than nothing. Although most of the items in this marketing plan are self-explanatory, some require elaboration:

ITEM 1: SEMINAR TITLE
The title of your seminar is important from a marketing standpoint. You may test several titles before you settle on the final one. You can list alternative titles in this section of the plan for future reference.

ITEM 2: SEMINAR DESCRIPTION
Make your seminar description concise. This particular description has two sentences and thirty words.

ITEM 3: POTENTIAL PARTICIPANTS
Who are your target groups? These are the people for whom the seminar will be designed. You may wish to designate primary and secondary target groups. The more specific you are in defining these groups, the easier it will be to focus your advertising.

ITEM 4: PARTICIPANTS' LOCATIONS
Identifying the locations of participants allows you to target advertising efforts to those areas. In this case, it makes sense to focus initial advertising efforts in the six states listed.

ITEM 5: PROJECTED SIZE OF PARTICIPANT MARKET
This information can be gleaned from sources such as census and other governmental records, professional association memberships and chamber of commerce estimates. Knowing the estimated size of your market will give you an idea of your direct-mail mailing costs.

ITEM 6: ASSUMPTIONS
This is a key question and requires some research. Questions to consider include the following: What do your participants want? What do they value? What are their needs? Will they spend money on a seminar? What motivates them? What problems do they have? What opportunities do they have? An important assumption in the example is that most members of the target audience have never attended a public finance workshop. If this assumption is erroneous, it will result in fewer registrations.

ITEM 7: PARTICIPANT BENEFITS
Why should participants attend your seminar? What problems will you solve? What specific benefits will they reap? Participant benefits should be expressed in results language. What specific outcomes can people expect from attending your seminar? Sample results include making money, increasing profits, reducing taxes, gaining recognition, improving health, saving time, avoiding criticism, protecting property, avoiding monetary losses and improving skills. Although not always possible, try to avoid terms and phrases such as *become familiar with, learn to appreciate, become aware of,* or *better understand.* These items are vague and do not express participants' tangible benefits.

ITEM 8: REACHING PARTICIPANTS

How do you intend to reach participants? E-zines? Direct mail? Newspaper ads? Radio or television? Before you decide, you should attempt to profile your target group. Do they read newspapers? Do they rely on computers? Do they access the Internet? What professional or trade journals do they read? What media is most likely to reach your target audience? What e-mail or direct-mail lists are available? What media is affordable? Although advertising on the *Pet Doctor* radio show may be a great idea for your dog-grooming seminar, it may prove too costly. Once you are able to profile your target groups you can focus on reaching them.

ITEM 16: EXCLUSIVE FEATURES

This question challenges you to identify those things that are exclusive about your seminar. In the market plan example, the author has written a book that he will provide to participants. The author also offers a one hundred-question survey that helps participants rank their own budgeting effectiveness. But you do not have to offer products. You could offer such things as a half hour of personal mentoring, a seminar in a desirable location where participants can relax, a hands-on demonstration, evening sessions or free follow-up consulting.

ITEM 19: TEST MARKET OBJECTIVES

In this case, the seminar will be tested in two test markets—Seattle and Chicago. The objectives for the test program are specific, citing that for every twenty-five brochures mailed, one registration will be received and for every fifty follow-up brochures mailed, one registration will be received.

If the test program fails to meet these thresholds, the seminar provider should modify the approach or drop the seminar.

ITEM 20: SEMINAR GOALS

What are your goals for the seminar? Do you intend to make

a profit? Do you want to acquire more customers? Laying out your goals beforehand will help guide your efforts in developing your program. Note that the goals are simply stated in one sentence.

TIP NUMBER 61:
Analyze Your Marketing Plan

Don't waste time designing a fluff piece that impresses friends but is useless to you. I have seen elaborate, multipage documents that have been prepared to obtain loans from bankers. The biggest problem was that these marketing plans were pure fiction. To be of value, your marketing plan must contain forthright, reliable information. Keep it simple but include all relevant background material. When honestly prepared, it will focus efforts and improve profits. It also can help you avoid financial disaster by raising red flags, such as the following:

- Your intended market is too small.
- Your competitor's price is too competitive.
- You cannot match your competitor's program quality.
- You don't offer anything special.
- Your intended advertising will cost too much.

After you have completed your seminar marketing plan, ask your friends and colleagues to critique it. Empower them to be honest—tell them to not hold back for fear of offending you. Do they think this seminar will be successful? What are its strong points? What needs to be improved? What is unclear? What parts seem overly optimistic? You should also ask yourself these same questions. If in doubt, dig into the issue until you have resolved your concerns.

TIP NUMBER 62:
Test the Market

Before you jump in with both feet, it is a good idea to test market your seminar. Unfortunately, there is no foolproof method for testing the market. A helpful indicator is whether other seminar companies are providing the seminar—how long has it been offered and how often? Do you see several offerings on the topic, even though they have different seminar titles?

If you know that people will attend your seminar, there is no need to test the market. Some seminar providers direct their marketing efforts to lining up companies and organizations that then arrange for audiences. If you do not have a group that is responsible for attracting participants, how do you determine whether people will, in fact, sign up and attend your seminar? This is the unknown, risky part of public seminars. Will you reap huge profits, modest returns or devastating losses?

The idea behind market testing is to get a fair test of your seminar's potential, while spending as little money as possible. Market testing is based on the assumption that if your seminar sells in one location, it will be successful in other places with similar demographics. You should select a test city that is representative of other cities. If you have a successful seminar with plenty of registrations, you then should market it in similar cities.

Another approach is to construct a questionnaire and distribute it to potential seminar participants. I am not enamored with this approach. Having surveyed and been surveyed, I have found the process flawed and responses suspect. It is one thing to say you will attend a seminar and quite another to decide to pay money to attend. Surveys can be expensive—whether you mail the survey, include it in another mailing or use the interview process. If you decide to use a survey, you might use some of the following typical questions:

---

1. **Would you attend a seminar or workshop on (pick a topic, such as making profits in a down stock market) if it was offered in your area?**

    Very Likely   Likely   Maybe   Not Likely   Very Unlikely

2. **Would you pay to attend this seminar?**

    Very Likely   Likely   Maybe   Not Likely   Very Unlikely

3. **How much would you pay to attend a one-day seminar on this topic?**

    $50 to $99 $100 to $199 $200 to $299 $300 to $399

4. **What topics would motivate you to attend this seminar?**

    _____

    _____

On the other hand, I have successfully used seminar market surveys within organizations. Employees are given a list of topics and asked to rate them as to their feelings of importance. Here is an example:

Dear Employee:

Here is a list of topics we are considering for next year's management training programs. Please indicate your feeling of the importance of the topic by rating it as a high, medium or low priority.

Topic	Priority		
	High	**Medium**	**Low**
Improving communications skills	___	___	___
Coaching employees	___	___	___
Conducting performance evaluations	___	___	___
Handling stress	___	___	___
Improving delegation skills	___	___	___

What other topics would you like to see provided?

1.
2.
3.

Comments:

_____

_____

_____

This questionnaire includes three parts--a rating for topics, ideas for other topics and comments. The comments section can provide some of the best information. The topic list itself is usually gleaned from interviews of key employees. Another approach to the high, medium and low ranking is to have employees numerically rank the topics from most valuable to least valuable.

TIP NUMBER 63:
Use Direct Mail as Your
Primary Marketing Tool

Brochures, catalogues, fact sheets, letters, postcards, Web cards and card decks are all examples of direct mail. Direct mail is the most popular advertising technique for obtaining workshop and seminar registrations. Direct mail is a highly competitive, trillion-dollar market. Analyze your own mail for a few weeks to get an idea of the various techniques direct mail advertisers use to get you to open their mailings. Free gifts, bonuses, limited-time offers, special sales and exciting savings to preferred customers are popular examples. Others resort to more aggressive eye-catchers, such as fake checks, coins, official notices and petitions. The conventional wisdom is that most people indiscriminately dump their mail without assessing its possible benefit to them. Direct mail marketers know better; people are not offended by junk mail and will open it if it appears to offer something of interest or value to them. According to the Household Diary Study, people read 68% of the direct mail sent to them. The same study shows that people read more than 50 percent of their direct mail immediately. When they go through their mail, that is the moment when you have their complete, undivided attention. In a way, you are speaking to them on a one-to-one basis.

Direct mail is expensive when you consider the cost per audience member solicited. It can cost from fifty to seventy-five cents or more to reach each potential participant when you take into account postage, material and labor. So why is direct mail so popular? It gets results because you can target a very specific group that may be interested in your seminar. Although newspapers and radio ads cost less per audience member to reach, 99 percent or more of the people reached are not interested in your seminar.

Direct mail also is popular because costs are controllable. You can decide how many direct mail pieces you want to send out. If you are on a tight budget, you can reduce costs by sending out five thousand instead of ten thousand direct mail pieces. Except for targeted e-mail and e-zines, direct mail is one of the most cost-effective marketing approaches.

TIP NUMBER 64:
Test Market Direct Mail

Direct-mail market testing involves limiting your mailing to a representative sample of your target population and determining whether enough registrations are produced to be profitable. The broad assumption is that if it works with small populations, the results can be duplicated in larger populations. You can then intensify your marketing efforts. Obviously, the larger the sample, the better the test.

Test marketing your direct mail program is critical for another reason. You will undoubtedly make mistakes the first time you offer your program. Why not make them on a small rather than a massive scale? After your first mailing, you also will learn things from registrants that can be incorporated in your brochure. When I got ready to market my seminar on budgeting for elected officials my first thought was to print forty-five thousand brochures and mail them all out at the same time. Fortunately, reason prevailed, and the first printing and mailing was reduced to fifteen thousand. It didn't take long to find out that the brochure was flawed. Even though several people had proofed the brochure, two significant spelling errors escaped detection. In addition, my phone number was only placed on the registration form. Once a person cut it out, others who came across the brochure would not know how to contact me. However, more important, I was able to take advantage of a great opportunity. Several people were not interested in attending the seminar but were interested in purchasing the *Elected*

Official's Little Handbook, which would be provided to every seminar participant. Recognizing the marketing opportunity, I made modifications and devoted one page of the four-page brochure to the book, including a book review, testimonials and a book order form for those who could not attend the seminar. This little change had a tremendous impact on my bottom line. Ultimately, book sales equaled 35 percent of seminar revenues.

TIP NUMBER 65:
Chart Your Direct Mail Results

It is a good idea to chart the results of all your direct mailings. Note the date that you send your mailing and then record the date of each registration received. As you build a database of experience, you will be able to predict the success of a mailing based on the initial registrations. When I use a first class mailing for my seminars, I begin receiving registrations within one to two weeks. My experience also shows that I will receive approximately 65 to 75 percent of my registrations within thirty-five to forty days after mailing. When using bulk mail, I get different results. I usually get my first registration within three weeks, and I obtain 65 to 75 percent within fifty to seventy days.

TIP NUMBER 66:
Obtain Quality Mailing Lists

The most critical variable in determining the effectiveness of your direct mail efforts is the quality of the mailing list. Jay Conrad Levinson in *Guerrilla Marketing* states: "Direct mail is more science than art . . . the science of direct mail is embodied in the 60-30-10 Rule. Sixty percent of your direct mail program depends upon your using the right list of people; 30 percent depends upon your making the right offer; 10 percent depends upon your creative package" (Levinson 1993, 99).

You can create your own mailing lists or rent them. Where do you get names for your own direct mailing list? Here are the more common sources:

- Telephone and other directories
- Advertising and direct marketing responses
- People who contact your organization for information
- Internet listservs and Web pages
- Names purchased from mail order companies or professional organizations
- Business listings in newspapers
- Chamber of commerce information

Some seminar providers begin developing their mailing lists early. They establish their database and find out that it is more work than they originally imagined. They also learn that they do not have sources that provide complete and timely information on address, name, occupation, phone, area code, fax, e-mail and zip code changes.

Keeping a direct mailing list up-to-date is time-consuming and labor intensive. However, it becomes more practical when you have one or all of the following:

- Other uses for the list
- The intention to rent it to others
- A very small target population
- A source for obtaining list information changes

Mailing lists can be rented from several sources. You can hire a list broker or search the Internet, the phone book or your local library. You also can employ a list compiler to put together a list for you. A list compiler assesses your needs and then consults several sources to put together a custom list for you.

Standard Rate and Data Service (SRDS) publishes the *Direct Marketing List Source*. This document is the Bible for the mailing list business. (SRDS is the leading provider of advertising information for mailing lists, newspapers, radio stations and cable stations.) The *Direct Marketing List Source* is published every two months with updates provided monthly. Although you can subscribe to this publication, it is usually available in the main branch of all public libraries. You can find out more about SRDS on the Internet at www.srds.com.

The *Direct Marketing List Source* provides 30,000 mailing lists in 222 market classifications, ranging from very popular to hard to find lists. You can get lists sorted by zip code, region, state, city, job title, occupations, professions, business classifications and subscribers of specific journals and magazines. Each list provider is profiled with the following information:

1. Contact person: Name, address, e-mail and fax number
2. List description: Types of people, groups or entities on the list
3. Quantity of names by category
4. Price: Price per one thousand names to rent or purchase
5. Date update: Date the list was last updated
6. Method of addressing: Cheshire labels, pressure sensitive or tape
7. Test quantities: Minimum number of names that can be rented for test purposes
8. List source: Where the names on the list were acquired
9. Credit policy: Terms for acquiring the list
10. Restrictions: Any conditions on the mailing list, such as sample mailing piece required and whether a rental contract must be signed

Most mailing list providers rent lists on a one-time basis and preclude the renter from copying or using the names more than once. Prices are usually quoted per one thousand names, such as $85 per one thousand. Most also have a minimum rental amount, such as five thousand or ten thousand names.

TIP NUMBER 67:
Be Aware of Mailing List Flaws

Quality mailing lists take considerable effort and expense to compile and maintain. List vendors estimate that mailing lists deteriorate at approximately 2 to 3 percent per month. Deterioration is inevitable as people change residences and jobs on a continuing basis. A poorly maintained list can easily result in 20 to 30 percent bad address returns. In this case, a seemingly inexpensive list may actually turn out to be a budget breaker. Some of the problems people find include the following:

Dated list.
How often is the list updated? Every incorrect address, name or title not only costs you money but, more important, is a lost opportunity. When your mail is delivered, you expect seminar registrations, not returns. Many list companies guarantee list accuracy. Be sure to ask the list owner what this means in terms of percentage of successful deliveries. Also, ask them what type of guarantee they offer. If they have a written guarantee, make sure you read the fine print. What does the guarantee say? Does it include all returns of mailings that were not delivered, such as forward time expired, returned for better address or undeliverable as addressed? You also want to determine what type of refund is provided. Do they credit your postage or just the proportionate rental cost of the returned name? Some companies will only provide you an additional name for every name that is not deliverable. Others will provide an incentive, such as two names for every undeliverable name returned to them.

Wrong list.

Does the list really match your target market? For example, you may want to target hospital volunteers for a workshop titled How to Become A Nurse, but 90 percent of the list includes experienced nurses. Although you may get returns from a dated list, you will not get returns from a mistargeted list. Most recipients will trash your mailing without a second thought.

Duplicate and inaccurate names.

Some lists include an excessive number of duplicate names because the list owners do not devote the time to purge them. Examine the seminar brochures that are mailed to you. I sometimes receive three to four mailings from some companies for the same-seminar. I receive mailings for Len Wood, L. G. Wood, Leonard Wood and L. Wood.

Overused list.

Some lists may include several names that are literally overused. It is akin to the overworked silver mine. It has passed its prime, and there is nothing more to be extracted. However, quality mailing list companies will attempt different techniques to keep the list viable, such as accelerated purging and even dividing the list and rotating names to prevent overuse.

TIP NUMBER 68:
Test Your Mailing List

Because mailing lists vary in quality, it is a good idea to test a new list before renting the entire list. You can test the list by acquiring a representative sample, using it for a test mailing and analyzing the responses. A test of one thousand to two thousand names should provide a good indication of the list quality. Most list providers have a minimum number of names you can rent, such as one thousand to five thousand. Even if the minimum is five thousand, it may be less expensive to rent five thousand names and then only use one thousand or two thousand for the initial test. A test mailing will provide information on (1) the number of requests for additional information and (2) the number of registrations. If you use first class mail on your test, you also obtain feedback on the number of undeliverable pieces.

Although you will need to develop your own experience, I offer the following results, for illustrative purposes, of my seminars on budgeting, management and commissioner training. Please note that I targeted each of these groups with high quality mailing lists.

Response Indicator	Budgeting	Management	Commissioners
Percentage requesting additional information per one hundred	2.5	1.1	4.0
Percentage of returned, undelivered pieces per one hundred	1.5	1.7	1.5
Registrations per one hundred	4.1	2.3	6.0

I receive higher registrations for commissioners' training and budgeting seminars because I am one of a few professional trainers who offers the topic and has actual experience in the field. In contrast, although I am a highly qualified and experienced public manager, there are hundreds of others who have extensive experience in public and private management.

TIP NUMBER 69:
Select the Right Mailing List Format

Mailing lists can be obtained in three common formats:

1.   *Self-adhesive labels.* As a new seminar provider, you may wish to use peel-off labels first. Adhesive labels are gummed on the backside and printed four abreast. I use peel-off labels for all my first class mailings.

2.   *Cheshire labels.* If you have the equipment or are using a mailing house, the most common label is a Cheshire. These labels are also printed in columns of three or four names on computer printout sheets.

3.   *Disk, tape or CD.* These lists are provided on disk, CD or tape. Disks are usually provided in 3.5- and 5-inch sizes. If you use Macintosh equipment, be sure that the medium can be read.

TIP NUMBER 70:
Decide between First Class
and Bulk Mail

What is more effective, first class or bulk mail? I use first class mail for most of my seminars, especially when I am introducing a new, seminar. However, bulk mail has a cost advantage. There is no one simple guide to this question. Factors to consider include your product, the target group you are soliciting (doctors, teens, seniors, etc.), the price of your product and the size of your mailing. Spending time to learn postal regulations will help you make this decision. Many U.S. Post Office bulk mailing centers hold two-hour workshops to familiarize people with bulk mail. This chart compares bulk mail with first class mail.

FACTOR	BULK MAIL	FIRST CLASS MAIL
Application	One-time application and $125 fee required; remains in force as long as it's used once a year	No application or fee required
Annual fee	Annual fee, $125, good from January 1 to December 31 (not prorated)	No annual fee
Cost per letter	Approximately 45 percent less than first class (twenty-three cents per piece).	Thirty-four cents per one-ounce letter, plus twenty-three cents up to two ounces
Delivery time	Local delivery approximately five to fourteen days; other areas from two to five weeks or more	Overnight within same metropolitan area; other areas three to five days
Returns	Nondeliverable pieces are discarded unless "Return postage guaranteed" is printed on letter	Nondeliverable pieces returned with reason indicated
Minimum mailings	Two hundred pieces or fifty pounds	No minimums
Preparation	Must be bundled by zip code; various prices depending on how packaged	No requirements

The following are other comments regarding first class versus bulk mail:

- First class mail is more expensive. If your budget allows for first class mailings, use it. But if you are mailing in large quantities, it may make sense to use bulk mail.

- First class mail costs more, but pieces that cannot be delivered will be returned to you, allowing you to correct your database and avoid wasting money on the next mailing, if you are doing multiple mailings.
- If you use theme stamps, make sure they are appropriate to your audience. Don't use National Rifle Association stamps for a Young Democrats group. Avoid cute designs; they may not be seen as professional (e.g., love stamps and flowers).
- There are no guarantees as to when bulk mail will be delivered. Bulk business mail moves between post offices on a space-available basis. Be sure that you never set a tight seminar schedule if you use bulk mailings.
- Improperly addressed bulk mail pieces will not be delivered or returned to you.
- The percentage cost differential between bulk and first class mail is approximately 45 percent.
- The more material you include in your marketing package, the more it makes sense to use bulk mail.
- If you use first class mail, put together at least two sample mailings with the exact items you will be mailing and weigh them. Don't use your own scale; it may be inaccurate. Go to the post office and use theirs. If the weight is close to the one-ounce limit, go to another post office and have them weigh your two samples. Labels, stamps and adhesive notes can take your mailing over the threshold. If you go over, it will increase your mailing costs substantially.
- Make sure you reweigh your packet if you change paper stock. I once changed to recycled paper, which took the weight over one ounce. The post office set aside the mailing for approximately one month and then returned the entire mailing to me. Although the mailing was sent out again, it was very late, and I wound up canceling the seminar.

- Send copies of your letters and brochures to relatives and acquaintances to check delivery times.

TIP NUMBER 71:
Determine Your Target Group's Enrollment Response Time

The timing of your mailing is important. You don't want to send your packet too far in advance. People may set it aside for later review and then forget about it. On the other hand, you do not want to send it out so late that potential participants cannot make adjustments in their schedules, process payments and obtain approvals to attend your seminar. If you have contacts in your target group, ask them how far in advance they need notice to schedule an off-site seminar. Among my target groups, local elected officials need from four to five weeks, whereas city managers need six to eight weeks. Participants for a basic management workshop need approximately four weeks.

The time of the year is also important. If you are mailing around holiday or election periods, allow extra time.

TIP NUMBER 72:
Evaluate Follow-Up Mailings

When you mail a brochure advertising your workshop, the first mailing usually produces the most registrations. Some people, however, can be wooed with another notice. Seasoned seminar providers find that a second and third mailing can produce additional registrations but not at the same level as the first brochure. Seminar providers estimate that a second mailing will produce approximately from one-third to one-half of the first mailing.

Should you use a second mailing? It may make sense if you have a limited mailing list and the revenues from the second mailing produce a profit after the cost of the second mailing is deducted. On the other hand, if you have a potential target market of fifty thousand people and you only mailed to ten thousand, you will get a better return on your investment by concentrating on the other forty thousand, rather than making a second mailing to the original ten thousand.

If you are considering a follow-up mailing, plan it beforehand. If you decide to do subsequent mailings, many mailing list brokers provide a 50 percent discount for duplicate lists (multiple-use discounts). To qualify, you must order duplicates at the same time as the original list.

Another decision relates to the content of the second mailing. Some providers print extra copies of the original brochure for the additional mailings. Others believe that a variation, such as a change in brochure cover or color, should be used to pique the interest of on-the-fence participants. Other variations include adding a letter, adhesive note, press release, list of testimonials or relevant article. If you are using multiple mailings, you may wish to use test mailings with and without the variations to determine cost effectiveness.

TIP NUMBER 73:
Consider Postcards as an Alternative

Postcards are an alternative direct mail medium. They are less expensive than first class letters. Seminar providers who use this method must recognize that there is limited information that can be included on the postcard. As a result, they usually direct the potential participant to an 800 number, an office address or a Web site to register. A typical postcard seminar ad contains an attractive picture on the front and basic seminar information on the back.

Before you decide to use postcards as a marketing method, you should use a sample mailing to test its effectiveness. I dropped postcards after trying two test cases of two thousand mailings each. In the first case, I received four inquiries and two registrations. In the second case, I received three inquiries and no registrations. Your target market has a lot to do with the success of postcards. I continue to receive postcards advertising how to invest in the stock market, how to incorporate and how to establish living trust seminars.

TIP NUMBER 74:
Be Wary of Card Decks

Card decks are sometimes suggested as another direct mail method for advertising seminars. A typical card deck consists of a packet of thirty to fifty index cards that contain similar service and product advertisements. Other decks will contain varying sizes of cards such as six by seven inch cards, as well as index-sized cards. For an additional fee, some companies will let you include a brochure and return envelope. You can have your card printed to include free return postage or a "place stamp here" box. Some companies will collect and tally the responses for you at no additional cost. They do this to help improve their mailing list. The card-deck company designs and produces the cards for you. Card decks are mailed using bulk mail.

If you are interested in using card decks, contact a card deck company and ask questions such as the following:

1. How many cards are in the deck?
2. Is there a general theme for the deck?
3. Is there an additional charge for design?
4. How many names are on the mailing list?
5. What is the cost per deck mailed?

6.   Is test marketing allowed or must I participate in the whole mailing?

You also should get copies of sample decks to see if the participating advertisers are targeting the same market as you.

Card decks may make sense as a way to expose your seminar company and your products to a particular target group. But they may not be effective in obtaining reservations for a specific seminar. Two seminar providers who have used card decks made the following comments:

> *My advice regarding card decks, after 15 years in the direct mail seminar business—Just say no. They are seldom profitable, except for the deck publishers themselves.*

> *I advertised with a company that mailed to a list of 200,000, and the cost to me was $1,500. Twenty people sent back response cards, and out of the twenty, I had three registrations.*

TIP NUMBER 75:
Develop a Web site to Anchor Your Seminar Marketing

I successfully marketed seminars several years without a Web site. However, that was before the Internet explosion. When I started writing this book, less than 50 percent of the big seminar companies listed Web addresses in their brochures. Today, all companies have at least one Web site and, in many cases, several. Although the Internet is still relatively new and the technology is evolving, it has become the indispensable marketing tool for the seminar business. Even more, this powerful device continues to evolve. As one seminar marketer states, "You do not exist if you do not have a Web site."

Software, such as Microsoft Frontpage and Adobe PageMill, is available that helps you author your own Web site. Many books are also available, including Peter Kent's *Poor Richards Guide to Web sites.* You also can find companies on the Web that will design your Web site. Some Internet providers, such as AOL, will let you develop free Web sites. Before you invest much money, you may wish to practice with a free service first to get familiar with Web site design and maintenance. Recognize that these sites have limited space and capabilities.

TIP NUMBER 76:
Establish Your Web site Goals

If you have not developed your Web site, you may wish to visit several Web sites that provide seminars, such as those listed in Chapter 4. This will give you design and content ideas. Before creating or employing a firm to develop your site, you should identify your goals. Goals for a seminar Web site may include a place that:

- promotes you and your products and services;
- allows participants to register for your seminars;
- provides additional information about a specific seminar you are promoting; and
- provides useful resource information to potential and former participants, such as articles and checklists.

TIP NUMBER 77:
Develop an Effective Web site

What is important about a Web site? Most people believe an effective Web site is one that not only attracts potential buyers but also brings them back. Use the following criteria to attract buyers to your site—and even bring them back:

USEFUL INFORMATION

When you surf Web sites, you find many variations. Some provide a great deal of valuable information. Others provide lots of information of little value. Still others provide little more than the basic information found on the company's business card. In this latter case, the company is not interested in providing information, only in providing basic address information. Whatever information you put on your site, make sure that it is of value to your Web site visitors. Why are you providing this information? How does it help you achieve your marketing goals? Remember this information is not for you; it is for your potential and past seminar participants. Low-value information can cast a negative image on your company and seminar offerings. If you want them to come back, make sure your information is fresh, accurate and useful to potential participants or purchasers of your products and services.

ACCESSIBILITY

All the effort you put into developing a Web site is futile if you cannot get your target group of potential seminar participants to visit your site. Unfortunately, you have a tremendous amount of competition. There are millions of Web sites, and the number is growing. So, how do you get people to come to your site in this very competitive market? According to Kimberly Judd, search engine placement expert and owner of CyberMark International, people find sites in the following manner:

METHOD	PERCENTAGE
Search engines and directories	46
Word of mouth	20
Random surfing	20
Magazine ads	4
By accident	2
Television, banner ads, other	8

There are several ways to notify participants of your Web site:

Self-promotion and marketing. You can list your Web site on your business cards, letters, seminar brochures, flyers and any other piece of paper you send out. You can list your site URL on the signature line of every e-mail you send. This is especially effective on the listservs and message boards in which you participate. Find a way to highlight your site at every event you attend and every seminar you provide. You also can get your Web address out by advertising. This, however, is more expensive.

Referrals and word of mouth. Word of mouth is considered one of the most effective advertising methods. One fifth of visitors find sites through word of mouth referrals. Find people who deal with those who need your services and encourage them to refer people to you. The key to the referral market is feedback. In some cases, it is a simple thank you to the person who was responsible for the referral. In other cases, it is a small gift that says thank you. And in big cases, it's a Corvette!

Search engines, directories and Web site linkages.
If people don't have your Web site address, the most
common way they will find you is through search
engines, directories and linkages to other Web sites.
There are companies that will help you maximize
your chances for attracting visitors to your site, such
as CyberMark International at www.cyber-mark.com.

FAST LOADING

How many promising sites have you wandered upon and
clicked away because it took too long for the first page to
load? People who have been directed to your site may wait
for it to load, even if it takes a bit more time, but surfers and
wanderers will not. They want your Web site to come up
quickly, and the experts tell us that eight to ten seconds is
the maximum tolerance limit in loading time. Don't
encumber your site with slow-loading features, such as
sound, filmstrips and moving objects. Although they are cute
and enjoyable, most viewers are gone before the first page
has a chance to display its brilliance. Surveys show that fast
downloading wins over bells and whistles every time.

CUSTOMER FRIENDLY

As you wander across the Web, you will find many boring,
if not annoying, Web sites. You also will find sites that appeal to you. As you find these sites, stop and analyze them.
Print a color copy of the main pages of these sites. What
makes them attractive to you? After useful content, here are
the features that appeal to me:

1. Not too cluttered, lots of white space and screens that
    do not have to be scrolled for too long
2. Attractive, yet simple design
3. A minimum of nonstop animation and no multi-
    media overkill
4. Easy-to-follow directions to other pages; no orphan
    pages that don't indicate whose site you are on or
    links that lead to dead ends
5. Easy to read; most important information up front to

keep me interested
6. Simple, functional graphics
7. Attractive, complementary colors
8. Easy to navigate to different parts of the site; follows both intuitive and logical sequence

TIP NUMBER 78:
Include a Full Description of Your Current Seminars

Your Web site is a great place to market your current seminars and to provide additional information on your offerings. Many of these topics are the ones you will be covering in your seminar brochure; however, you do not have the space limitations that a hard copy brochure has. The important topics to consider covering include the following:

Seminar description. You can describe the seminar in a short, crisp narrative with bullet points. What topics will be included? You also might wish to include a copy of the actual seminar agenda.

Seminar attendees. This section should identify what groups and people the seminar will benefit.

Participant benefits. This section should present the benefits your participants will receive by attending your seminar.

Resources provided. This section should include a short description of the materials provided, such as a workbook, handouts and other documents.

Price. The cost of the seminar should be highlighted. As with seminar brochures, do not make people hunt for the price.

Otherwise, they will get the impression that you are trying to hide it.

Schedule. If you are offering the seminar at different locations, you should show the schedule along with the specific locations of the seminar.

Frequently asked questions (FAQ). Include a section on frequently asked questions (FAQ). You will begin getting questions as soon as you send out your first direct mail piece or post your first ad on the Internet. As you receive these questions, you should record them and your responses.

Your bio. Here is your chance to shine. Present your bio to emphasize your presentation and training abilities. Items to address include the following: What is your background? What gives you the credibility to present this seminar? How long have you been presenting it? What books and articles have you written? Do you have any academic achievements? Here is a place to put your photo. People like to see who will be the presenter.

Articles. If you have written articles of interest to those who will visit your Web site, you should consider including them. Some trainers include quizzes, survey results and polls to get people to return to their site. If you collect important statistical information from your seminar participants, you may wish to display this information on your site. Check the American Management Association (AMA) Web site to see surveys they list (www.amanet.org/research/stats.htm). National Seminars Group (www.natsem.com) has several examples of quizzes. Listed quizzes relate to seminar topics and provide instant feedback to users.

Testimonials. Select your most relevant testimonials and list them on your site.

Products and services. If you offer other products, such as newsletters, books, audiotapes and videotapes, CDs, workbooks and pamphlets, you should not miss this marketing opportunity. A photo of these items will help sell them. If you offer in-house seminars, descriptive information should be included.

Your guarantee and cancellation policy. If you have decided to provide a guarantee, place it in a prominent location on your Web site. Your cancellation policy also should be included.

Registration instructions. Be sure to include instructions on how people can register. When setting up your Web site, you may wish to design it to accept registrations online. If you do so, make the process simple and painless. If you request information that is not essential to the registration process, you may lose potential registrations. Don't risk it. You always can follow up with a supplemental questionnaire for those who register.

Privacy policy. You need to assure people that you will not share their e-mail, phone or fax number with other companies. Be up front. Some people will not share any information for fear of being spammed. A statement such as, "You have our personal guarantee that the information you provide will not be shared with anyone. We don't like being spammed any more than you do." This will help alleviate such fears.

Some seminar promoters believe that each seminar deserves its own Web site. They have a main site and then develop other sites for specific seminars.

TIP NUMBER 79:
Advertise in E-Zines

E-mail newsletters, commonly referred to as e-zines, are prov-
ing to be an effective way to market seminars. E-zines are
Internet newsletters that provide valuable information for a
group of subscribers who have common interests. E-zines
are popular advertising mediums because rates are relatively
low and ads can be aimed at a very specific group. They are
sent out on a weekly, biweekly, monthly, quarterly or even
semiannual basis. Other e-zine providers send them out on
a schedule at the author's discretion.

Most of the established e-zines with dedicated read-
erships include a limited number of advertisements with each
issue. Advertisers select e-zines because they believe their
product or service will appeal to the subscribers. For example,
www.speakersnet.com provides an e-zine for professional
speakers and seminar providers. This electronic newsletter
is sent to subscribers every two weeks, and within every issue are several relevant tips for speakers and seminar providers. Every issue includes service and product advertisements that are specifically targeted for this market. This is
my favorite e-zine because it provides relevant, valuable content for seminar providers.

Reputable e-zines do not fall into the spam or unsolicited e-mail category. Every single subscriber has made a
request to receive the newsletter. Reputable e-zines publish
easily located instructions on how to unsubscribe. These factors make e-zines one of the most cost-effective advertising
mediums. Before you decide to advertise in an e-zine, determine all the subscriptions of your target group and select
the best. Here are some issues to consider:

1. How many opt-in subscribers does the list have?
    Don't fret if the figures are not large. Remember, the
    right list includes your most promising prospects.

2. Look for e-zines that provide quality information. Some e-zines exist for the sole purpose of advertising. They provide one or maybe two ideas or tips but are filled with lots of commercial garbage.

3. Look for e-zines that are tied to a quality provider. Whether it be a single person, company or non-profit group, it does not matter. What matters is the quality and usefulness of the information provided. Examine the provider's Web site. Determine the reason for the e-zine. Why does it exist? Does it have a mission statement and, if so, is the mission compatible with your message?

4. Check the e-zine contributors' Web sites. Are the contributors high caliber? Do they have good credentials? Do they provide valuable content?

5. Determine if the e-zine provides an archive of past issues. If so, scan past articles to determine the relevance to your audience.

6. Determine the reliability of the e-zine. How long has it been published? Has it been published on a consistent basis as promised?

7. What are the advertising rates? What are the rates per issue? With the subscriber information, you can develop the cost per person reached.

8. What do past advertisers say? Will the e-zine give you references from current and past advertisers?

TIP NUMBER 80:
Create Your Own E-Zine

If you have the time and like to write, you may wish to create your own e-zine. Patricia Fripp (www.fripp.com) provides a free e-mail newsletter in which she shares business insights and strategies that she has gleaned over the years. "Register here to receive a free membership, including special mailings for MentorU.Com, and a two-month subscription to *Mentor Insights* by Patricia Fripp." She also includes notices of her upcoming events and products. Joan Stewart (www.jsteward), creator of the *Publicity Hound,* puts out an e-zine that contains both her ads and other people's ads.

If you use an e-mail newsletter, it is a good idea to use an opt-in sign-up form for your subscribers. Accumulating e-mail addresses from various sources without getting permission may subject you to charges of spamming. You can avoid this by having potential subscribers sign an opt-in form before letting them subscribe. Your form should offer people the option of receiving updates on your products. This will give you an opportunity to send directed e-mails to your subscribers. Store opt-in forms in a safe place because people tend to forget that they opted for your newsletter and products and service notices.

TIP NUMBER 81:
Use Listservs to Establish
Connections and Credibility

Several years ago, my wife June and I boarded a crowded bus in New Orleans to get to the convention center. To our bemusement, the rider across from us opened a box containing a beautiful chocolate cake topped with four large candles. He then took out a barbecue type lighter and methodically lit every candle. While he was doing this tedious job, other riders pulled out forks, plates, napkins and little paper cups. What floored us was the punch bowl that the passenger on the back seat of the bus pulled out of a large cardboard box. He then began mixing a bowl of Hawaiian punch. After everyone, including us, received a piece of cake and a cup of punch, the passengers all sang *Auld Lang Syne* to a somewhat embarrassed young lady. She had just gotten married and was moving to another part of the city, so she would no longer be riding the bus. These friendly passengers had become very close over the years and were celebrating the marriage while saying good-bye to a dear fellow passenger.

A good listserv is like the New Orleans bus. It brings together several people heading to a common destination. To make the journey easier and more fun, they get to know each other through casual and then meaningful conversation. Over time, they establish bonds. Good listservs bring people together who share valuable information.

Topica, a mailing list directory (www.topica.com), provides over ninety thousand discussion group lists. You can locate a group of people on the Internet who have common interests with you. Subscribe to those lists that are in your market niche. But don't stop there. You need to become a participating member who shares valuable information with members. The trick is to subtly market your services and products while sharing. By not trying to sell directly, you will gain people's confidence and trust. When they need help, they will seek you out.

TIP NUMBER 82:
Just Say No to Bulk E-mail Lists

An Internet advertiser offers two million Internet addresses for only $19. Another offers five million Internet messages for $49. The appeal of reaching an overwhelming number of prospects by e-mail is tantalizing. How else can you reach so many seminar participants at such a negligible cost? Although the lure is great, the payoff is not. The Internet term for unsolicited commercial e-mail is *spam.* Recognize that most people despise spam and react very negatively to the message. They consider it intrusive, and they don't like the time it takes to open and trash the message. Is there a successful way to use bulk e-mailing? Sites offer free subscriptions to commercial e-mail lists. Surfers are told that these lists were created so advertisers could target ads to this specific group. People then sign up for the topics they are interested in. People also willingly sign up for e-mail newsletters, reports and messages. In these cases, the distinction is that people want them. Unless the people you send such messages to have knowingly invited such messages, don't do it. Junk or bulk e-mail is a loser. Most people consider spam an intrusion and uncivil. If you engage in spamming, you also run the risk of your Internet service provider removing you from their list. Use spam mail at your own risk.

TIP NUMBER 83:
List Your Seminars on the Internet

Explore the idea of listing your seminar offerings on the Internet. There are several Internet sites that list seminars. Some are free, and others are provided for a fee. One of the free seminar sites is www.freeseminar.com. This site allows you to list your events in the seminar database for free. Unless you have a very popular topic or you have established your credentials, don't expect lots of registrations from these sources. Most seminar Internet sites are relatively new and need time to establish themselves.

TIP NUMBER 84:
Investigate Newspaper Advertising

Newspapers offer another way to market your seminars. In general, newspaper advertising is not considered an effective medium for most seminars because of the high cost. Have you noticed the full-page newspaper ads that are run in the *Chicago Tribune* or the *Los Angeles Times* to advertise a seminar? At this writing, the cost of a full-page ad to run once in the *Times* (circulation 1,200,000 subscribers) costs approximately $40,000. If you charge $300 per seminar participant, you need 134 registrations just to pay for the advertising. Smaller newspapers have significantly lower costs, but they have much lower circulation figures. The *Santa Barbara New-Press* charges $3,900 for a full-page ad and $500 for an ad of one-eighth page. However, the *New-Press* circulation is less than 10 percent of the *Times*.

There are advantages to using newspapers for advertising your seminars.

- Newspapers do not require the same lead time that a direct mail campaign demands. With a newspaper ad, you can advertise on Monday and give the seminar on Friday or the weekend.

- Newspaper ads make sense if you are advertising a seminar that appeals to a general audience. The more general the seminar, the more attractive a newspaper ad becomes. Examine your newspaper for a few weeks and you will be able to identify the types of seminars that use newspaper advertising. I have found that the typical programs include How to Incorporate, How to Buy Stocks, How to Create Living Trusts and How to Purchase Foreclosed Properties.

- Another circumstance when newspapers make sense is when a mailing list does not exist for a large group that is forming around a phenomenon. For example, it would have been impossible to get a complete list of Harry Potter fans, even after the first four books were published.

Many libraries carry a copy of Standard Rate and Data Service's *Newspaper Circulation Analysis*. This publication provides excellent demographic information about newspaper readership, including advertising rates, copy deadlines and circulation figures.

Newspapers base their advertising rates on circulation; the greater the number of people reached, the higher the rate. When advertising in a newspaper, you want an ad that is large enough to attract the attention of potential registrants, yet not too large as to consume your entire budget.

The section you advertise in is important from the standpoint of connecting to your target market. In his seminars, Howard Shenson used to advise, "Placement is very important. You need to ask, 'If no other section of the newspaper were read that day, what section would my potential participant be most likely to read'?" (Shenson, personal communication, 1987). Newspaper inserts offer another option. Most seminar providers report that display ads generate a better response than newspaper inserts. Many people view inserts as junk mail, and as a result, they have a lower success rate. People toss flyers.

TIP NUMBER 85:
Market Test Newspaper
Advertisements

Market testing for newspaper advertising is different from direct mail testing. If you are using direct mail and are measuring costs, it does not matter where you test. First class and bulk mail costs are the same for New York as for Jefferson City, Missouri; Myrtle Beach, South Carolina; Pawtucket, Rhode Island and Juneau, Alaska. Newspaper testing is more sensitive, and location is very important. What you want to find is a representative newspaper for your target group. An ad run in San Francisco may attract many registrations, whereas the same ad will bomb in Dallas. They are different communities with different demographics. Use the Standard Rate and Data Service newspaper information to select your test market newspapers.

TIP NUMBER 86:
Use Magazine and Journal Advertising

Advertising in magazines and journals can be effective if your seminar appeals to the same people who subscribe to the journal or magazine. You can reach mass markets with magazines like *People, Time* or *Readers Digest*, but most of the readers will not be interested in your seminar. On the other hand, you can reach very specialized markets with publications such as *Cat Fancy, Bon Appetit* or *Field and Stream*. If you offer other products and consulting services, magazines have an additional benefit—they have long shelf lives. I still get book orders from an ad I put in *Public Management* eight years ago!

Will subscribers read your ad? Perhaps. I subscribe to several journals and magazines. I skim vocational magazines but read every line and classified in my hobby magazines.

TIP NUMBER 87:
Postpone Radio Advertising

Radio advertising offers another marketing opportunity to seminar providers. On my way to work, I often hear commercials about upcoming seminars, mostly focused on business, personal improvement and health seminars. Before you get too carried away with the possibilities, check the prices. Although radio has the potential of reaching a large audience, it is relatively expensive. Radio advertising costs vary, and they are negotiable. When you are ready to consider different types of advertising, call several radio stations and get their rates.

On an average day, over 160 million Americans tune in to the radio. They typically listen for two hours, and radio's largest audience is homemakers, followed by commuters. Each audience has its own interests; with homemakers' interests are family care, children, education, health, music and other community service topics. Commuters' interests are business, politics and sports. If you have a business-related seminar, such as how to make money in the stock market, a good time to promote it over the radio waves is during the early morning and late afternoon commuting times.

Radio advertising can be targeted to a local or national audience. The *Radio Advertising Source,* which is published by Standard Rate and Data Service (SRDS), provides a comprehensive listing of all AM and FM radio stations in the country. It provides information on the following:

1. Where the radio station is located, along with the station's phone, fax, e-mail and URL
2. The listening audience profile and demographic makeup
3. Key contacts, including general managers, general sales managers and program directors
4. The program format to help you determine if your seminar is targeted to the listening audience
5. Operating information, including station call letters, power, time zone and hours of broadcasting

If you use radio advertising, a prerecorded message can be prepared, or the announcer or host will read your script. The former requires that a tape be created in a sound studio with professionals. This can be an expensive process. The latter approach is less expensive, but you want to make sure that the announcer will do justice to your message.

Radio has the potential for reaching a large audience; however, it assumes that people are listening to the station at the times your ad is aired. Recognize also that listeners may switch stations as soon as the commercials begin. Because there are several competing stations, you must select the one that most appeals to your target audience. Be sure to get a media kit from each of the radio and television stations you are considering. These kits will tell you the cost of the time offered for sale. The media kit also delineates the demographics of the audience and the reach of the station. If you are considering using radio in your local area, you should obtain a log of radio stations from the newspaper and spend time listening to them to determine which ones broadcast commercials similar to your message. Remember, once a commercial airs, it vanishes into the air never to be referred to again. For this reason, you should consider running your radio ad several times. Here is another thing to consider: You also should repeat your phone or Web site as often as possible. Listeners, especially commuters, may not have a pen and paper immediately available and will need to hear your contact information several times to remember it.

TIP NUMBER 88:
Negotiate Radio Advertising Rates

Many radio station rates are subject to negotiation. Nanette Miner, a seminar provider and President of The Training Doctor (nanette@trainingdr.com), was promoting a seminar on business etiquette in Hartford, Connecticut. She contacted the sales manager at a local radio station and proposed a trade. Instead of paying a fee, she offered to train the station's sales staff in exchange for free commercials. The sales manager liked the idea and accepted her offer. The station sent eight participants to Nanette's seminar, and she wound up with a total of sixteen radio spots, each lasting thirty seconds and broadcast during commute times. The fact that the local radio station sent eight station employees added prestige to her seminar.

TIP NUMBER 89:
Publicity is Free—Seek it Out

Publicity is free advertising from the print media, radio and television. They are always looking for features and programs. The key to gaining their attention is to present your seminar's significance in a way that will grab their audience's interest. You must convince the editor or program director that your topic is timely, important and interesting. Enterprising seminar providers gain free publicity by linking their topic to a current event.

Alex Carrol (www.radiopublicity.com) has mastered the art of obtaining free radio publicity. While working as a courier, he obtained several speeding tickets, which threatened his job. He studied the problem and learned how to legally contest tickets and win. This led to his book *Beat the Cops: The Guide to Fighting Your Traffic Ticket and Winning.* Alex's book has sold approximately 140,000 copies, primarily through radio interviews. His technique is to identify the radio show with large audiences and pitch the producer directly. He convinces them that he has an interesting and controversial topic—two things radio stations love. Carrol has done over twelve hundred radio interviews that he values at over $4 million in free publicity.

Mark Victor Hansen and Jack Canfield co-founded the best-selling *Chicken Soup for the Soul* book series. Since 1993 they have sold over fifty million copies that have been translated into thirty-eight languages. How did they become so successful? Part of their secret was publicity: "We made a habit of doing a minimum of one radio interview a day, seven days a week, for two years," relates Hansen. They also worked closely with the print media. According to Hansen, "We gave newspapers and magazines free reprint rights to all our stories" (Hansen, personal communication, 2000).

TIP NUMBER 90:
Develop Your Press Releases
and Media Kit

A short press release should be prepared for each seminar. Your release should be well written. It should identify who is issuing the statement and the name and phone number of the contact person. A good approach is to prepare your release like a newspaper article and include the journalistic basics—who, what, where, when, why and how. It should have a headline that grabs the audience's attention. Why is your seminar important to the media's audience? The first paragraph should contain facts and examples supporting the headline. Your press release will be much more effective if you remember that editors and producers do not particularly care about you or your seminar. They care about creating a good story or showing that it appeals to their audiences. Above all, make sure that your message is not self-serving—that is the fastest way to get it canned.

Some word processing programs now have press release templates that can be used as guides to develop your release. It's not a bad idea to create several different releases for the different audiences you have.

Once you have developed your press releases, you have the lynch pin for a media kit. The kit might also include the following items:

• Brochure describing your company
• Brochure describing the seminar
• List of questions and answers about the seminar
• Seminar leader biography and photograph
• Testimonial letters about this or other seminars
• Information on your products and services

The media kit can be a very useful and versatile publicity aid. Although you may have a master media kit, the actual contents of individual media kits can be varied, depending on the purpose and needs of the person or group being sent the information.

TIP NUMBER 91:
Be Prepared for Media Calls

A few years ago, a $1.4 billion bankruptcy, the largest municipal financial disaster in history, had just occurred in Orange County, California. Seizing an opportunity, I quickly reworked one of my seminars on budgeting to take advantage of the marketing opportunity. My new title, Avoiding the Fiscal Nightmare—Lessons from Orange County, drew hundreds of elected officials to my series of seminars. Unfortunately, I did not anticipate that two major newspapers and a radio station also would be attracted by the workshop advertisements. By not being prepared with succinct, crisp statements about the seminar, I lost free publicity from a major newspaper and radio station before I developed a script. This script helped me get prominent coverage in the *Los Angeles Times*.

Don't be caught unprepared. Whether you are contacted by newspaper, radio or even television, you should be ready for a telephone call or an in-person interview. One of the best ways to prepare for spot interviews is to develop a list of questions and answers about your seminar. Do not make your questions and answers too technical or detailed. Make the questions of interest to a large audience. Also, make your statements somewhat provocative, if possible. One of my best lines that was quoted in the *Los Angeles Times* was "Many Elected Officials are amateurs at finance, yet they're dealing with millions of your dollars." Several people who ultimately attended my seminar mentioned that quote. Prepare yourself for questions like the following:

- Why should people spend money to attend your seminar?
- What is the purpose of your seminar?
- What real benefits will participants get?
- Why did you create your seminar?
- Who will benefit from your seminar?
- Can people get the same information out of a book?
- What makes your subject matter unique?
- What are your credentials?
- What actual experience have you had with this topic?
- What effect has your seminar had?

You also should be aware that newspaper reporters may show up at your seminar to write a follow-up story. In the case of my elected officials seminar, the *Los Angeles Times* followed up and attended my seminar. They listened to the presentation for a short period to get the flavor of the seminar and then began interviewing several participants on why they were there and what they thought about the presentation. Although it was somewhat disruptive, it resulted in another great article.

Creating an Enticing Brochure

If the ad has a well designed brochure or eye catching headline—it gets three to four seconds to grab me. If the topic is of interest, then I'll give it a good look and read most, or all of the message depending on the quality of the information being provided.
Seminar participant Toni Perichini

The seminar brochure or flyer is the most popular seminar-marketing format. The purpose of the brochure is simple. Its primary intent is to get people to sign up for your seminar. This suggests that you must get your prospective participants to notice and read your brochure. It also suggests that you should only include the information that is necessary to convince people to sign up. It is used alone or in combination with a transmittal letter. It provides all the pertinent information about your program in a coherent, appealing presentation.

Deciding what information to include in your brochure requires you to finalize several critical decisions, such as determining price, location and seminar topics. Once printed in a brochure these items cannot be easily changed. People interpret your seminar offering as your promise to them. At this juncture you cannot wing it; you are at the point of making firm decisions about these critical seminar items and then putting them in writing.

This chapter begins with tips on developing your seminar brochure. You will note that many of the brochure tips apply to the other advertising mediums.

TIP NUMBER 91:
Develop Your Brochure Copy First

Don't decide on the size, layout and graphics of your brochure until you have developed the content. Deciding on the size before the amount of copy may force you to include unnecessary information to fill space. Or worse, force you to leave out important items because of a lack of space. Once you complete the copy, you can develop the format to convey your message. Many word processing programs, such as WordPerfect, have brochure and newsletter templates that can be used to layout your copy.

TIP NUMBER 92:
Use Your Competitor's Brochures to Stimulate Thought

In Chapter 3, I suggested that you collect copies of competitor's brochures. You will get numerous ideas by analyzing these brochures. A good technique before you design your own brochure is to lay out all your acquired brochures on the floor or table and rank them from least appealing to most appealing. You should then select the bottom three to five and ask the following questions:

1. What don't I like about these brochures?

2. What features detract from these brochures?
3. Are there common negative features that they all have?
4. What could make these brochures better?

After this exercise, I select the three to five best and ask the following questions:

1. What made me select these brochures?
2. What features do I like?
3. Are there common positive features that they all have?
4. What features can be incorporated into my brochure?

As you make judgments, make notes on Post-it notes and attach them to the brochures. Aspects to consider include graphics, format, size, complexity of design, photos, cartoons, illustrations, typeface, headlines, subtitles, color, color combinations, stock, fonts, ink color, language, white space, margins and print quality.

TIP NUMBER 93:
Make a Final Decision on Your Seminar Title

Tip number ten in Chapter 2 discusses the development of a tentative title. Now is the time to finally decide on the title of your seminar. Select a title that tells people what your workshop is about. Try to keep your title short, descriptive and crisp, such as How to Delegate, Troubleshooting the Macintosh, Finance for Nonfinancial Managers, Surfing the Web, or How to Prune Roses. This is especially important for how-to seminars. You should also avoid run-on titles such as How to Find, Hire and Promote People in a Tight Job

Market While Retaining Your Own Employees with a Great Benefit Program. Remember, most people make an instantaneous decision whether or not to read beyond your title—so put thought into hooking them with a compelling title.

TIP NUMBER 94:
Focus on Benefits, Not Features

The seminar description closely follows the title in importance. If the title is meant to hook them, the description is designed to actually land them. The description should be concise and provide an appealing portrait of the seminar. Too often, workshop descriptions mistakenly focus on seminar features, such as the following:

- This seminar will be presented with state of the art presentation equipment.
- You will be learning in a comfortable setting in the beautiful Rockies.
- Case studies will be used throughout the seminar.

Although the above examples present useful information, they are features and not benefits. Features have a place in the brochure—as supporting information, not the main focus. Features do not convince people to attend your seminar. To grab people's interest and induce them to attend, you must offer tangible benefits. "What's in it for me" is the participant's hot button. "Participants will use the latest, most powerful computers" is a feature, whereas "You will learn how to implement seven security measures to protect your network from hackers" is a tangible benefit; the seminar promises you protection if you implement the suggested security measures.

A good question to address is, What tangible benefits or results will the workshop participants take away with them? Benefit examples include increased profits, personal improvement, greater efficiency, new skills, protection of assets, greater savings, improved health, higher esteem or tax savings.

TIP NUMBER 95:
Decide On the Description Format

Brochure writers use different formats when writing the workshop description. One approach is to describe the program in paragraph form. If you use this format, use short, concise sentences. Descriptions in this format should not be long, rambling paragraphs. Here is an example of the paragraph approach used for a program entitled How to Design a Training Program (So That Anyone Can Present It Successfully):

A TRAINING WORKSHOP THAT FOCUSES ON TRAINING PROGRAM DESIGN . . .

That's right, introducing a workshop that will help you design and develop training programs—without wasting your time on presentation skills and techniques you don't need.

Chances are, if you've read this far, this program is just what you need. Maybe you're an experienced trainer—give you the right program, and hey, you've got learners balanced on the edge of their seats. Or maybe you're a computer whiz—you can effortlessly teach your techniques to anyone, anytime . . . as long as it's one on one. Or maybe you're a top-notch supervisor with proven skills on the job.

Whatever the case, now you've been asked to do something different with your valuable skills and irreplaceable knowledge. You've been asked to write it down.

In fact, it's your job to see that these skills are unilaterally transferred—and transferable—to every member of the work team so

*they can continue to grow the success of your company. But . . .
while you may have had training in sales or presentation techniques, you've probably never received the kind of training you
need to actually develop training programs.*

That's where we come in . . . .

Another approach is to use the bullet format. For a
new supervisor's workshop the description might appear
as follows:

A powerful, one-day seminar that will:

- *Provide immediate payback through reduced turnover,
  fewer grievances, lower absenteeism and fewer customer
  complaints.*
- *Increase your promotability by revealing seven leadership
  secrets of the pros.*
- *Slash employee-turnover costs and hassles by using
  specific hiring and interviewing techniques.*

Benefit 2 promises the most value for an ambitious person.
It promises to reveal secrets on how to climb the corporate
ladder.

A bullet format for a Customer Service Seminar might
appear as follows:

You will learn skills like these to make your job easier and
customers happier:

- *Five techniques to help you keep your cool when confronted
  by the customer from hell.*
- *How to handle the seven most common customer
  complaints.*
- *How to say "no" when you have to without arousing
  anger and resentment.*
- *How to use words that trigger positive, good feelings.*

Other suggestions for your description include the following:

1. Avoid wording such as "If you attend" or "If you decide to attend." Show confidence in your written words—assume they are going to attend.
2. Suggest urgency, using wording such as "Fax your reservation now or reserve your seat by acting now."
3. Use wide margins and plenty of white space. White space is a design feature that makes copy more attractive and easier to read.

TIP NO. 96:
Focus on Who Should Attend

It is now time to zero in on your target group. This is the group at which you will be aiming your marketing efforts. They are people with common characteristics that set them apart from other groups. The more information you have about your target group, the more precisely you can focus your marketing efforts.

The trick is to be specific enough to appeal to your primary audience without excluding others who may wish to attend. Who do you want to come to the seminar? The more specific you are, the smaller the audience. The more general, the more basic the participants may feel it is. You need to target who the workshop is intended for. This can be done by identifying particpants by function or title, such as "This seminar is for employee relations managers, human resources managers, personnel managers and labor relations specialists." Or it can be done by identifying specific needs or deficiencies, such as in the following example:

"You should attend our design seminar if:

- You're responsible for developing printed materials.
- You're an experienced desktop publisher who wants to brush up on the fundamentals.
- You're new to the "ins" and "outs" of desktop publishing.
- You need to recharge your batteries.
- You simply want to learn about desktop publishing. "

Bottom line, you don't want to attract participants who will find your seminar too basic or participants who will be in over their heads.

TIP NUMBER 97:
Use the Scan Test for the Big Three

Once you have grabbed the attention of potential participants with your topic, they immediately search for the price, location and date in that order.

> *Price.*
> If a person is interested, they look for the price. Don't hide it. I recently received a brochure on how to be a tough negotiator. I liked the title and immediately began searching for the price. After quickly leafing through the brochure, I failed to find it. I started over again and scanned more closely. Then, on page seven of the eight page brochure, I finally found the elusive price of $159 per person printed in small type in a corner nestled between two other items that were in bold type. The price was reasonable, but for whatever reason the price was placed in an obscure place. I could have just as easily given up and discarded the brochure. Don't take the chance. Place the price in a noticeable spot and use large bold colors.

Location.

Once the price is found, potential participants look to see where the seminar is being offered. The address of the facility where the seminar will be held should be included. This, of course, requires that you make arrangements with the facility beforehand. You don't want to advertise a location and then find that it is booked with no meeting rooms available. If the place is deemed convenient, they then look for the date.

Date.

Potential registrants then determine if the date works with their calendar.

Although not every person follows this sequence, many do. Don't risk losing them because they cannot find this basic information. A good technique is to have friends apply the PLD (price, location, date) scan test to your brochure before it is finalized. The test involves timing them while they look for the PLD. If it takes more than five seconds, you should consider modifications to make the PLD more easily and quickly located.

TIP NUMBER 98:
Make it Easy for People to Register

Make the registration process simple without making people go through hoops to register. To do this, provide an easy to use, simple registration form that requires only the information that is absolutely necessary. Here are the basics:

* Seminar name, city and date
* Names and titles of those attending
* Organization, address and phone number

- E-mail address and fax
- Method of payment (credit card information)

You may need additional information but make sure that it is absolutely necessary. Some of it can be gathered later, such as answers to the questions How did you hear about us? or Do you have special dietary requirements? Above all, avoid such items as approving manager's name and title. Some seminar companies will send out a follow-up letter to the supervisor telling them all the good things the employee learned. In fact, this is nothing more than a marketing ploy to get another name for their mailing list. What they don't realize is that this turns away some people, who wonder "Why do they want my supervisor's name? Are they going to check up on me?"

It is a good idea to put your phone number on all pages. Brochures are passed around. If it is only on the registration form and someone has cut it out, you may lose potential registrations.

TIP NUMBER 99:
Include an Outline of the Program

Most program outlines are similar. They consist of a series of statements supported by bullet points. Here is a typical section, with a leading statement supported by bullet points:

Get Acquainted with Microsoft Office Fundamentals
- An overview of Office and what it's designed to do
- How to simultaneously start an application and open a new document
- Lost a file? How to use Find File to search for missing files
- Why using long file names isn't always a good idea
- How to set up the Office shortcut bar

An outline may consist of several of these sections. Another approach is to use a standard outline approach. This format is not as eye-catching as the statement bullet approach.

Some seminar providers include a detailed outline with times printed at the beginning of each section or topic. I have tried this approach and found that some people will get upset if you do not keep to the printed times: "You promised a break at 10:30, and we didn't get it until 11:15." A better approach is to show the beginning and ending times. This leaves you the flexibility to adjust the seminar to your audience's interests.

TIP NUMBER 100:
Include Your Bio and Photograph

This is where you may have a definite advantage over the big seminar companies. Many do not identify the actual presenter because they do not know who will be conducting the specific program. Another approach they use is to list several presenters with the notation: "Meet our faculty. One of these capable experts will present your seminar." You, on the other hand, can highlight your bio and photo and indicate that you are the presenter and that there will be no substitutes.

If you use guest speakers for segments of the program, be sure to include them in your brochure. They will help sell your program. Sometimes I will bring in colleagues who are experts and have them do a one-hour segment during a two-day or three-day workshop, and then I pay them a small honorarium. This permits me to include their names and photographs in the brochure. This results in a win-win situation for everyone. Participants benefit from the additional points of view. My colleagues appreciate the opportunity to share their ideas and enjoy the chance to be on stage. It provides me a break during a long workshop.

TIP NUMBER 101:
Include Testimonials

When I first started giving seminars, I did not think about testimonials. When someone told me it was a great seminar, I didn't ask if I could quote them. Don't make this mistake. Aggressively pursue testimonials that are offered. My four testimonial rules are:

1. Never blatantly solicit a testimonial; you do not want to create the impression that you are trolling for testimonials.
2. Always humbly receive a compliment and then figure out a way to get permission to use it as a testimonial. Get the participant's name, position and company. People that are known and hold prominent positions have the greatest value.
3. Offer to put their comments in writing, if they don't have time to write one. Or, send them a follow-up e-mail with their comment and ask whether you can use it.
4. Maintain a file that documents testimonials. You should not use a person's name without obtaining their written permission. However, if you cannot get their permission, you can list general statements, such as "A state senator proclaimed this as one of the best seminars to teach people how to obtain federal loans."

Here are some examples of wording used to introduce endorsements in brochures:

Is this seminar worth one day of your valuable time? Yes! But don't just take our word for it. Read what past participants have to say:

Most enjoyable professional seminar that I have ever participated in. On a scale of 1-10, I give it a 10+!

John Wilson
Human Resources Director, the Wilson Companies.

Customer Service must be continually reinforced. Your seminar hit at the gut reasons companies need to practice quality customer service. Thank you.

Henry Wood
President, All Car Automotive.

Another approach is to list the companies that have sent people to your seminar.

Alcoa, AOL Time Warner, Boeing, Carnival, Coca-Cola, Disney, IBM, Microsoft and Xerox have sent employees to our Customer Etiquette seminar.

One seminar provider printed twenty thousand brochures for a series of five seminars he was presenting in different cities. He printed them all at once to get a printing price break. Because he had not given the seminar when he printed the brochure, he did not have any testimonials. However, after the first session he received two valuable endorsements, which he wanted to include in his brochure. But he had over fifteen thousand brochures remaining. He solved the problem by taking the brochures to the printer and having them overprint the testimonials in purple ink. Fortunately, he had left enough white space on the original brochure that he was able to include the additional information. He now leaves space on his brochures so that he can insert late-breaking information and make it look like it is part of the original design. If you intend to use this approach, do not have the flyers folded at the time of the original printing. Most printers do not have the capability to print on folded flyers.

TIP NUMBER 102: *Check into Continuing Education Credits*

Some seminar providers award eligible participants Continuing Education Units (CEUs). CEUs are nationally recognized units of measure for continuing education and training programs that meet the criteria of the International Association for Continuing Education and Training (IACET). You will see messages, such as the following, about CEUs in brochures:

- *Our programs are authorized for 7 contact hours (7 CEUs) as set forth in the guidelines of the International Association for Continuing Education and Training (IACET).*
- *Many national, state and local licensing boards and professional organizations will grant CEUs for attendance at our seminars when you submit the course outline and your Certificate of Attendance. You may want to contact your own board or organization to find out what is required.*
- *At the completion of the seminar, you will receive a CEU certificate, which acknowledges that you have earned .3 CEU's for a half-day seminar, .6 CEU's for a one-day seminar.*

Many professions require members to continue their education by accumulating a specified number of CEUs each year. They achieve this by attending workshops that award CEUs. If your target audience includes members who must acquire CEUs, contact IACET to determine their certification requirements for your program. IACET now offers two options for recognition of programs, the Single Event Approval Program and the Authorized Provider Certification Program. Their Web site (www.iacet.org) describes these programs, outlines the requirements and includes applications. Their address is

IACET
1620 I Street, NW, Suite 615
Washington, DC 20006
Phone: (202) 857-1122
E-mail: Iacet@monic.com

TIP NUMBER 103:
Be Careful with Tax Advice

Many seminar brochures mention tax deduction possibilities:

- *Training taken to maintain or improve professional skills is usually tax deductible. Consult with your tax advisor. Your seminar expenses—including instruction fee, travel, meals and lodging—may be tax deductible according to the Treasury Regulation 1.162-5 Coughlin vs. Commissioner, 203F 2d307.*
- *The expense of continuing education, when taken to maintain and improve professional skills, may be tax deductible. Please contact your accountant for verification.*

Note that in both cases, the advice is hedged. In the first case, the word *usually* is used, and in the second case, the word *may* is used. In both examples, the participant is advised to talk to their tax advisor. I question the need to include statements about tax deductions in the brochure. Most people are aware of the general rules. They also know that their situation is probably unique. If you do use wording regarding tax deductions, make sure you include the qualifiers.

TIP NUMBER 104:
Seriously Consider a Seminar Guarantee

You should include a guarantee in your brochure. Seminar guarantees establish confidence. They are so prevalent today, people consider it a warning sign if you do not offer one. A guarantee is a cost of doing business. Sure, some people may ask for their money back. But, the fact is, very few, if any, will do so if you offer a quality program.

Here is the AMA Guarantee:

Your satisfaction is guaranteed! At AMA we guarantee the quality of our programs. It's that simple. More than 98% of our attenders say that they would recommend AMA events to their colleagues. But if for any reason you are not satisfied with the program, AMA will give you credit toward another program at a comparable price or refund your fee. That's it! No hassles. No loopholes. Just excellent service. That's what AMA is all about.

Fred Pryor has taken it further:

Results or Else! That's our guarantee. If you are not completely satisfied with this seminar, we will refund your tuition in full, at any time, no questions asked. Only Fred Pryor Seminars offers this comprehensive, lifetime guarantee.

If you are going to provide a seminar guarantee, do not hassle people when they apply for it. It creates bad feelings and gains nothing but bad will.

TIP NUMBER 105:
Let Them Know What Materials Will Be Provided

Seminar participants expect to be given a workbook, which includes such items as copies of slides, handouts and the latest information. Let them know that is not an ordinary workbook; it is a precious commodity that you have put a lot of energy into developing. Here are two examples of workbook descriptions:

Yours Free! A Valuable Workbook

We've created this special workbook for you to bring back to the office and use as a quick-reference guide. It contains important tools to help you confidently tackle problems head-on. It includes surveys, checklists and case studies.

You'll Leave With More Than Great, New Ideas

As a participant in our seminar you'll receive a hardbound workbook filled with tips, techniques, shortcuts and how-to's you learned at the program. Your workbook will serve as an invaluable desk reference, as you turn to it again and again for help with your questions.

TIP NUMBER 106:
Use Quizzes and Self-Tests

Some brochures include quizzes to increase interest. I call them teasers. The typical quiz includes three to five multiple-choice or true or false questions. These tests can be an effective technique if the questions are relevant to the seminar topic and are somewhat challenging. The trick is to make them challenging so that a person says, "I know I should know the answer, but I am not quite sure." If you use quizzes make sure that you include the answers somewhere in the brochure.

TIP NUMBER 107:
Devote Space to Marketing Your Other Products

Many brochures devote a portion of the space for promoting in-house training:

- *If you'd like to see productivity really skyrocket, train your entire employee group—at the date and location you choose. This seminar can be brought to your location and customized to meet your employees' specific training needs—at a surprisingly affordable cost.*
- *If you prefer to arrange for group training or consulting in your own setting—at your own schedule—call our in-house Training Consultant.*
- *Much of our in-house training business comes from referrals from employees who have attended our public sessions.*

  In-house sessions:

  —Save precious time away from the office
  —Provide quality training to your employees at considerable cost savings
  —Customize the program to your needs
  —Deal with real company problems
  —Prevent sensitive issues from becoming public knowledge

You also can market books, booklets, tapes, CDs and consulting in your brochure. These are all part of the back-end sales that will increase your seminar receipts.

TIP NUMBER 108:
Decide on Your Cancellation Policy

Your brochure should let participants know how to cancel. Here are some typical cancellation provisions:

- *Cancel up to 7 days before the seminar and your registration fee will be refunded less a $25 enrollment charge. If you need to cancel less than 7 days prior to the seminar, you may send a substitute or transfer your registration to another seminar of your choice within 12 months.*

- *Cancellations received up to five working days before the workshop are refundable, minus a $50 registration service charge. After that, cancellations are subject to the entire workshop fee, which you may apply toward a future workshop. Please note that if you don't cancel and don't attend, you are still responsible for payment. Substitutions may be made at any time.*

Cancellations can affect your bottom line, especially if you have met the bare minimum and people cancel at the last minute. If you are providing meals, you must guarantee the count within 24 to 72 hours of the session. If people do not show up, you most likely will be stuck with the extra meal costs. Bottom line, don't penalize registrants for canceling, but try to recapture your costs. In both the examples listed above, the cancellation fee represents less than 15 percent of the cost of the seminar.

TIP NUMBER 109:
Develop Your No-Show Policy

All seminar providers are plagued by seminar phantoms. Phantoms promise to show up but fail to do so. They call or register by fax or e-mail and usually promise to send payment later. Prepayment reduces the number of no-shows. Many seminar providers will not refund the registration fee if the participant does not show up and did not call beforehand. Others will let the registrant enroll in another workshop of equal value.

TIP NUMBER 110:
Consider Including an
Act-Now Provision

People may respond favorably to your brochure but put it down to peruse later. Unfortunately, when they put it down, it gets buried or forgotten. Here is an example of act-now language that some seminar providers put in their brochure:

Please Note: This special workshop is offered only a few times each year and class sizes are limited (or fill up), so please enroll early to ensure your place.

Are there incentives that you can offer to entice them to sign up at the time they review the brochure? Seminar providers offer a variety of incentives to accomplish this.

If you sign up for John Kremer's three-day program on book marketing, he throws in a thirty minute on-site, personal consulting session for each participant. Fred Pryor has established the Fred Pryor Club, which offers free seminars.

If you attend three seminars, you receive a fourth registration free. Pryor also provides a newsletter that contains information on professional and managerial issues. If you attend a seminar you get four issues free.

Seminar provider Fred Gleeck offers the following for his book publishing boot camp:

1.   Half hour consulting time
2.   Substantial discount on future seminars
3.   A print on demand (POD) book on marketing
4.   Discounts off products and books

One of the most popular incentives is the group discount. Many seminar providers offer a discount for multiple registrations from the same organization. A good technique used to encourage participants to respond immediately is to add this phrasing to your brochure: "Send your registration in now. Encourage others to register later. We will keep track of all registrations from your organization," or "Send in your registration now. We'll keep track of your company's team, you don't have to bother with the detail." If you ask them to all register at once, they may put off registration until they convince friends to attend. During this process, they may decide the hassle is too burdensome and decide to forgo the seminar.

TIP NUMBER 111:
Practice the Three Proofing Rules

You guessed it: The three most important rules are proofread, proofread and proofread.

Mistakes in your brochure can be killers—especially if they are made on dates, locations, price or other contact information. Moreover, brochures that contain spelling or grammatical errors create a negative impression with your participants. Don't make the mistake of running your brochure over to the printer as soon as you finish drafting it. Put it aside and wait for a day or two. Then read it over at least three times. Another technique is to read your brochure aloud to someone else. Have them stop you when something sounds awkward, wordy or stuffy.

A better check is to have other people proof your brochure. They are not as close to it and will more likely spot errors that you overlooked. They can also check to see if your ideas make sense and whether the brochure focuses on benefits rather than features.

Mary Miller developed a great brochure for her Breaking the Upper Management Glass Ceiling seminar. Miller was so pleased, she spent over $2,500 to print 16,000 copies. Unfortunately, she forgot to include the date of her seminar in the brochure. Although some of those who were interested in the seminar called to get the date, many did not. Mary would usually attract approximately 1 percent of the target market on her mailings. Instead of getting the expected 160 participants, she only received 45. If you are listing seminars at multiple locations in your brochure, take the time to verify every date with the meeting facility before you order a print run.

If you have tied your seminar date to a specific event or conference, make sure that you mention it in your brochure, for example, "This is a preconference workshop one day before the National Real Estate Brokers Association annual conference."

TIP NUMBER 112:
Don't Discount the Shelf Life
of Your Brochure

You will find that people will keep your seminar brochure much longer than you would have ever imagined. Out of the blue, I have had people call for an in-house seminar two or three years after the event. My record is seven years. A senior administrative analyst from the County of Los Angeles Chief Administrator's Office called and wanted to attend the next performance measurement seminar I was going to give. Unfortunately, I had discontinued the seminar two years before because of a lack of registrations. After several phone calls, she convinced me to give a seminar on performance measurement to the Los Angeles County Management Team. Los Angeles County is one of the largest local governments in the world, and her arm twisting led to a complete series of performance measurement seminars for every department in the County.

Your printed brochure is evidence that you are a pro. Very few seminar providers have the confidence to spend their own money to put on their own seminar. Once you print a brochure showing that you are putting on your own seminar, keep extra copies for promotional material. Show them that you have enough confidence in your seminar to put your own money on the line. It works.

TIP NUMBER 113: Get a Brochure Critique

You should have someone critique your brochure before you print it. I have found that family members and friends can be recruited at relatively low cost. However, you get what you pay for.

If you want a professional critique, LERN critiques seminar brochures for approximately $100. Appendix E includes a critique of one of my seminar brochures. Contact LERN at:

Learning Resources Network (LERN)
Attention: Brochure Critique
P.O. Box 9
River Falls, Wisconsin 54022

9

Setting the Price for Your Seminar

Underpricing seminars and workshops is one of the most common mistakes made by people just getting into this business.

Training Shoppe Vice President June Wood

Many seminar providers don't charge as much as they should for their seminars and workshops. This is especially true for beginners. So, how do you price your seminar?

Pricing a seminar is tricky, especially if you have not given the seminar before. Recognize that the fee-setting process is subjective, and there are no commonly accepted formulas. However, there are several factors to consider when establishing your seminar price.

TIP NUMBER 114: Determine What the Market Will Bear

As a first step, examine your market. A little research will give you an idea of what the market will bear and help you avoid underpricing or overpricing your seminar. Collect seminar information from every organization and person providing a seminar similar to yours. After you have accumulated the information, record it and analyze the results. The following tables present a sample comparison of prices for basic supervision workshops.

Seminar Title	Company	Length	Total Price	Per-Day Price
How to Supervise People	Seminars for Fast Fooders	1 Day	$159	$159
The First Time Supervisor's Workshop	London, Lloyds & Associates	1 Day	$459	$459
How to Supervise Problem Employees	Jennifer Ames	2 Days	$379	$190
How to Delegate	The American Supervisors Association	2 Days	$895	$448
How to Coach Employees	The Learning University	1 Day	$399	$399

Average Per Day Price (1,655/5 = $331)	$331
Median Price (The median is the middle number): $159, $190, $399, $448 and $459.	$399
Highest Price	$459
Lowest Price	$159

The highs and lows of the market establish the broad parameters in which you can establish your price. In this case the high is $459, and the low is $159. However, you should not be constrained by the range. If you have a reason to go higher, such as a higher-quality seminar, you may decide to exceed the range. Or, you may wish to do a one-day, no frills seminar for $99.

TIP NUMBER 115:
Relate Your Seminar Fee
to Your Seminar Goals

Before you set a fee for your seminar, think about your goals. Why are you offering this seminar? A corporate trainer may wish to go into the public seminar business to make money. In this case, profit is the motive, and efforts will be directed at maximizing profits. You may have another purpose that is just as important as, or more important than, making a profit. A real estate developer may have acquired considerable development experience and has decided to share some of his knowledge with others. A successful consultant may want to use seminars to promote her business and obtain consulting contracts. Again, she may forgo some profit just to fill seats at her seminar. An author, on the other hand, may use the seminar as a way of selling books and tapes. In each of these cases, the seminar provider may sacrifice some profit just to get participants to attend their seminars.

TIP NUMBER 116:
Determine the Image You Wish
to Create

Where do you want to price your seminar? Do you want to position it at the high end, in the middle or at the low end of the market? The general rule is that price is inversely proportional to the number of participants. Higher prices mean fewer participants. Lower prices mean more participants. It does not follow that you should necessarily price your seminar at the lower end of the market. You may make more money by charging near the higher end and limiting attendance. With fewer participants, your costs are less. It also allows you to provide more quality time for your participants. When you charge at the higher end, participants expect higher-end amenities. Higher-end seminar providers usually produce an expensive looking brochure and use a first-class meeting facility. Some even provide meals. Many of the large seminar companies have carved a market niche at the lower end of the market. They make their money from the large number of people who attend as well as the additional products they sell, such as books and tapes. Their disadvantage is that they must make their seminar information very general because they have such a varied audience. The amount of interaction is also limited because of the large number of participants. This assembly line training leaves a market niche consisting of participants desiring a higher quality experience with more personalized attention.

TIP NUMBER 117:
Estimate the Cost to Develop, Market and Present Your Program

Although the market will ultimately determine the price at which your seminar will sell, you want to know what the costs are to produce your seminar. This becomes your price floor, the price at which you should not offer your seminar if you want to make a profit from registrations. In some cases, seminar providers will take a loss on registrations to sell products at, and after, the seminar.

START-UP COSTS

When you first begin your seminar business, you will incur start-up costs that should be considered as capital investments. There are four categories of start-up costs to consider:

1. Hardware items used in the creation of your seminars, such as computers, printers, copiers, photographic equipment, and scanners
2. Software, such as word processing, spreadsheet, graphics and presentation programs, used in developing seminars
3. Presentation equipment, such as easels, slide projectors, overhead projectors, VCRs, monitors, screens and LCDs
4. Business equipment and software, such as faxes, postage meters, scales, folding machines and accounting software

Before purchasing presentation equipment, you may wish to try rental equipment first. Just before I started providing seminars, I purchased a large, expensive overhead projector. It was a top of the line unit at the time. Since then I have only used it two times, even though I have given hundreds of presentations. Overhead projectors, even the portable ones, are bulky and awkward to carry, especially on airplanes. I also purchased an overhead projector attachment that automatically feeds overheads. I am still waiting to use this unit.

Much of the hardware and software acquired for the development of your seminars can be used for your business operation. Once acquired, these items can be used for the development and delivery of other seminars, so the costs can be amortized. One way to do this is to attribute a percentage of your start-up cost, such as 5 percent, to each seminar. Another way is to consider these as overall business costs and not attribute any portion to seminars. If you use start-up costs in calculating your break-even point, they are considered fixed costs.

DESIGN COSTS

Design costs are the direct expenses incurred in producing your seminar. They include all items needed to create your seminar, such as slides, overheads, handouts, notebooks and demonstration material. Although sometimes overlooked, design costs also include items purchased for research and background purposes, such as books, magazines, audiotapes and videotapes, survey instruments and even travel expenses related to creating your seminar. Design costs are considered fixed costs because they do not vary with the number of participants.

My wife and I love to collect and show the little, lighted Dickens Village houses sold by Department 56 of Minneapolis. If we were to design a seminar on How to Create a Realistic Dickens Village Display, we could expect to spend money during the design phase for the following items:

- Photography materials expenses (we would want to obtain photographs of outstanding displays)
- Source books describing Dickens Village pieces
- Articles and books on display techniques
- Several Dickens lighted houses and accessories for display purposes
- Material to make sample roads and landscaping
- Slides and overheads
- Master participant workbook
- Travel expenses, telephone and other costs incurred while creating the program

PROMOTION COSTS

Promotion costs are all your expenses incurred to convince people to attend your seminar. When analyzing promotion costs, you need to determine if the promotion is for the seminar or your business. A general brochure on your business that does not contain specific information about a seminar is not a promotion cost for your seminar. Promotion costs are fixed costs, are expended up-front and are lost if you decide to cancel the seminar because of low registrations. Promotion costs include such items as:

- Mailing list rental
- Brochure design and printing
- Envelopes (if used)
- Postage
- Newspaper and magazine ads
- Internet advertising

DELIVERY COSTS

Delivery costs are the monies you spend delivering your seminar. Other than deposits, most delivery costs can be avoided if you cancel the seminar. Delivery costs include the following:

- Room deposit and rental
- Equipment rental
- Workshop materials and notebooks
- Food and beverages
- Other items provided to participants, such as books

Most delivery costs are variable costs in that they increase with the number of participants. The more participants you sign up, the more notebooks, handouts and beverages you will need to provide. Equipment rentals and room deposits and rentals are fixed costs. The following tables compares the different types of costs.

COST CATEGORY	COST ITEMS
Start-Up Costs (Fixed Costs)	Computer Laptop computer Copier Ink jet and laser printers Scanner Digital camera Zip and jag storage Internet and Web site fees Letterhead Word processing, graphics, spreadsheet and presentation programs Easel and pads Overhead projector Slide machine Screen VCR and monitor LCD or other projector Business equipment Accounting software Automatic hole punch Postage meter, scale and folding machine Toll free number fees Answering machine Credit card processing equipment and fees
Design Costs (Fixed Costs)	Periodicals, books and magazines Copier fees Clipping service fees Research fees Audiotapes Transparencies Slides Canned training programs Management instruments Surveys Demonstration material Travel expenses Duplication expenses Other costs incurred when researching and designing your program
Promotion Costs (Fixed Costs)	Brochure design and printing Mailing list rental Direct mail letters and envelopes Postcards and Web cards Bulk mail application and permit fees Postage Newspaper and magazine ads Internet advertising fees E-zine advertising Radio advertising Television advertising
Delivery Costs (Variable and Fixed Costs)	Meeting room rental Food, coffee, tea and other beverage costs Workshop notebooks and materials Duplicating costs Office supplies and other demonstration materials Flip chart pads and pens Equipment rental

TIP NUMBER 118:
Develop Your Break-Even Point

The break-even point is defined as the point where seminar revenues equal expenses. There is no loss incurred or profit made at the break-even point. A break-even analysis is an important planning tool that can help you establish the price of the seminar or the number of registrations needed to recover costs.

To develop a break-even analysis, you need to compile and then separate variable costs from the fixed costs of your seminar. The following table and calculations illustrate a sample compilation of costs.

FIXED COSTS	AMOUNT	VARIABLE COSTS	AMOUNT
Portion of Start-Up Costs (5 percent)	$250	Workbooks	$ 8
Design Costs	$300	Materials	$ 5
Promotion Costs	$4,750	Beverages	$10
Room Deposit and Rental	$500	Food	$27
Equipment Rental	$125		
Total Fixed Costs	**$6,000**	**Total Variable Costs Per Participant**	**$50**

You can determine how many participants are needed for you to break even with the following analysis. The formula to calculate the break-even point for seminars is:

Registrations (R) = $\dfrac{\text{Fixed Costs (FC)}}{\text{Seminar Price (P)} - \text{Variable Costs(VC)}}$

Using this formula, you can test several scenarios. If you peg our seminar registration fee at $200 and have fixed costs of $6,000 and variable costs of $50 per participant, you will need to obtain 40 registrations to break even.

$$R = \frac{\$6,000}{\$200 - \$50} = 40$$

If you raise the cost to $250, you will need a registration level of 30 to break even.

$$R = \frac{\$6,000}{\$250 - \$50} = 30$$

You also can test levels of participation to determine the break-even point. Assume you have $5,000 in fixed costs, $75 per participant in variable costs and you expect to obtain between forty and fifty registrations. What is the minimum you can charge to break even? The formula to determine price follows:

$$\text{Price} = \frac{\text{Fixed Costs}}{\text{Registrations}} + \text{Variable Costs}$$

The seminar price needed to break even with fifty registrations would be $175:

$$P = \frac{\$5,000}{50} + \$75 = \$175$$

The seminar price needed to break even with forty registrations would be $200:

$$P = \frac{\$5,000}{40} + \$75 = \$200$$

However, the price may need to be higher if you provide a discount for multiple registrations.

The break-even analysis enables you to test several scenarios related to price or number of registrations needed. From the results you must make judgements as to what appears to be achievable and what does not. In one of my first seminars on supervision, I wanted to put a bare-bones program together and only charge $79 per participant. After calculating the break-even point, I determined that I would need to attract two hundred participants to break even. I decided that this was an unrealistic number for a first-time seminar. I instead opted to charge $149.

TIP NUMBER 119:
Identify All Your Estimated
Revenues

Although we have been focusing on registration fees, seminar providers make money from seminars in several ways—registration fees, back of the room sales and backside revenues.

Fees.

How much are you going to receive from seminar registrations? Seminar providers can receive money from a sponsoring organization or from participants. Registration fees are also known as the front side.

Back of the room sales.

Seminar providers soon learn that they can multiply returns by offering products and services for sale at their seminars. Called back of the room sales, they include such items as books, pamphlets, audiotapes, videotapes, CDs and consulting services.

Backside revenues.
Seminar providers also reap returns by selling services or products after the seminar. Backside items may include consulting services, newsletters, access to specialized databases, books, audiotapes and videotapes. Some providers will sell copies of the course workbook to people who cannot attend.

From the very beginning, you should begin developing products and services to sell at and after your seminars. If you haven't developed any yourself, another alternative is to partner with people who provide complementary products. You can strike a deal where they sell you books or other items at a substantial discount, such as 50 to 60 percent off, and then you resell them at full cost. Or you can negotiate a commission for selling their products.

TIP NUMBER 120:
Compute the Return on Your Promotional Investment

One way to determine the success of your seminar marketing efforts is to compute the return on your promotional investment. Promotion costs represent an investment. You spend marketing dollars to attract participants to your seminar. Your promotion costs produce your income, and income determines whether your seminar will be a success. A ratio used by seminar providers is the return on your promotional investment (RPI).

This ratio is computed by dividing the seminar income by the promotion costs. Assume you received $4,600 in registrations fees, and you spent $2,300 in marketing activities:

$$\frac{\$4,600}{\$2,300} = 2$$

Thus promotion costs result in a 2 to 1 return. Another way to express it is that every dollar spent on promotion produced two dollars in income. A 2 to 1 RPI is marginal and after production costs and trainer time are taken into account, leaves little profit. A more acceptable return on your promotional investment is 3 to 1 or better.

TIP NUMBER 121:
Recognize the Psychological Price Breaks

Kent Hutchinson, Associate Director of Continuing Education at Stephen F. Austin State University, raised the price of a computer applications seminar. He needed additional funds to compete with an adjoining institution that had increased their fees and began an aggressive marketing campaign. He raised the price from $40 to $49 on all computer application seminars. With the additional revenue he was able to increase marketing. This resulted in a 20 percent increase in enrollments. Flush with success, Hutchinson increased the fee of all seminars to their natural price breaks, such as from $50 to $59 and $70 to $79. Although he did not see a 20 percent increase in registrations for these other seminars, he had modest increases. More important, he did not lose any enrollments. The additional income generated by this change enabled him to increase publicity for the entire program.

There appears to be thresholds at which people take note of a change in price. As long as you don't exceed these thresholds, people do not appear to notice. The key is to identify the thresholds and set prices close to the bar. Instead of charging $40, charge $49. Instead of $179 charge $199. People do not perceive a difference between $79 and $99, but they do at $100. This is especially true if the employer is paying the tab. What are the thresholds?

$49	$99	$149	$199	$249
$299	$349	$399	$499	$999

Psychological price levels are understood by retailers. Drive down the street and notice the prices posted in the windows. Most prices end with 95 or 99 cents.

TIP NUMBER 122:
Determine Your Capture Ratio

The capture ratio is defined as the ratio between number of pieces of mail sent and the number of people signing up for the advertised seminar. It is the response rate to your mailing.

Dividing the number of participants signed up for your seminar by the number of pieces mailed results in the capture ratio. For example if you mail 7,000 brochures and you get 35 participants, your capture ratio is .005 or 1/2 of 1 percent. With a capture ratio of .005, a mailing of 25,000 will produce 125 participants.

Knowing your capture ratio helps you determine the size of the mailing you need. For example, if your are aiming for 150 participants and your historic capture rate is 2 percent, you would mail approximately 7,500 pieces (150 divided by 0.02 equals 7,500). Capture ratio can also help you determine the size of the room you will need for the seminar. Knowing your capture ratio, however, does not help you determine profitability.

TIP NUMBER 123:
Determine Whether to Proceed with
Your Seminar

You've designed your seminar, sent out brochures and the registrations begin to trickle in, but not at the rate you expected. You have made a deposit on a hotel room, and the hotel manager is calling to get the rest of your rental fee. You have incurred costs for all of these activities. Your investment will be lost if you do not proceed. On the other hand, is it prudent to spend more money? It is time to determine whether to proceed or pull the plug. What do you do? Here is a questionnaire to help you decide whether to proceed with your seminar.

1. How does the money situation look at this point?

   Slight Profit   Break Even   Slight Loss   Large Loss

2. How many more registrations are needed to break even?

   0 to 9%   10 to 19%   20 to 29%   30 to 39%   Over 40%

3. How many additional registrations will you likely receive?

   0 to 9%   10 to 19%   20 to 29%   30 to 39%   Over 40%

4. If you proceed with the seminar, what is the probability of making back of the room sales?

   Very Likely   Possibly   Unlikely

5. If you proceed with the seminar, what is the probability of obtaining back-end revenues, such as consulting contracts or in-house training opportunities?

   Very Likely   Possibly   Unlikely

6. If you proceed with the seminar, will you gain valuable training experience?

   Yes   Possibly   Unlikely

   Explain:
   _____
   _____
   _____

7. If you cancel the seminar, what damage will be done to your reputation?

   None   Little   Considerable

   Explain:
   _____
   _____
   _____

8. Can you reduce costs without reducing the quality of your seminar?

   No   Perhaps   Yes

   Explain:
   _____
   _____
   _____

9. What were your original goals? Is it worth it to proceed with the seminar to achieve these goals?

   Most important goal:
   _____

   Explain:
   _____
   _____
   _____

10. Sum it up with the following decision chart:

Top Three Reasons to Proceed	Top Three Reasons to Not Proceed
1.	1.
2.	2.
3.	3.

My decision:

Seminar Partners Need Prenuptial Agreements

I have found that having a written agreement is perhaps the safest way to preserve friendships. What seems to destroy them is the "I thought you said . . ." or "I misunderstood what you wanted" stories. With a well-drafted written agreement, each party knows what was intended.

Author and publisher Dean Barrett

Martha and Mike were good friends. They had worked together several years at a Fortune 500 investment firm and decided to jointly develop and present a seminar on profiting from high-risk, high-gain investment opportunities. Both were experienced presenters, having given workshops and seminars through the American Management Association.

Because they were such good friends, they decided against a written agreement. Mike summed up their feelings, "Why ruin a good friendship?" Instead they spent their time talking about how much fun it would be to work together on such an exciting seminar and "get paid for it, too." Although they were discussing the new seminar, Martha mentally noted how much Mike loved to talk. This tendency, she thought, would be a definite plus for their seminar.

The seminar venture started out well. Martha, who had a little more experience than Mike, planned and outlined the program. Mike supported Martha by conducting the research that was necessary to fill in the information gaps. They both worked on the notebook and handout materials, with Mike volunteering to pull everything together.

Martha organized the seminar into one-hour modules. Rather than attempt a joint presentation, they decided that the best approach would be to take turns presenting the individual modules. Martha would kick off the seminar with a short introduction, and Mike would follow with the first module. They would continue the alternate presentations as follows:

High-Gain Investments for the Not So Timid			
Agenda			
Time	Item	Presenter	Ending Time
8:30 A.M.	Coffee & Registration		8:45 A.M.
8:45 A.M.	Introduction	Martha	9:00 A.M.
9:00 A.M.	Module 1	Mike	10:00 A.M.
10:00 A.M.	Module 2	Martha	11:00 A.M.
11:00 A.M.	Module 3	Mike	12:00 noon
12:00 noon	Lunch		1:00 P.M.
1:00 P.M.	Module 4	Martha	2:00 P.M.
2:00 P.M.	Module 5	Mike	3:00 P.M.
3:00 P.M.	Module 6	Martha	4:00 P.M.
4:00 P.M.	Close	Mike	4:30 P.M.

The day of the seminar finally arrived. Although Martha agreed to arrive early and check on the equipment and room setup, she did not get to the hotel until 8:45 A.M. Not to worry, Mike arrived at 7:30 and checked on the room and equipment. It was fortunate that he had arrived early because he had to oversee the rearrangement of the seating. The room was set up classroom style, instead of their requested cafe style with five people per table.

Both presenters were anxious, excited and energized. Both graciously greeted participants as they entered the room. Although Mike said he would sign in participants as they arrived, he forgot to do so.

Martha's introduction to the seminar went as smooth as silk. Having captured the audience's interest, she handed off to Mike as planned at 9:00 sharp. It was clear that Mike had done his homework as he easily picked up where Martha left off. The audience was enthralled, and Mike was energized from their response. He did a great job presenting his module.

Martha checked her watch at 9:55 A.M. and anxiously awaited the closing of his session. She also was invigorated by Mike's presentation and couldn't wait to jump back in. Mike, however, showed no signs of winding down. He seemed oblivious to the time. It's like he was in a time warp. "Oh well," Martha thought, "I am sure he will wrap up soon." At 9:10 Mike was still going strong. Because they had no prearranged signals, Martha tried to get Mike's attention with subtle facial and hand signs. Having failed, she tried clearing her throat and then audibly shuffling papers. At 9:24 with still no indication of a let up, Martha stood up and told Mike to end his module. Stunned, and somewhat miffed, Mike reluctantly relinquished the stage.

Martha was now in the unenviable position of trying to condense a one-hour presentation into thirty-six minutes. To get back on schedule, Martha rushed through her presentation. She also skipped several overheads she had intended to present. Unfortunately, Martha's frantic attempt to catch up was not lost on the participants. They appeared bothered with her hurry-up approach, compared with Mike's relaxed style. But her efforts put them back on time.

Mike began presenting the last module before lunch. Martha was confident that Mike would keep on time because even he knew the importance of letting people out before the noon rush. As lunchtime neared, Mike was still going strong. Finally, at 12:20 Martha broke in and announced it was time for lunch. Mike apologized and told the participants that they could come back twenty minutes after one. Martha was angry. Not only had he stolen precious minutes from her first module, he now set her back another twenty minutes after lunch.

Martha began her after lunch presentation at 1:20. Having recognized that rushing through her material was not the thing to do, Martha decided to take her full hour and end at 2:20. "Let him see how it feels," she thought. At 2:00 P.M. Mike ceremonially stood up and jokingly demanded that Martha finish her module. (Hadn't she done the same thing to him?) Angry, Martha stammered and hastily concluded her remarks.

Mike's hogging of the limelight forced Martha to leave out critical information. This was information participants really needed to truly understand high-risk, high-gain investments. So, Martha decided to bring in the information by piggybacking on Mike's statements. When Mike talked about going short during a bull market, Martha suggested that the practice was too risky. When Mike suggested three high-risk, high-gain investments, Martha trashed all three. "Their price earnings ratios are too high to qualify for high-risk, high-gain status."

Both fumbled through the remainder of the seminar. When it was time to close, Mike began summing up by talking about the necessity of prudence even with high-risk investments. At this point, Martha decided to tease Mike on his risky investment portfolio and how he had yet to reap even a small profit. Mike was devastated. As he later told her, "In one simple quip you undermined my credibility and the whole program."

Shaken, Mike hastily gathered up the evaluation sheets, telling Martha, "I'll copy them and send you a set." Unknown to Martha at the time, she would never see the workshop evaluations.

The next week, Martha presented the seminar to the Rotary Club. She used some of Mike's material and didn't think anything of it because she was doing it for no fee. Five weeks later, a colleague gave Martha a brochure advertising the highly successful High-Gain Investments for the Not So Timid Investor seminar. Not only was her name left off, her modules were being presented by Jerry Croskrey, a renown securities advisor! Martha got a lawyer.

TIP NUMBER 124:
First, Decide Why You
Want a Partner

Talking about the seminar partnership from hell, Martha and Mike could write several chapters for the book. Their experience raises the following question: Is it worth it to work with a partner? Here are some of the reasons people decide to work with partners:

> *Knowledge and expertise.*
> You may need the person's expertise for part of the program. Perhaps that person wrote a book and will bring great drawing power to the seminar. It may be that you cannot give a comprehensive seminar without another person's expertise.

> *Credibility.*
> The person is articulate, well-known in the field and will enhance the credibility of the program. Naming a credible person in the brochure usually increases enrollments.

> *Contacts.*
> The person may have contacts that you do not. Perhaps they can help penetrate markets you could not without their help.

Money.
You may need financial help for the initial invest-ment required to market and present the seminar.

Time.
You may not have the time required to develop the seminar, workbook and handouts.

Comfort level.
You may want moral support before you take on your first seminar.

Business knowledge.
Another person may have business knowledge that you do not possess.

Whatever the reasons, before deciding on a partner, consider the alternatives. For example, if you need financial assistance, have you tried to obtain a loan? It may be much easier to get rid of or refinance a loan than disengage from a bad seminar partner.

TIP NUMBER 125:
Determine Whether You
Are Compatible

Before you form a partnership, ask yourself very honestly whether you like the person and can get along with him or her. Are you compatible? Your relationship will undoubtedly be strained at different points during the development, mar-keting and delivery of the seminar. Will business decisions fray the relationship? What will conflict do to it? Can you take criticism from this person? Can you give criticism to this person? It is said that the test of a good manager is whether the manager can fairly evaluate and constructively criticize friends. This applies more so to seminar partners.

TIP NUMBER 126:
Recognize the Deadly Sins
of a Partnership

If you have ever partnered with someone on a project or business, you are undoubtedly familiar with the partnership scenario—things start out well and then something stresses the partnership, and all of a sudden the partners are at war. Why does this happen? When potential partners first begin talking about a venture, very little if any of the discussion is devoted to interpersonal relationships. Budding partners, for whatever reasons, continue to make the same mistake. They just don't want to talk about the difficult issues or, more important, what they should do if the partnership starts to sour.

David Gage of Business Mediation Associates has helped many business partners resolve conflicts before they evolve into outright war. He marvels on how little quality time is spent on recruiting business partners and working on relationships. "People will interview receptionists more carefully than they will a potential partner. It's much easier for partners to work on a business plan or a marketing plan, rather than sort out how they're going to treat each other" (Gage, personnal communication, 2000).

TIP NUMBER 127:
Be Wary of Partners from Hell

Forget about getting the perfect seminar partner. Every person brings his or her own strengths and weaknesses to the partnership. You want to be wary of the following partner prototypes:

The Procrastinator. You know who they are. They promise the world but just don't get around to doing it. You must check on the procrastinator at all times, or you will find that they will let you down on critical items.

The Promoter. This partner does a great job selling the seminar. If selling a seminar is equivalent to poetry and presenting the seminar is equivalent to prose, these people are the poets. This can result in an effective partnership if their job is restricted to marketing. Don't expect them to do the designing or presenting. They view those jobs as mundane. The promoter's strength is also their weakness. Exaggeration may work well in the marketing phase but not in the seminar.

The Dominator. This seminar partner loves to take charge. Given a chance, they will take over the entire enterprise, and you will wind up working for them. They love to move things along, and they have a great deal of confidence in their decisions. It is easy to follow the flow, but the problem is they may begin to exclude you from the decision-making process.

The Orator. This partner loves to speak. Give them the floor, and they will grudgingly relinquish it. When presenting, expect them to use all their allotted time plus a good portion of yours. You really need the Vaudeville hook for this character.

The Whiner. Nothing is ever right for this person. In some ways they are perfectionists, except that even when things are perfect, they still whine. At first the whiner helps you fine tune the seminar, but after a few outings, the whiner wears thin. After all, wasn't the idea to have some fun?

The Lavish Spender. Nothing is too costly. They will insist that you buy the latest in projection equipment, cameras, computers and the latest versions of software. Moreover, every item needs all the bells and whistles. They have to have the best and do not think about the seminar's profitability.

The Miser. The miser is used to providing seminars on a shoe-string. But do you really have to collect the five by eight name tents and use them again by folding them inside out? Make sure the miser does not keep your seminar partnership from expanding because of stifling frugality.

The Forgetter. The forgetter is a very lovable partner. They don't procrastinate; they simply forget to follow through on assignments. The forgetter is one of the most deadly partners. If you assigned them a critical task, you may find out too late that they failed to carry it out.

The Bore. Bores come in many varieties. There are the ones who read their presentation to the audience. There are those who never use voice inflections. There are those who focus on the detail at the expense of the big picture. Although they may be an expert in their field, they simply don't know how to capture the audience's interest. If you let a bore go unchecked, people will not sign up for your seminar.

So how do you deal with potential partners who show some or several of the characteristics of partners from hell? One approach is to forget about the partnership and find an alternate approach. Another approach is to recognize potential problems and deal with them beforehand. Here are four steps that can be taken to establish your partnership on a firm foundation:

1. Fix partnership work responsibilities
2. Develop partnership protocols
3. Agree on dispute resolution methods
4. Develop a written agreement

TIP NUMBER 128:
Fix Work Responsibilities

A critical first step is to identify work responsibilities and then assign the responsibilities to each partner. The list can be as broad or detailed as you desire. the Responsibilities Checklist that is listed below contains a Joint category, make sure that one partner is the lead. Otherwise, some of these responsibilities will fall through the cracks, accompanied by the inevitable comment, "I thought you were doing it."

RESPONSIBILITIES CHECKLIST			
Task	Partner A	Partner B	Joint
PREPARATION AND DESIGN PHASE			
Coordinate seminar notebook			
Create notebook cover			
Create content for seminar notebook			
Print seminar notebook			
Develop seminar handouts			
Develop slides and overheads			
Develop flip charts			
Arrange seminar locations			
Determine room layout			
Negotiate facility agreement			
Coordinate equipment needs			
Coordinate room setup			
Arrange beverages and food			
Receive seminar registrations			
Oversee banking and accounting			
Other			
MARKETING PHASE			
Obtain mailing lists			
Write brochure copy			
Coordinate brochure design			

Task	Partner A	Partner B	Joint
Obtain envelopes and stamps			
Mail brochures			
Acquire e-mail lists			
Write newspaper ads			
Place newspaper ads			
Arrange radio show spots			
Do radio shows			
Handle seminar inquiries			
Other			
Other			

PRESENTATION PHASE

Task	Partner A	Partner B	Joint
Make contact with the person in charge			
Resolve preworkshop problems			
Check room setup			
Monitor temperature			
Greet at door			
Kick off seminar with introduction			
Present module one			
Present module two			
Present module three			
Present module four			
Present module five			
Present module six			
Present module seven			
Present module eight			
Close			
Collect and compile evaluations			
Distribute or mail evaluations			
Other			

BUSINESS ITEMS

Task	Partner A	Partner B	Joint
Reconcile expenses and income			
Prepare tax information			
Be available for participant follow-up questions and information			
Distribute or mail certificates of completion			
Other			
Other			

TIP NUMBER 129:
Establish Partnership Protocols

Beyond assigning responsibilities, you must also develop partnership protocols. Protocols are understandings with your partner about specific behaviors that can affect your working relationship. Examples of behaviors that must be discussed if you are to avoid partnership meltdown include the following:

- Whose name is listed first on seminar brochures, notebooks and other materials?
- What if a partner fails to follow through agreed upon tasks?
- Are partners expected to be in the room when not presenting?
- Are partners expected to participate in breakout groups if used?
- Can one partner interject when the other is speaking?
- Can one partner add to the other's statements?
- Can one partner give a contrary view during the other partner's presentation?
- What if a partner goes beyond his allotted presentation time?
- Can partners use the seminar without the other's permission?
- Can partners use the material for presentations to community and other nonpaying groups?
- Can partners use their own contributed material for other seminars?
- Can partners use some of the other partner's material for different seminars?

When you work alone, you can make independent decisions. A partnership requires a collaborative approach. It is much easier to talk through these items before the inevitable blowup occurs.

TIP NUMBER 130:
Consider Alternate Dispute
Resolution to Resolve Problems

Sometime during the relationship, the luster will begin to wear off and you will notice things about your partner that escaped your attention before. It can be a series of things or one big event. I call this the moment of truth. You now have a potentially terminal disagreement with your partner. What now? Although the court system is the method by which disputes have traditionally been settled, there are less expensive ways of resolving partnership conflicts. Conciliation, mediation and arbitration are forms of alternate dispute resolution (ADR). Each of these processes requires the services of a third-party neutral.

Conciliation.
This is the informal process in which the third party assists in resolving the dispute. In most conciliation cases, the parties do not meet together. Instead the conciliator acts as a go-between for the parties.

Mediation.
This is a more formal process in which the third party person facilitates a meeting of the partners so they may reach a mutually acceptable solution to their dispute. A good mediator can elicit frank dialogue.

Arbitration.
This provides the most power to a neutral person. In this role, the third party does not attempt to facilitate agreement. The arbitrator hears arguments by the parties and makes a decision. Arbitration can be binding or nonbinding, depending on the parties.

Mediation is the most common method selected and if partners are willing to negotiate in good faith and work out a solution, the results are generally favorable.

Alternate dispute resolution processes generally provide more control over the outcome to the parties. It is less expensive and may be faster than waiting several months for a court trial and possible appeals.

TIP NUMBER 131:
Develop a Written Seminar Partnership Agreement

Have a lawyer draw up your seminar partnership agreement. Do not rely on a verbal understanding, especially if the seminar partners are making significant commitments. An agreement will spell out expectations.

Donald Brenner, a self-proclaimed business divorce lawyer, advises potential partners to hold frank discussions on the partnership before agreeing to undertake a seminar venture. "Business partnerships are as fraught with perils as a marriage. You need both a business pre-nuptial and post-nuptial agreement in order to protect yourself and your business" (Brenner, personal communication, 2000).

The purpose of a partnership agreement is to spell out the expectations of the respective partners. You save time and money if you decide on the division of responsibilities, protocols and dispute resolution methods before you even see an attorney. Some of the issues you may wish to work out before seeing an attorney include the following:

- Term of the partnership. How long is this partnership? Is it for one seminar, a series of seminars or a period of time such as three years?
- Purpose of partnership. Why are you partnering?
- Parties involved? What role do spouses, children and other relatives play? What rights do they have?

- What are the responsibilities of the partners?
- How will the seminars be valued?
- How are profits and losses determined and shared?
- Who maintains the books and accounting documents?
- Who receives the money and how is it accounted for?
- What type of reporting—when and how often?
- Hiring of contract services—who decides and what is their dollar limit?
- What happens if one of the partners dies or is incapacitated?
- How do partners get out of the agreement? What is the exit process?
- Can one partner buy out the other?
- How will books and other products arising out of the seminar be handled?
- How will forbidden acts, such as taking out loans in the name of the partnership without the written consent of partners, be handled?
- Can partners be added?
- Can one partner conduct the seminar without the other?

11

Arrive Early and Avoid Disaster

You get all dressed up to do your training session and the first thing you wind up doing is rolling up your sleeves and rearranging tables and chairs.
Trainer and Author Jane Holcomb, Ph.D.

You wake up early in the morning and think about the day ahead. Preparation is behind you, and you are now ready to deliver the workshop you labored so hard to create. Arriving late to meetings may be fashionable in some instances. Don't try it with your own workshop. It will prove fatal. There are too many things that can and will go wrong, such as the seating arrangement. Although you may have specified a cafe style layout, you find that the room is arranged in a perfect theater style arrangement.

Former city manager and trainer Joe Baker sums it up this way, "Mentally prepare yourself for problems. No matter how much you plan, expect something to be wrong. I have never gone to a site and found everything in order. That is why you get there early—to find the problems and fix them. I have avoided numerous disasters by following this simple rule"(Baker, personal communication, 2001).

Such things as lighting, temperature and room configuration are critical to the success or failure of a workshop.

I have seen it occur repeatedly. A person bothered by the temperature becomes distracted or even confrontational. Although you may not be in charge of the cooling system, you are the seminar leader. Seminar participants expect you to resolve problems.

TIP NUMBER 132:
Be Prepared for Surprises

The following are just some of the surprises that I have encountered:

Surprise #1: Room too small for the number of participants. I was told that the room would comfortably hold eighty people. I had thirty-five participants, so I felt comfortable taking it sight unseen. When I got there, I found that the room was unusually small. Although it conceivably could hold eighty participants, they all would have to be standing up.

Surprise #2: Noisy band. The adjoining room had a five-piece band for a wedding reception. Even though the buffering appeared to be adequate, there was no way the walls could contain the blaring music.

Surprise #3: Distracting view. The golf course view was so breathtaking, I spent the whole day competing with it. Participants were constantly distracted by golfers teeing off. Unfortunately, there were no drapes to close off the view.

Surprise #4: Intruding pillars. The room was rectangular and had adequate square footage. Four wide columns sat prominently in the middle portion of the room, obscuring several participants' views of the screen and trainer.

Surprise #5: Narrow room with low ceiling. The meeting room was of adequate size, but it was so long and narrow that only two round tables could be placed side by side. Because I needed ten tables, they were lined up five deep. The ceiling was only eight feet high, so the participants in the rear six tables could not see the screen.

Surprise #6: Useless space. Although this room had adequate square footage to hold my meeting comfortably, over 30 percent of the space was behind a corner wall, which obscured views and rendered that space unusable.

Surprise #7: Microphone. The adjoining room had two hundred participants, dwarfing my group of twenty-five. The facilitator needed a mike to be heard by his large group. Unfortunately, the room dividers were not sufficiently buffered, resulting in obnoxious noise spilling into my meeting room.

Surprise #8: Air conditioning. Although the room had a central air conditioning system, it could not be adjusted to a single meeting room. When the air was turned on, heat came out. This made for a very uncomfortable session.

Surprise #9: Room lighting. The lighting control did not work. Lights flooded the area, making it impossible to see what was displayed on the screen.

Surprise #10: Room location. The room was located next to the kitchen. The swinging doors created a continuous disturbance throughout the session.

Surprise #11: Room change. I unloaded and set up the room. Then I found out that the room had been changed to one at the other end of the hotel.

Surprise #12: Lost notebooks. The notebooks that I had shipped two weeks before the session were lost and could not be located. They were finally found two hours after the session started.

TIP NUMBER 133:
Stay Overnight

Whenever I have to fly or drive more than one hundred miles, I plan to stay overnight at the hotel of the seminar or as close to the seminar site as possible. This way I avoid the stress associated with travel. Your day is going to be full of anxiety, tension and adrenaline rushes, so it is a good idea to eliminate some of the unnecessary stressers. Arriving early also permits you to check out the meeting room the night before your session.

TIP NUMBER 134:
Inventory Personal Items
Before You Leave

Before you depart for your seminar destination, check to make sure you have all your personal items, such as eye glasses, watch, wallet, purse and keys. Not too long ago, I left my glasses in the car before I hopped onto a plane for Dallas. I got to my downtown hotel very late, and the gift shop was the only place open. They had one pair of reading glasses in the entire store—women's designer glasses costing over $100. I had no choice except to buy them here because my seminar started at 7:00 A.M., and I cannot see without reading glasses. Participants seemed not to mind. I thought I had gotten away with it until one person left the following comment on the evaluation sheet, "You did a great job, but dump the glasses. Men wearing women's items doesn't work here."

The old maxim that you should carry the important items with you makes a lot of sense. This is especially true when you fly. If you carry on all of your luggage, you should not have a problem. But if you check your baggage, carry those essential items that will permit you to give a seminar even if your baggage is delayed or lost.

It is a good idea to carry a portable clock, just in case the hotel does not have one. Although you can always request a wake-up call, anticipating that call in a dark room when you don't know the exact time can cost you valuable sleep time. I have tossed and turned over two hours anticipating the wake-up call on the morning of the seminar. I find that a clock with a luminous face lets me check the time and go back to sleep.

TIP NUMBER 135:
Carry Backup Supplies

They are referred to as meeting kits, diddy bags or tool kits. I call them emergency kits, but they all serve the same purpose. They contain critical items that allow you to take care of minor problems that inevitably arise when you put on seminars. For example, I once watched a maintenance person cut off the third prong of a heavy-duty electrical cord that I had just purchased. The facility had old-fashioned electrical outlets, and no three-prong adapters were available. I now carry a fifty-nine cent adapter in my emergency kit.

I maintain two emergency kits—a smaller one for airline travel and a more complete one when I drive. My small one contains the following items:

- Small roll of masking tape and scotch tape
- Scissors
- A fifteen-foot lightweight extension cord
- Five new felt-tip markers
- Five blank overhead transparencies and marking pen
- Pliers
- Philips and standard screwdrivers
- Small stapler and staples
- Staple remover
- Duct tape to tape cords to the floor or carpet
- Box of paper clips and push pins
- Pack of large (5 by 8) index cards for name tents
- Pack of small (3 by 5) index cards for exercises and data collection
- Packs of various color Post-it notes
- Small ruler for drawing charts
- Small writing tablet for ideas and notes
- Assorted pens and pencils
- White correction fluid
- Hand sanitizer

You can expect one or two participants to come up to you and request a pen or pencil. I also carry a supply of business cards and brochures. The larger emergency kit, which I carry in my car, includes additional items:

- Hammer
- Heavy-duty twenty-foot extension cord
- Staple gun
- Three-hole punch
- Tape recorder and blank tapes
- Fish wire for hanging items
- Extra flip charts
- Full set of marker pens

If I am using my slide or overhead projector, I take backup bulbs. LCD projector bulbs are expensive, but when

I replaced my last one because it became a little too dim, I began carrying it as a backup. I can use the older bulb to get through a seminar if the main one goes out. My thought is that a dim bulb is better than no bulb.

It is a good idea to periodically check your supplies, especially the tape, Post-it notes and markers to make sure they have not dried out. A somewhat risky alternative to carrying emergency items is to purchase items if needed. This strategy requires you to locate an office supply store beforehand. Office Depot, Staples, Kinko's and Office Max all have Web sites that list store locations.

TIP NUMBER 136:
Get Into the Habit of Checking Traffic, Parking and Directories

I make it a rule to arrive sixty to ninety minutes before the start of the seminar. Even if it is the third day of a seminar, there is always something that crops up that must be dealt with. Arriving early gives you the time to resolve problems and mitigate the stress that accompanies the problem.

TRAFFIC PATTERNS

As you drive to the hotel or meeting facility, check the traffic patterns. Is the traffic flowing satisfactorily or is there a problem? Although it may be too late to do anything about the traffic, if there are problems, you will be alerted to the fact that people may be late. You can then decide whether to adjust your agenda to take this problem into account.

PARKING

When you get to the hotel, check out the parking situation. Is the parking lot full? Is there a parking fee? I have arrived at meeting facilities and found that there was no free parking available—something that was not pointed out to me beforehand. In this case, I found it prudent to pick up the parking fee for all the participants.

DIRECTORIES

As you walk into the hotel or meeting facility, locate the directory and examine the posted information. The directory may be on a television monitor, on a printed list under glass or on a reader board. The directory lists all the meetings, luncheons and seminars being held in the facility for the day. Check to make sure that the title of your seminar, your name, the time scheduled and the room location are correct. Hotels are notorious for getting names and times wrong. If it is incorrect, get the staff to correct it right away. I have found that you have to check back to make sure that the changes have actually been made.

Inquire at the front desk to see if they are aware of your seminar. Do they know where to direct people? I have gone into a hotel and found that my meeting was left off the list. If front desk personnel have not received the room assignments for the day, your inquiry will force them to obtain a copy.

If your meeting room is in an obscure place within the facility, create your own signs or ask the meeting personnel to post signs to direct participants to the meeting room.

TIP NUMBER 137:
Make Contact with the
Person in Charge

Many problems can be dealt with if you can find the person in charge. This person may carry the title of banquet manager or facilities manager. You want the big kahuna—the person who has authority to change rooms or make refunds. In many cases, he or she will come by and check the meeting room to make sure everything is satisfactory. Get the manager's business card and then ask where he or she can be reached later in the day. Try to get the manager's direct office number and pager number. Find out who to call if the manager is not available. I have found that although the manager may be available in the morning, he or she is more difficult to track down later in the day.

TIP NUMBER 138:
Check the Room Setup

One of the first things I check is the room arrangement. Are the tables and chairs set up as you specified? Even if you have sent a detailed diagram, you may find that the setup is not correct. On more than one occasion, I have sent a cafe style seating diagram only to discover upon arrival a theater style seating arrangement. Failure to follow your specifications is one of the most common oversights. Following are some other problems:

- The arrangement is as specified, but there is no room for you to move about. Participant tables are too close to the front.
- The arrangement is as specified, but the participants are too far from the presenter.
- Unstacked chairs are left at the back of the room. This not only looks sloppy, but also it offers seats for reluctant or shy participants.

If the setup is not satisfactory, ask the hotel staff to arrange it the way you need it. Don't accept an inadequate room configuration just to be polite. If meeting room personnel are busy elsewhere, you may have to roll up your sleeves and start moving furniture. (Be careful, though, you may run afoul of the union.)

Get rid of the lectern. Lecterns are the equivalent of training wheels, and too many presenters still use them. Wean yourself off of it. Ask that it be moved out of the room. However, if you are going to use it, check to see if the microphone and reading light work.

Look for your materials at this time. If you mailed notebooks and seminar material out prior to the session, search the room and hall for them. Efficient hotels and meeting facilities staff will have already delivered them to the room. If not, track them down. This may mean calling the person in charge of deliveries at home.

TIP NUMBER 139:
Inspect the Equipment

After you have checked the room setup, focus on the equipment. Some items to examine are discussed in the following sections.

FLIP CHARTS

Check how many pages are left on the flip chart pads. Are there enough for your seminar? Some meeting facilities will provide you recycled charts yet charge for a new pad. Insist on new pads. Notice how the flip charts are fastened to the easel—are pages easy to change? Check the condition of the easels. Make sure the legs on the easels are even. Do they stand up squarely? Can they be adjusted for maximum viewing by participants? Do you have enough marking pens? Do the marking pens still have sufficient ink?

OVERHEAD PROJECTOR

Place a transparency on the glass and turn on the projector to check the focus and centering on the screen. Make sure the transparency fills the screen. Walk to the back of the room to make sure that participants can see transparencies. Find the backup bulb switch and check to make sure that there is a backup bulb that works. Check to be sure that the table holding the projector has enough room to hold your transparencies.

SLIDE PROJECTOR

Place slides in the carousel and turn on the projector. Check the focus and centering. Examine the remote control. Play with it. Make sure it turns on and off and goes forward and backward. If the remote control is on a cord, determine its length and how far you can walk in each direction. Check how to set and remove the carousel. Figure out how to remove a jammed slide. If needed, check to see if the projector has a reading light for notes. If the slide projector has an automatic timer, learn how to turn it off. There is nothing more embarrassing than watching a carousel take off on its own, with the presenter watching in helpless horror. Find out the procedure to follow if a bulb burns out.

LCD PROJECTOR

Make sure the table is large enough to hold the computer and LCD projector. Turn the machine on and check the image focus and the color. Test the forward and backward modes. Find out how to freeze a frame and put the projector in standby mode. Find out what to do if the LCD goes down. Insist that the provider have immediately accessible backup equipment available. When using the LCD, make sure the laptop computer is plugged in. I learned this the hard way during a seminar. I was moving along very well when all of a sudden, the screen went blank. I spent several minutes checking until I found the problem. I had not plugged in the laptop, and, as a result, I had drained its battery.

SCREEN

Is the projection screen large enough for the group? Make sure that the screen is centered. Walk around the room and check to make sure that every seat has an unobstructed view of the screen. I have found that room arrangers will set up tables or chairs outside the viewing area of a screen. Your walk around will also allow you to check projector focus from different viewing points. If you notice a problem, change the seating arrangement or location of the screen.

ELECTRICAL CORDS
Make sure all cords are taped down. Although you may think you can navigate over a cord, during the height of a presentation, you may forget where it is and trip.

MICROPHONE
If you will be using a microphone, become familiar with it. Does it have a cord or is it cordless? If it has a cord, check the length. Get used to walking around with it. If it has a fastener, clip it on beforehand to make sure it fits and looks right. Know how to turn the microphone on and off. There are too many horror stories about speakers who failed to turn off their mike during breaks and lunch periods.

LASER POINTER
If you are going to use a pointer, check it now. Does it jump around? Can it be viewed on the screen?

TIP NUMBER 140:
Examine the Room Infrastructure
The next thing I check are the utilities and other support systems.

VENTILATION SYSTEM
Check out the heating and cooling system. I get more complaints about the heating and cooling system than anything else. Most of the morning complaints come from participants who are too cold. Rooms are usually icy cold in the morning. As people enter, the room warms up. Remember that in performing your role as workshop leader, you are moving around and may not feel the cold. Afternoon complaints come

from people who are too hot. Inevitably, as the day progresses, the room heats up. I have walked into a room and sweated, even though there was snow outside. At this point, air conditioning may no longer keep the room cool.

Unfortunately, I have found that this problem is not easily remedied. In some cases, the complaining participant may be sitting under a vent. See if moving helps. Another way to deal with the problem is to put a statement in the seminar information advising participants to wear layered clothing. Whatever you do, don't attempt to fix the temperature yourself. You cannot win with this approach because some will begin complaining as soon as you change the thermostat.

LIGHTING

Finding and learning how to operate the controller is the biggest lighting challenge. Find a staff member who can show you how to dim, turn on and turn off the lights. Other lighting issues include checking to make sure lights are not shining directly on the screen and that drapes can be closed to keep outside light from obscuring anything displayed on the screen.

NOISE

Check both adjoining rooms. How is the buffering between the rooms? What type of equipment is being set up in the adjoining rooms? Take note of microphones, video recorders and musical instruments. Go over to the adjoining rooms and introduce yourself. Establishing an early rapport usually helps if you have to go over later and ask them to control the noise.

Have the room phone turned off or request that no incoming calls be put through to the room while the seminar is being conducted. You also may want to make an announcement that cell phones and pagers should be put on silent or vibrating mode. Also make sure that the sound system is turned off. There is nothing worse than public announcements or music interrupting your program.

TIP NUMBER 141:
Check Food and Beverage Services

Prior to booking the facility, you probably entered into an agreement for beverage and perhaps food service. Now is the time to confirm the arrangements. Check to see what they have on their room checklist. On more than one occasion, I have been surprised to find that the menu is not the same as I ordered. Specify the time you want items delivered. If it is a busy facility with several meetings taking place, try to get your items delivered before the big rush. Otherwise, you may lose valuable seminar time waiting for food delivery.

It is also a good idea to have beverages and pastries set up in the meeting room rather than the hall area. All too often, goodies left in an unobserved area are too tempting for nonparticipants, who will partake of your unintended hospitality.

If you are serving lunch or dinner, confirm the number with the facility. Meals are expensive, and you do not want to pay for unneeded ones. This assumes that you have met the previously agreed upon minimum number of meals.

Be prepared for food and beverage items to be delivered late. I always try to call just before to confirm that they will be delivered as specified.

If the facility provides candies, writing pads and pens, make sure they have been set up. At a minimum, make sure each participant has water and a glass.

TIP NUMBER 142:
Use Name Tents

Make sure you have name tents. Having a person's name in front of you allows you to use their name when asking or answering a question. "Remember that a person's name is to that person the sweetest and most important sound in any language," said Dale Carnegie.

You can use folded five- by eight-inch index cards for name tents. Or, you can have them professionally printed with your name and logo. If you do not have many partici-pants, you can print them on your computer. There are sev-eral software programs that produce attractive name tents.

TIP NUMBER 143:
Create a Presentation
Announcement

Consider making a transparency, flip-chart page or slide with the title of your presentation and other important informa-tion. You can display it while the audience arrives and gets settled. I usually prepare a flip-chart page that says:

Welcome
Civil Engineers of Southern Florida
Being a Better Supervisor
By Len Wood

I sometimes add a happy face, depending on the group. This announcement also can be done on a transparency or slide.

TIP NUMBER 144:
Put Yourself in Participants' Shoes

Now that you have checked all the essentials, switch gears and put yourself in your participants' shoes. It's time to think about what is important to them. I get myself in the right

frame of mind by selecting a participant location, closing my
eyes for ten seconds and, when I open my eyes, I am a participant who has paid good money for Len Wood's seminar.
What are the things that are important to me? Here is a list to
consider:

Water
Coffee and tea
Decaf
Comforatable chairs
Room to take notes
Elbow and knee room
Unobstructed view
Adequate Lighting
Pencil and pad
Name tags or tents

TIP NUMBER 145:
Be Prepared for Walk-Ins

If you advertise the location and time of your seminars, you
should be prepared for walk-ins. Accommodate walk-ins but
don't let them denigrate the quality of your program. If additional people will crowd your prepaid registrants, you may
want to turn them away. Similarly, you may have to send
them away if you don't have the capability of printing more
materials.

Talk to your hotel beforehand. Can they handle un-
planned participants? This includes beverages, food and seating. You also want to make sure that you can provide materials to the unexpected arrivals. If you have a limited number of participant packets, be very cautious about giving
walk-ins materials until you have provided them for all of
the preregistrants. Before your seminar, check with the hotel
to see if they can duplicate materials. You also want to check

the price for this service. I have been charged up to $1.50 per page.

Be prepared for last minute cancellations. With a large crowd this can be a blessing, but with a minimum crowd it can make a difference in how you conduct the seminar. For example, if you counted on a certain number of participants for a group exercise, you may have to eliminate it from the program. If you are serving food and beverages, you should get a more accurate count to the banquet people.

TIP NUMBER 146:
Wear What You Think
You Should Wear

There are plenty of books on proper dress. Versions include dressing for success, power dressing and smart dressing. My experience is that a person who is putting on a workshop has a pretty good idea of what they think they should wear. Seminar provider Fred Gleeck says he always wears a colorful but smart and expensive sweater. "I don't want to be like other presenters. The bright sweater is my trademark" (Gleeck, personal communication, 2001).

Wear what you feel is right, depending on your topic, audience, location and time of year. With that thought, I have four other suggestions:

- Dress a notch above your participants. As Mina Bancroft says, "Dress one level up, unless they are dressed like slobs, then two levels. Stay simple and use clean lines, and solid colors. Add layers for authority—vest, sweater, jacket" (Bancroft, personal communication, 2000).
- Carry backup clothes just in case they want you to dress down. This lesson came after the group insisted that I get rid of that tie and long sleeved shirt.

- Dress to match the perception you wish to convey. In control? Casual? Knowledgeable? One of the guys?
- Wear one new item of apparel, whether it be socks, shoes, underwear, blouse, shirt or coat. I find a new piece of clothing gives me a feel-good energy surge.

TIP NUMBER 147:
Be Concerned About
Personal Security

With everything going on, you must not forget about your own personal security. I was once giving a seminar in Oakland. It was in a rear room that had access from the back of the hotel. The room was set up, and coffee and rolls just had been delivered by hotel personnel. They left, and I was alone. While I continued to set up my equipment, a scraggly looking man walked in the back door toward me. He said, " I'm not here to hurt you. I just got out of prison, and I am hungry. Can I have something to eat?" I, of course, said, "You bet." After loading him up with coffee and pastries, I sprinted out of the door and did not return until hotel security had spirited the man away.

TIP NUMBER 148:
Plan How You Will Distribute
Handouts

Although it may seem like a small issue, handout distribution should be planned beforehand. If you need to refer to a handout during your session and find that it must be distributed, it can take what seems like forever for the items to get into the participants' hands. You have several options, including the following:

1. Place materials on a table before session begins. Participants can pick up all the items as they enter the room, and you don't have to worry passing them out. Some participants, however, will take more than one copy of each item. If you use this approach, make sure you have extra copies.

2. Place handout items at each participant's table. This is usually done before the session. With a large group, this can take time.

3. Put handouts in the workshop notebook. Notebooks are assembled before the session so that you do not have to worry about distribution during the session.

4. Distribute to participants during the session. Distributing items during the session consumes valuable time, especially with large groups. If you use this approach, obtain help from the participants to distribute your materials.

When using handouts, make sure they relate to the point you are making. In a job recruitment seminar I attended, the leader handed out a list entitled "Three Most Important Reasons Employees Remain Loyal to a Company." The three reasons were career growth, challenging work and making a difference. The leader proceeded to ignore these topics and spent the next twenty minutes talking about dry cleaning as a perk for busy employees. While he talked, people scuffled around looking for where it appeared on the handout only to find out that is was not listed.

It's Show Time: Presenting Your Seminar

There are two types of speakers: those that are nervous and those that are liars.

Mark Twain

Several years ago, the *Book of Lists* identified speaking in public as the number one fear among people. It trounced such phobias as fear of snakes, flying, drowning and falling from high buildings (Wallechinsky 1977, 469-470). No matter how many seminars, workshops or presentations I make, I still am anxious before the start. I subject myself to horrendous mental torture, asking myself questions such as "Why am I doing this?" "Why not turn around and go home?" "What if they don't like me?" "What if I make blunders?" I always go through this self-doubt and now believe that it is a necessary phase of preparing oneself mentally for the session. If I didn't worry, I would probably be too confident and prone to make mistakes.

Even highly paid professional speakers get nervous, so expect to feel some anxiety yourself. Preparation and stage time will help you manage nervousness. There are several things that you can do to reduce your anxiousness. This chapter addresses opening and presenting your seminar and the things you can do to overcome the jitters.

TIP NUMBER 149:
Visualize

Take a few moments, close your eyes and visualize yourself leading your seminar. You are in charge. As you scan the room, you see participants nodding their heads, while there are others busily taking notes. You are self-assured and knowledgeable. All of them are hanging on to your every word. Then someone asks a question, and without hesitation, you impart words of wisdom. Not only are you imparting information, you are entertaining them.

   Visualization works. It is one of the most effective techniques for getting mentally prepared and for overcoming anxiety. Professional athletes use this technique to get prepared for a sporting event. You can use it to get ready for your seminar.

TIP NUMBER 150:
Carry Seminar Fire Insurance

One of my mentors, Burbank City Manager E. Robert Turner, took me along when he gave a speech to the City of Fresno Library Board. As we sat in a restaurant and had a leisurely lunch before the session, he started jotting notes on his napkin. I asked him why, since he was a great impromptu speaker. He said, "Len, I probably don't need these notes, but they help me organize my thoughts. But more importantly, I'm contributing to Churchill's fire insurance policy." He left me hanging on that comment. Later on, I learned that

Turner was referring to one of Winston Churchill's famous comments. When asked why he prepared notes for most speeches but did not use them, Churchill exclaimed, "I carry fire insurance, but I don't expect my house to burn down."

Regardless of how you prepare to open your session—impromptu, key words or memorization—it is critical that you carry fire insurance for the beginning part of your seminar. Although I have never had to use it, I have a written script that I can follow for the first five minutes of my seminar. Just preparing this safe script and having it makes me feel much more confident.

TIP NUMBER 151:
Open Up and Get Over the First Hump

When I played competitive basketball and tennis, I was quite nervous before I started playing. Warm-ups helped relieve the tension, but there was nothing like getting out there and competing. So, too, with presenting. I still have lots of nervousness before the session, but once I begin, all my nervousness is channeled into making it one of the best ever given.

TIP NUMBER 152:
Expect the Unexpected

The inescapable rule: Seminar presenters must be prepared for the unexpected. Patty Hendrickson of the Hendrickson Leadership Group, Inc. recalls the time when she fell off a ten-foot high ladder, and her skirt came up over her head. "What a lovely view for the audience members in the first few rows!" she now jokes. In another instance, Patty was conducting a workshop in an auditorium when all of a sudden bats started flying around. "That was just a small distraction," she recalls (Hendrickson, personal communication, 1999). Paulette Ensign, author of *110 Ideas for Organizing Your Business Life,* narrowly avoided serious injury when "the screen for projecting the overheads fell off the wall and barely missed hitting me on the head." Paulette faced another challenge when she presented a workshop on getting organized that was held in the furniture department of a Staples store. "Throughout the whole session, the public announcement system kept interrupting with various announcements for store employees" (Ensign, personal communication, 1999).

Whenever such freak events occur, the presenter must make up his or her mind on what to do. If the problem can be fixed, great. If not, it means continuing, despite the distraction. Jeanne Harper provides a wonderful example of thinking on her feet when calamity struck. Within sixty seconds of beginning a half-day mandated workshop on suicide prevention, intervention and postvention for the entire school district staff, she became very ill. At that point, she could have explained her situation and requested time to deal with the problem. Standing in front of an audience of over 150 teachers, administrators and staff members who were not enthusiastic about being there in the first place, she chose another approach.

Knowing how important the beginning of the seminar is, she decided to quickly put participants into small groups. "I asked them to share with each other what they expected or wanted to get from the mandated workshop" (Harper, personal communication, 1999). When the participants began sharing, Jeanne ran to the bathroom to take care of her sickness. Returning to the room, she took command and conducted a brilliant seminar, even though she continued to visit the bathroom. Postsession evaluations lauded Jeanne for listening to what the participants had to say. "We finally got a speaker who realizes we have wisdom to share with each other." Since that day, Jeanne begins all workshop seminars with groups of two or three people, who are given the charge of defining what they want to learn from the seminar.

As a postscript, Jeanne went to the hospital after the seminar and found out that she was hemorrhaging from the intestinal lining. Surprisingly, participants did not know she was ill. "I let the counselor at the school know what had been happening that day. She said they never suspected" (Harper, personal communication, 1999).

TIP NUMBER 153:
Review Your Presentation

Nervousness also can be mitigated by reviewing your presentation material—notes, overheads and handouts. Think about or, better yet, review what you have prepared. The simple act of mentally scanning your prepared material is very effective. It reassures you that you have a first-quality program with excellent material.

TIP NUMBER 154:
Work the Room

Another helpful technique is to engage participants in conversation as they enter the room. Experienced seminar presenters try to have a brief conversation with every participant prior to the beginning of the session. They exchange pleasantries and even joke. While doing this, the presenters impart information about themselves and gather important information about the participants—their backgrounds, experiences and expectations. These polite discussions help the seminar leaders determine why people are attending and if they know each other. This technique is very soothing. Presenters who are fully engaged in meeting people as they come in the door find that their anxiety quickly dissipates.

TIP NUMBER 155:
Be Prepared with an Opening

Create a seminar opening. Here is a sample opening to a seminar on seminars:

> *Ladies and gentlemen, good morning and thank you very much for being here. I think I have had the pleasure of meeting just about every one of you. If I missed someone, my name is John Sheldon. Our subject today is seminars, how to build and maintain your own full-time or part-time seminar business while having fun in the process and, of course, make money.*
>
> *We will spend today talking about all of the strategic aspects of building and maintaining a viable, profitable seminar business. This is a fascinating business; the opportunities abound, and what I will attempt to do today is to share with you everything I have learned in the last 20 years—what works and does not work in the marketing of seminar services, what I have learned from working with other providers, either in seminars like these or in other capacities, and what I have learned from my research.*
>
> *Let me give you a little bit of background information about me, and then we will get right down to work. I have been in the seminar business for about 20 years—the last 12 on a full-time basis—but I began putting on seminars on a part-time basis when I was at Harvard University. That part-time seminar experience convinced me of two important things. First, that the seminar business was substantially more interesting and a good deal more lucrative than the University business. Secondly, that seminars provided the opportunity and the chance to test one's ideas in the real world in a true profit orientation. So*

after eight years of part-time academically based workshops, I left the University and went into the full-time seminar business, which is where I have been ever since and haven't regretted it for one moment.

Our schedule today will have us concluding the session by 5:00 this afternoon. There will be time at the end of the day for questions and answers, but please don't hesitate to raise questions at any time during the seminar as you have them. They add to the program, and I am more than happy to entertain them. Also, with respect to questions, you all have my telephone number. It is on virtually every page of my seminar material, so please don't hesitate to give me a call at anytime following the seminar if you have any questions on the subject of seminars that you think I might be able to be of some assistance. I can't promise to answer all questions for you, but I will do my best to give you at least an answer or to direct you to another source.

As far as materials go, you should all have a workbook. The pages in this book will correspond directly to the overhead transparencies, which I will be using. There are a lot of pages in this book. I am not going to spend the day reading it to you. However, I will point out things that you may want to look at in more detail once you have left the seminar. Some of the pages are copies of the transparencies I will be using, and you may wish to put your notes on them.

All right, we will get started now by taking a look at page 3.

TIP NUMBER 156:
Develop Your Own Opening

The opening in Tip 155 establishes the speaker's credentials with an overview of his background and experiences. It also tries to get participants excited about the seminar business.

After this introduction, he jumps into the workshop.

The presenter is a very successful presenter. He fills the room wherever he decides to present his seminar on seminars. His opening, however, may not work for you. It is a little bit long and may be considered trite and self-serving. He gets away with it because he is very successful. You need to develop your own approach.

TIP NUMBER 157:
Topics to Cover in the Opening

When you first start giving seminars and whenever you give a new seminar, it is a good idea to plan your opening. I find it helpful to jot down the key points I need to cover in my opening. Possible topics to include in the opening of your seminar include the following:

1. *Who you are.*
   Introduce yourself and establish your credentials.
2. *Overview of agenda.*
   Acquaint participants with the subjects to be covered.
3. *Timing of program.*
   Indicate general timing for breaks, lunch and adjournment.
4. *Workbook.*
   Familiarize the particpants with it and indicate how it relates to the seminar. Is it a fundamental part of the seminar or is it supplemental material that can be used for a reference or study guide after the seminar?
5. *Logistics.*
   Indicate the location of phones and restrooms.
6. *Food and beverages.*
   Explain how lunch will be handled and where coffee and other beverages are located.
7. *Icebreakers and warm-ups.*
   You may want to open with a short exercise to get the

group involved. For example, I sometimes open with a simple true-false or multiple-choice test. Here is an example of a test that I use for a seminar on leadership:

Leaders are born not grown.	True ___ False ___
Leadership can be learned.	True ___ False ___
Leaders are charismatic.	True ___ False ___

After administering this simple test, I provide the answers and then go into introductions and a description of the course.

TIP NUMBER 158:
Use Icebreakers and
Warm-Ups Sparingly

When used properly icebreakers and warm-ups can get participants involved early. Sue Bianchi, author of *Warm Ups for Meeting Leaders* states, "Based on years of experience in using warm ups, sessions were more dynamic, participants were more motivated and the level of enthusiasm was elevated beyond our imagination"(Bianchi, personal communication, 1999). Although icebreakers can be helpful, I suggest two caveats. First, if you use them, be sure they do not backfire and embarrass the participants. I once attended a high-powered, well-funded, government-sponsored seminar. The facilitator decided to use an icebreaker to get the participants to know each other. The icebreaker consisted of an exercise in which sixteen participants were asked to form a semicircle. Participants were then asked to introduce themselves and relate their first name to an object or trait, such as "Hello, I am Alice Apple" or "Hi. I am Fred Friendly." The first person in line was then asked to repeat her name.

The second was asked to introduce the first person, Alice Apple and himself, Cool Charlie. The third was asked to introduce Alice Apple, Cool Charlie and herself, Daring Darlene.

As the introductions moved around the semicircle, it became more difficult for some participants to remember all the names. The ninth person was Randy Results. Randy remembered the first three names and then froze. He simply couldn't remember any more names. People started joking and then laughing about Randy's lack of results. His confusion turned to humiliation. Without raising his head, he gathered up his materials and walked out the door. What was intended to be a lighthearted, get-acquainted exercise turned into a disaster.

My second caution about icebreakers is that they can consume too much time if you do not monitor them closely. When I first began providing seminars, I used an icebreaker entitled Murder on the Orient Express. I was giving a somewhat technical seminar and wanted to loosen up the participants by getting them to interact in a fun exercise. They loved the exercise, so much so that it took 110 minutes, instead of the thirty I had planned. I had to cut approximately eighty valuable minutes from the planned program to get the seminar back on track. Needless to say, I dropped the Murder on the Orient Express icebreaker from my program.

I like to use a get-acquainted icebreaker for programs that are scheduled for more than one day. My favorite is a variation of bingo. Participants are given a handout that has a bingo card printed on it. Instead of numbers, it has specific characteristics listed in each cell. A bingo card for a program on seminars might appears as follows:

SEMINAR BINGO

Designs Own Seminars	Uses Flip Charts	Has Never Given a Public Presentation	Uses a Slide Projector	Does Multiday Seminars
Evaluates Seminars	Presents to Groups of Fewer Than Fifty People	Sells Books at Seminars	Has Developed a Seminar Brochure	Uses Radio for Advertising
Has Developed a Seminar Tape	Has a Book on Tape or CD	**FREE SPACE**	Has Presented to Groups of More Than 100 People	Uses Infomercials
Uses Newspaper Advertising	Uses Software Other Than PowerPoint	Develops Charts in Excel	Has Authored a Book	Is Proficient in Using an LCD Projector
Designed Own Brochure	Has Authored More than Two Books	Has Given Seminars for Less Than a Year	Uses Overheads	Markets Others' Seminars

Participants are asked to find a person in the room who matches the characteristic. The person identified must then put their initials in the cell. Because some participants can match more than one cell, they are instructed to sign only one cell. The first participant to fill the bingo card is the winner. Although there is no need to give a prize, I have provided a book or modest gift certificate.

A variation of bingo is the game Find the Person in the Room. In this exercise, participants are given a handout with several statements. They must find a person who matches the characteristic and have them sign on the adjacent line. The following is a shortened version:

FIND THE PERSON . . .

- Who has given a seminar before   _____
- Who has never given a seminar   _____
- Who has participated in an icebreaker   _____
- Who has taken an online seminar   _____
- Who served as a panelist for a seminar   _____

The two important keys to the success of icebreakers are make sure that they accomplish the purpose you intended and that they do not consume too much time. These goals you can verify through close monitoring. Recognize that if the exercise takes longer than anticipated, you can end it before participants have completed it.

TIP NUMBER 159:
Establish Your Credentials

In John Sheldon's opening, he focused on his credentials right away. It helped build his credibility with the audience. There are some instances in which you may wish to wait until later before talking about your background and experience. First, if people are arriving late, you might want to wait until they have all arrived, otherwise you will get questions about your experience throughout the seminar. Second, if people know you or about you, there is no need to give a detailed recital of your qualifications. In this case, you want to provide examples of your experiences that relate to the program topic.

TIP NUMBER 160:
Consider Self-Introductions

Eric Baron of Consultative Resources Corporation believes that the overall tone of your seminar is set within the first minutes of the seminar. In his sales management seminars, he believes self-introductions help to ease nervousness and set the stage for learning. He begins his workshops by asking people to introduce themselves by focusing on such things as their likes, avocations, or famous people with whom they'd like to dine. He usually introduces himself first to provide an example.

If you are dealing with a small group (up to thirty people), have participants introduce themselves. People like to talk about themselves. People also like to know something about the others who are in the workshop. Knowing something about each other makes it easier to initiate conversations during the breaks. It also facilitates future networking. I usually create a flip-chart page entitled self-introductions. The page has four bullet points:

SELF-INTRODUCTIONS
- Your Name
- Your Organization
- Your Position
- Why You Are Attending

The last item reveals the topics that are important to participants. The presenter wants to be sure to cover these items or to state why they will not be covered. Some presenters will write these topics on flip charts and post them. Near the end of the seminar they will go over the list to make sure all items have been covered. Asking why you are attending can also lead to welcomed levity when people respond with quips, "It was either this or mowing the lawn."

If you have a large audience, avoid self-introductions. It will consume too much time and will turn off many of the participants. Likewise, make sure that participants do not become too talkative. Some people love to talk and will use this opportunity to hijack your seminar. Do not hesitate to politely cut off ramblers.

TIP NUMBER 161:
Use a Version of the Donahue
Approach When Presenting

Phil Donahue was one of the first talk show hosts to use the technique of walking into the audience to establish and maintain rapport. If you get a chance to see an old *Donahue* show, observe how he darted from one participant to another. People loved the special attention and closeness of Donahue. This can be an equally effective technique for workshop presenters. In his book *Energizing the Learning Environment*, William A. Draves discusses the Presenter's Space and the Participant's Space (Draves 1995). Audience members subconsciously recognize their own space and that of the presenter. The Presenter's Space is a circle approximately ten feet in diameter. According to Draves,

1. Moving forward three to five feet inside the Presenter's Space focuses audience attention, resulting in increased retention and learning.
2. If the presenter moves farther out into the audience, he or she then enters the Participant's Space. This results in intense interest and attention. "Invading of Participant Space is seen as an intimate act, bringing speaker and

audience very close together" (Draves, personal communication, 1999).

3. Speakers should not invade Participant's Space too often. Save it for very special moments when important points are to be conveyed.

4. Moving horizontally across the room does not have the same impact. In fact, it creates a physical distraction.

Some other thoughts: When moving out into the audience, be careful about disconnecting a microphone or tripping over a wire. When I first used the walking into the audience technique, I moved out into a large audience without thinking about the twenty-five-foot cord on my mike. After stumbling and disconnecting the mike, I learned to predetermine how far I could go into the audience.

What should you do with your hands? Your hands are very important presentation tools. People observe your hands. If things are going well, you will not even notice your hands. They are out in front of you, and you are using them to emphasize important points. Put your hands where they feel natural. Just don't let them become a detractor to your presentation. Have a trusted person give you feedback on your use of your hands. If you are answering questions, it is appropriate to put your hands behind your back and walk forward to the audience. Carol Burnett used this technique very effectively to establish rapport with her audience.

TIP NUMBER 162:
Decide How to Handle Audience Questions

Should you take audience questions? I encourage audience questions; they help create involvement and build rapport. To encourage questions, I advise participants at the beginning of the session that I will take questions at any time. "If you have a question or comment, please don't hold back. Ask it."

If I get questions early, it tells me I have gotten their interest. It also says that they feel comfortable and not threatened. Your response to the first question is critical. Acknowledge the question, give it a receptive response and signal that you appreciate it. Make the questioner feel like this was the most brilliant question ever asked—even if it wasn't. I like to respond, "That's a good question."

Get into the habit of repeating participant questions. Questions from the back of the room may not be heard in the front. Likewise, questions from front-row participants may not be heard in the back. People get frustrated when you begin answering a question that they did not hear. Repeating questions also gives you time to think of a good response and permits you to rephrase the question if necessary. The larger your group, the more important this is. If you are recording the session, repeating questions is mandatory because the tape does not pick up questions from participants.

You will also have instances where you do not want questions or when a question does not produce a positive effect. A question such as, "I know I'm talking to a very sophisticated group, but does everyone here know what a Skelly hearing is?" will produce a silent room. In no way will you get a person to admit that they don't know what it is, especially in front of a large group. In some cases, you may not want questions. Perhaps one person is dominating the session with rhetorical questions. Or perhaps you are running out of time. A way to deal with this problem is to advise participants that you are running tight on time and request that they hold their questions to a specific time, such as at the end of the module or at the end of the workshop.

Some questions pertain to just one person rather than the whole group. Handle these quickly or try to broaden the scope of the question so that it applies to the entire group. Likewise, be wary of getting into a conversation with a single participant. This usually occurs when the person asks a question and then asks several follow-up questions. You can lose the interest of your audience if you do not open the conversation to them. Most of all, do not ask a critical question unless you know the answer.

Management labor attorney Mike White was doing a great job mesmerizing his audience. At a critical point, he directed what seemed like a simple question to the human resources director of the organization he was addressing. Mike didn't get the simple answer he expected. Instead, he got a long rambling explanation that he could not gracefully cut off. This killed the momentum he was building with the audience and sidetracked the seminar. He could have avoided this problem by calling the director beforehand and alerting her to the questions to make sure the responses worked into his seminar. It also would have been common courtesy. Later, as Mike examined his performance he found that he was using questions as a crutch.

What if you don't have an answer? There are a couple of strategies. One is to admit that you do not know the answer but that you will research the matter and get back to the person. This assumes that you can get the answer sometime during the session. Another approach is to throw the question back to the audience. If all else fails, get the person's e-mail address or card and indicate that you will have to do some research and get back to him or her.

TIP NUMBER 163:
Establish Audience Rapport

You need to establish audience rapport right away. A speech class professor once told me to always smile and project an open face. He said that too often speakers forget this because of initial stress. His advice? Draw a big happy face in the left-hand margin on every page of your notes, overheads or flip-chart pages. This little technique works. As you glance at your material, you cannot help but notice that bright smile that beckons you to do the same.

First impressions are very critical in a workshop. Successful presenters use a variety of techniques (for example, shyness, humbleness, arrogance) to get participants involved. Getting a quick laugh out of them goes a long way. I am not talking about a joke, but rather a quip that relates to the subject matter of the seminar. In fact, don't use a joke if you are not skilled at delivery. I can't think of a worse start than opening a seminar with a misfired joke or forgetting the punch line.

Don't forget that people decided to attend your seminar because you have preestablished credibility with them through your reputation or brochures. Consider the opening as your honeymoon period. A seminar honeymoon lasts for a very short period; however, you can extend it by smiling and making eye contact early. The following table illustrates some of the things that increase and diminish rapport.

THINGS THAT INCREASE RAPPORT	THINGS THAT DIMINISH RAPPORT
Act confident in what you do	Act diffident in what you do
Open face	Blank, poker or closed face
Face the audience	Look away or talk to visual aids
Establish brief eye contact	Stare at or rapidly scan audience
Converse with audience	Read material
Move about	Remain at podium
Walk toward audience	Stand in fixed position
Respond to questions	Put off questions
Varied voice pitch and tone	Monotone

Comedian George Burns, reflecting on his and Gracie Allen's Vaudeville success, said, "Our audience made us successful. As the audience responded, we watched their faces. And we adjusted according to what we saw."

Don't be caught looking at your watch too often. And

most important, don't tell your audience this is your first seminar. Imagine a pilot saying, " Welcome on board. By the way, this is my first flight. So sit back and enjoy it."

TIP NO. 164:
Let Participants Establish
Ground Rules

Many train-the-trainer courses emphasize the need to establish ground rules at the beginning of a seminar. Ground rules, they argue, are necessary to lay out seminar expectations to the participants. A typical list might appear as follows:

1. Listen
2. Participate
3. Be openminded
4. No smoking
5. Turn phones and beepers to vibrator mode
6. Be on time

In one of my first seminars, I brought in a flip-chart page similar to the above list. It was a management seminar for police captains and lieutenants. I ended my seminar honeymoon period very quickly by attempting to lay out ground rules for this group. They were in no mood to be told how to behave, especially to be on time. During the entire seminar, they didn't say a word, nor did they ask questions. The message was clear: don't ever try to tell a seminar group what they must or must not do. If you decide to use ground rules, have participants suggest them and only use those that they agree on.

TIP NUMBER 165:
Be Continually Alert to Boredom

Mark Twain admonishes us that "No sinner is ever saved after the first 20 minutes of a sermon." Don't get hung up like the proverbial professor who gets carried away and bores students to tears. People like an informative, fast-paced presentation. If you are using a personal computer and PowerPoint, you can use the timing feature to practice your pacing.

Continually scan the room to determine whether participants are bored. Look for boredom signs by viewing their body language. Faces, positions and movements provide important clues that can help you assess the level of interest or boredom. Here are some important signals you can check to determine if your audience is bored:

• **Faces:** returning eye contact versus avoiding it; smiling versus blank face or frowning; eyes open and alert versus glazed, vacant or droopy eyes

• **Limbs:** arms at sides versus crossed; looking at you versus checking body parts or watches

• **Actions and movements:** paying attention versus reading; sitting still versus constant squirming or getting up and walking around

When assessing your audience, consider them as a whole. Within every group you will find some who are bored or distracted easily. You also will find some who believe that you can do no wrong. Don't overreact. What are the majority of your participants doing? Learn to recognize the signs in total. How many participants are displaying bored behavior? Learn also to interpret what is happening. You may be giving a great workshop, but you have gone into lunch-time, or the reason people are squirming is that the chairs are uncomfortable.

If one person is acting bored, engage him or her in a friendly conversation during a break. I like to use the direct approach by asking the person how things are going. You will usually draw out the person's issues. Once, while I was giving a seminar on management, a participant was acting very bored and fidgety. She just couldn't stay still more than two minutes. During the break, I walked over and began a conversation. She asked when we were going to get into the seminar topic. She said she was a chemist by training and wanted to learn how to manage so she could get a promotion. She wanted something precise, tangible and scientific. Taken aback, I explained to her that I had just presented some of my best material and that the remaining program would be conducted similar to the morning session. She just couldn't believe that good management was based on judgments, intuition and the situation. "How can management be so intangible?" she demanded. Failing to satisfy her, she decided to leave. Although I did not like losing a participant, I was relieved to be rid of her distracting actions.

In another seminar, I had a table of sheriff's captains, with folded arms across their chests, frowning at me. They appeared downright hostile. Although I didn't really want to do so, I decided to sit with them during lunch. As it turned out, I was not the reason for their anger. "Len, we are sorry for the way we have been acting today. But the newly elected sheriff just fired the undersheriff, and we are really upset."

When you observe boredom in the audience, don't ignore it; deal with it. Some techniques you can use include:

- *Speed up the pace.* Although you may feel you are moving too fast, your audience may feel otherwise.
- *Take a break.* Allow people to get up and stretch.
- *Invite questions on complex issues.* Ask, "What is your feeling about this?"
- *Challenge participants.* Ask, "Do you really believe this?"

- *Move on.* Quickly conclude the topic you are covering and move on to another.

Don't misinterpret confusion for boredom. In fact, participant boredom may be due to confusion over an issue. Frowning, fingers on chin, vacant stares and puzzled looks all signal confusion. If you observe these signs, consider using examples or stories to clarify your point. It's okay to ask if a point was understood, so long as it's done in a nonembarrassing way.

TIP NUMBER 166:
Recognize Contentment

People let you know when they are enjoying the presentation. They return your eye contact, they smile back at you, they take notes, they lean forward, they fold their hands behind their heads. Other than applause, there is no better feedback. Your audience is tuned in and enjoying the session.

TIP NUMBER 167:
Use Corporate Buzz Words Judiciously

Every field has its own jargon, consisting of words, phrases and even signals that only the individuals within a group know. If some people are using buzz words and you know the meaning, define them for the audience. Although you and the questioner may understand the word, many of your participants may not. Some people deliberately test you. They make the assumption that you should know what particular words mean. Don't fall for it. If you don't know what they mean, ask them to define the terms they are using.

TIP NUMBER 168:
Announce Whether People
Can Record Your Seminar

You will get requests from participants to record your seminar. You should decide on your policy before you begin giving seminars. Many of the national seminar companies will not permit recording and say so in their promotional brochures. They also reinforce the ban at the beginning of their sessions. Their feeling is that seminars are a very competitive business, and they do not want someone stealing their material. If you intend to sell audiotapes, you may wish to ban recorders.

TIP NUMBER 169:
Adjust to Your Audience's Level

Early on you will get a feel for the audience you prepared for and the audience you actually got. Generally speaking, you want to aim higher than the current information level of your audience, but you cannot go too high. Don't forget that you not only have experience in this area but you also have thoroughly researched the topic. Don't make the mistake that they are as familiar with the topic as you are. (If they were why would they be attending your seminar?)

You also should not assume that participants will tell you when they don't understand what you are presenting. I once partnered with an expert in reengineering, who was very well respected in the field. He presented his portion of the session, and although he didn't get any questions, it appeared like the attending managers comprehended what he said. Wrong. The postsession evaluations stunned the expert. Written comments such as "too foggy," "too technical," "meaningless drivel," "needs to come down out of his ivory tower" peppered the forms. One incensed participant signed her name and listed her phone number. I called her, and she gave me an insight into what had occurred. She indicated that the company managers considered themselves at the cutting edge of reengineering, and although they didn't understand what the expert was saying, there was no way in the world that they would admit it.

On the other hand, don't aim too low, such as at the elementary level, because the audience may feel like you are talking down to them.

Don't get carried away with displaying your great knowledge about the topic. They are not paying for you to obtain ego gratification. They want relevant, meaningful and useful information.

TIP NUMBER 170:
Dealing with Challengers

With any audience, you will inevitably face problem people. For whatever reason, they decide to challenge you. They do it for various reasons. They didn't like what you said before. They had a bad night, they don't like being at the seminar or they think that they know more than you. Don't lose your cool. Your task is to deal with them without losing your concentration or, more important, the audience.

When there is a challenge, there are three parties: You, the challenger and the audience. Never forget this because there is a delicate balance that must be maintained. The presenter's most important rule is "Solve the problem but never lose your audience." So, how do you do this? First, recognize that you are in charge. In that respect, the audience views you as an authority figure. People expect you to use your authority judiciously.

Second, recognize that seminar participants do not like someone who is disruptive. You have to be careful not to make participants uncomfortable when you handle the disrupter. The key is to firmly deal with challengers without escalating the situation. You have three options when dealing with a problem person:

1. *Ignore.* This strategy works as long as the challenger does not push it too far. This works well with the person who asks too many questions or interjects too often. My approach to these people is to call on them until it becomes obviously distracting. Ask yourself, what are they adding to and what are they taking from the seminar? If the minuses exceed the pluses, it is time to ignore them.

2. *Confront and manage.* This is the area in which you can show your best balancing skills. Merely ignoring may not be enough. Some participants need to be confronted. A mild rebuke may be enough. Don't be brought down to their level. Don't be pushed into looking defensive. Don't let people see that they are getting to you. Don't get personal or take it personally.

3. *Remove.* Removal is very rare. I once observed a past participant from a How to Buy Stocks seminar show up at a free seminar used to solicit new recruits for the How to Buy Stocks program. He paid over $4,000 for the workshop and then lost several thousand more in the stock market. He was livid. He yelled and screamed about the fraud and ran toward the stage, chasing the seminar promoter out a side door. The promoter's assistants finally subdued the angry man and hustled him out the door. After sitting in stunned silence for five minutes, most of the participants got up and left the building. Obviously, this was not a pretty sight.

Know When to Quit

The secret of being a bore is to tell everything.
Voltaire

When starting out, most seminar presenters don't appreciate the importance of or plan for the close. In fact, many do not think about the seminar close until they are confronted with it. "I did not think about it. So when I got to the end, I said thank you—we are adjourned," recounts Wilma Thompson after presenting her first seminar. "It was like I had used a stun gun on the audience. People stared at me in awkward silence. There was only 20 feet to the door, and I had a fleeting thought about running for it. Fortunately, one person broke the silence by getting up and walking toward the door. You know, I never let it happen again. The next time, I transitioned into the closing. I let them know it was nearing the end, and I received a standing ovation for the seminar" (Thompson, personal communication, 2001).

Wilma didn't get the standing ovation for her close. She received it for an outstanding presentation. People want to give an ovation for a good presentation, but they have to be given the opportunity. An inadequate close, however, can rob a presenter of a well-deserved applause. This chapter suggests ways to transition into a smooth close.

TIP NUMBER 171:
Master the Seminar Clock

Good chess players plan several moves in advance. Some even can predict the end of a game after a few moves. Seminar presenters need to learn how to project the ending time of their seminar. Experienced presenters have developed their own seminar clock. They know how to avoid running out of time. They also know how to avoid finishing too early. They know where they are timewise throughout the seminar. They recognize when they have gotten off course and make adjustments when this occurs. They manage their time by using the following techniques:

1.   Shortening or stretching material
2.   Calling strategic breaks
3.   Extending or shortening lunch and breaks
4.   Using group exercises
5.   Stimulating or subtly discouraging questions

TIP NUMBER 172:
Cover Everything Promised

As you near the end of your seminar, you may be forced to choose between what information you cover and what you omit. As a general rule, you should cover all topics outlined in your advertisements and promotional material. Consider these as your commitments to participants. One or several of these topics have influenced them to attend your seminar. I learned this the hard way. Things were going very well with my budgeting seminar. Participants were really into the subject and were asking lots of questions. Unfortunately, we were running out of time. I only had covered four of the seven advertised topics. With the time left, I figured that I could cover two of the remaining three topics. Judging from the participants' questions and interest areas, I decided to cover taxes and performance measurement and forget about budget cutbacks. What a mistake! After I concluded the session, the assistant librarian from the Glendale Public Library came up and indicated that she was very disappointed that I did not cover budget cutbacks. The workshop promotional material highlighted budget cutbacks as a topic, and this was the only reason she had attended the session. Although it was too bad that she did not mention it to me sooner, the fact was I had erred. To make up for the oversight, I offered to put on a free mini-seminar for the entire Glendale Public Library management staff. She willingly accepted.

I learned the lesson that it is much better to summarize or shorten an advertised topic than to delete it. I now cover all the topics I advertise—even if I must extend the seminar time. If I must drop something, I get the group's concurrence. Also, if you are asked whether you are going to cover a particular topic, don't say yes and then forget about it. On the other hand, you do not have to cover all the material in the course notebook. In fact, some presenters place extra material in the notebook for later reference by participants.

Should you end the program even if it is before the published ending time? In most cases, yes! I have found that participants appreciate it when you wrap up your workshop, if it is not too early, and you have satisfactorily covered the promised material. There is nothing worse than listening to a presenter drone on or ad lib to adjourn at the prescribed time.

When making a decision to wrap up early, try to read the group's composite body language. Are they ready to go? Are they worried about traffic? Have some left already? Or, are they glued to their seats, enjoying themselves and wanting more? In cases of early dismissal, you can offer to stay afterward to discuss topics with interested participants. It is a good idea to offer to stay around to answer any questions that participants may have in all your seminars.

TIP NUMBER 173:
Keep Material in Reserve

One of my greatest fears is to run out of material before the workshop is over. Each group attending a seminar has its own distinct personality. Some are very participatory, and you must balance continued interaction with the need to cover the essential topics. Other seminar groups are very quiet. In this case, I worry about sprinting through the material and being stuck with nothing more to cover. This is the worst feeling in the world. What if you have covered all your material ninety minutes before the scheduled end of the seminar? Answer: Keep material in reserve, you can use it if needed. Have handouts available or put reserve material in your course notebook. That way you can pull it out and use it if necessary.

TIP NUMBER 174:
Offer to Answer Any
Lingering Questions

Leave time near the end of your session to answer any lingering questions, either about the topic just completed or a previously covered topic. If someone asks a multifaceted question that you do not have time to adequately answer, suggest that the person talk to you after the session. If you take questions near the end, be sure that you do not conclude with a hastily crafted response to a question.

Recognize that you can encourage or discourage

questions by the way you ask for them. If you say, "Well, it's getting late and traffic is building. However, are there any last minute burning questions?" Obviously, you will not get any questions. The reality is that if you have taken and answered questions throughout the session, you will not get many final questions.

TIP NUMBER 175:
Leave Time for the Wrap-Up

Make sure that you leave time at the end for your seminar summary and conclusions. Too often presenters use up all the time and short shrift the recap. Your wrap-up could include the following:

- *Thank you.* The wrap-up may include thank yous for listening and participating, if they have been working on group exercises.
- *Action plans.* You can have participants develop personal action plans on what they intend to do, create or change after leaving the seminar.
- *Summary of important points.* A summary of key points or conclusions is a good way to end the seminar. When I use this approach, I create a one-page handout for participants.
- *Review of opening expectations.* If you developed a list of participant expectations at the beginning of the workshop, use it to conclude the session. You can go over each item listed and indicate how it was covered. Review these expectations beforehand to make sure you have covered all of the items or have an answer for not doing so.

TIP NUMBER 176:
Mean It When You Say,
"In Conclusion"

If you use the phrase, "One last point," or any variation, such as "and finally," don't introduce more than one point and end it on the introduced point. Your audience expects you to wind down the session after you make this pronouncement. Participants, even if they enjoyed the seminar, count the issues you introduce after you make this terminal statement. Bill Wilson, director of the Virtual University of the Independent Insurance Agents of America, offers this thought: "Many speakers announce that they are nearing the end of their presentation by saying, 'In conclusion. . . .' The problem is, rarely do they actually conclude with the trailing statement! I once observed a speaker who said, 'In conclusion' seven or eight times during his ending comments. If you really want to make busy people angry, say 'in conclusion' and keep going for ten to fifteen minutes"(Wilson, personal communication, 2000).

TIP NUMBER 177:
Expect Off-the-Wall Reactions

Although rare, you also should be prepared for what I call off-the-wall reactions. Management Consultant Jane Dillon had a disconcerting experience near the end of one of her workshops. "One participant was enthusiastic and participating very positively throughout the entire workshop, seeming to get every penny's worth of value from the class. During the very last five minutes, she blurted out, "What a waste of time the whole thing was" (Dillon, personal communication, 2001). Dillon never found out what set the participant off. However, she sent a letter two weeks later, demanding a refund.

I had a similar experience. I was wrapping up what I felt had been a very successful seminar. A man, who sat quietly and attentively throughout the whole day, startled everyone when he blurted out that the seminar was a crock and that "you don't know what you are talking about." He continued to get worked up, waving his arms and making threatening gestures. The only coherent part was that he wanted his money back. Fortunately, someone had summoned hotel security, who calmed him down. Later, I sent his money back, which he promptly returned to me with an apology.

When confronted with these types of situations, don't get upset. Ask what they believe you didn't cover. Offer to return their money. It is a lot better than being verbally or physically assaulted.

TIP NUMBER 178:
Help Them Stay in Touch

If you have a group that has become close during the session, you can enable participants to network after the session. In addition to providing a copy of a list of registrants with standard information, such as name, phone, fax, e-mail and Web site, other headings may include areas of expertise (that is, participants can list information or resources they can provide) and help requests (that is, participants can identify resource or information requests).

There are different ways this can be accomplished. One way is to make a large flip chart for participants to write their needs or expertise during the workshop. You can also circulate an information sheet. This will require someone to duplicate the sheet for participants. Another technique is to have each person leave several business cards with requests for information printed on the back. Whatever process is used, be sure to explain the purpose and process.

TIP NUMBER 179:
Check the Bill Carefully

If you have not paid the entire bill, meeting facility personnel will present the final bill for the room, equipment, food and beverage right after you adjourn. I have had several experiences in which they wave the bill in my face while participants are gathering around to ask questions.

Don't just sign the bill. Take the time to examine it carefully. On several occasions, I have found errors on the bill, such as higher than agreed upon fees for the meeting room, double coffee charges and extra meals. Most will add the gratuity to the bill. Make sure it is not applied to the sales tax. Likewise, make sure the sales tax does not include the gratuity amount.

TIP NUMBER 180:
Don't Forget the Certificates
of Completion

If you provide certificates of completion, don't forget to distribute them. I have found that most participants value these certificates. Participants show them, they frame them and, if relevant, they request that they be put in their personnel files. Some presenters stand at the door and hand out the certificates. This allows them to say goodbye to each of the participants. Appendix F includes a sample letter used to transmit certificates to your participant's place of employment.

TIP NUMBER 181:
With Seminars, It's Over
Before the Fat Lady Sings

Lord Birkett said it best: "I don't object when people look at their watches while I'm speaking, but I strongly object when they start shaking them to see if they are still running."

The best advice on concluding your seminar is to end it when it is time. When things are going bad, it is easy to end the session. But what about when things are going well? Should you end it as scheduled? Yes. If you take it beyond the scheduled time, you are doing it for your own gratification and not your participant's benefit. People plan to get out on time. Don't hold them there while you continue to pontificate, no matter how they appear to enjoy it.

And finally, super presenter Patricia Fripp tells us how to make them feel that they got their money's worth every time. She suggests, "Greet attendees at the door and shake their hands. At the beginning of the session, ask the audience if they have a philosophical problem with rating you excellent. Then inquire what ingredients are needed for them to feel it was excellent" (Fripp, personal communication, 2000). According to Fripp, most audiences say:

1. Cover the points promised in the description
2. Be energetic and entertaining
3. Don't be monotone
4. Don't read your talk
5. Before you close, make sure you ask them if you covered every point they wanted covered
6. Get them to complete the evaluations before you close
7. End on a high
8. Go to the back of the room and shake their hands again.

Feedback Is Brutal and Usually Accurate

You cannot tell if you are winning unless you keep score.

Several people, including Yogi Berra

Feedback is painful, especially for beginning presenters. But it must be solicited if you want to become a first-class seminar provider. It's sort of like eating your vegetables to develop strong bodies and minds. For my first seminar, I developed a simple one-page written evaluation form. I passed it out at the end of the program and was somewhat bemused by the things people did with them. After furtively filling them out, some turned them over and literally darted out of the room. Others guardedly folded them in half or in quarters and slid them in the middle of the stack. Few said goodbye, and even fewer looked me in the eye as they departed.

I knew my performance that day was not sterling, but I didn't know just how bad it was—until I read the reviews. I was devastated. Nothing escaped the participant's wrath: the seminar content, my delivery, how I answered questions and even the seminar workbook. How could people be so cruel? Didn't they know I was considered an expert on the topic? Didn't they know how hard I had worked putting the program together? What did they expect for a first-time performance? Like a participant on the first *Survivor* television show, I felt like I just had been voted off the island by the tribal council.

My reaction was defensive, but I reconciled that it was my first time out of the gates. Things would be better next time I thought. I used a different evaluation form for my second seminar, but again the comments were painful. Each one seemed to be like a dagger in the heart. Unlike *Survivor* participants, I realized that you could be voted off the island more than once.

Because changing the evaluation form didn't seem to matter, I decided to eliminate it from the program. Why subject myself to this needless torture, I rhetorically asked? For the next two seminars, I was relieved that I did not have to read those stinging evaluations. Although I had improved somewhat, it was not enough. I had given the workshop four times, but I still stumbled through the program and participants still avoided eye contact.

Fortunately, my wife June attended my fifth seminar, and she had lots of suggestions after it was over. Because I couldn't employ the same approach I used with the evaluation form, I was compelled to listen to her. Actually, she was very sensitive to my anguish, and after giving some compliments, she made several suggestions on things I might do to fine-tune my seminar. Her understanding approach worked. She disarmed my biggest impediment, my ego! Although I still feel agony whenever a negative criticism is made, I now view criticisms as opportunities to improve. Which brings up the critical point of this chapter: you need to collect, assess and use feedback to improve your seminars. If you are not ready to deal with feedback, you're not ready to give seminars.

TIP NUMBER 182:
Conduct a Critical Self-Evaluation

You can evaluate the overall success or failure of your program by conducting a critical self-evaluation. You will have a general idea of how you did after the seminar. To be of any value, the self-evaluation must be brutally honest. After completing your seminar, you will probably have competing feelings. You may feel relief from getting through without being bloodied. At the same time, you may feel elation for pulling it off. Don't let these feelings mesmerize you. While the experience is still fresh, make a self-evaluation chart with two columns—what worked and what needs improvement.

WHAT WORKED	WHAT NEEDS IMPROVEMENT
Good introduction	Ice-breaker took too much time
Up to date and relevant information	Need better answers to questions
Good workbook	More frequent breaks

Do not limit your focus on the things that went wrong or need improvement. Spend time on the things people liked. Think about why they liked them. What did you do that elicited positive participant reactions?

Overall, how did you do? I always give myself a grade from A to F for each section or module of my seminar. I have never given myself an F, but I have bestowed Ds. The Ds led to significant improvements or the outright elimination of the topic. If you are going to put seminars on for profit, nothing less than an A is acceptable. What lessons did you learn? What can you do better next time? Even if you scored a home run, how can you do better next time? Do a module-by-module analysis. Think also of participant questions. Were you surprised by any questions? Were you able to answer all of them? Should topics from participant questions be incorporated into the seminar?

TIP NUMBER 183:
Make Yourself Available
to Participants

An effective way of obtaining feedback on how things are going is to talk to participants during the breaks and lunch. Staying around after the session also can produce useful feedback—both positive and negative. People will stay around and talk if you make it comfortable. Be careful though. Don't let one person dominate your attention. Occasionally, you will get the participant who wants you to solve all their problems. They want to dominate your time, and they don't care if other participants are waiting to talk to you. Give them one question and then politely move on to the next person.

If you were giving a persuasive, sales or motivational type of workshop, you may have a more concrete way of measuring your success. For instance, you may be able to determine your success by measuring how many people bought, acted or did what you were trying to get them to do.

TIP NUMBER 184:
Use Written Evaluations

Just what were the participants' attitudes toward your program? Questionnaires or evaluation forms are one of the most common ways to obtain audience feedback. They provide immediate feedback and are inexpensive and easy to administer. Typical evaluation forms are distributed near the end of the seminar and they cover such questions as the following:

- What part of the workshop was most beneficial to you?
- What changes would you suggest?
- Would you like to give specific feedback to Len Wood?
- What topic would you like for another workshop?
- Did the program achieve the promised objectives?
- Was the information conveyed clear and understandable?
- Was the pace of the presentation satisfactory?
- Was the presenter prepared?
- Did the presenter answer questions adequately?
- Did the presenter involve the participants?
- Was the meeting room comfortable?
- Was the information conveyed valuable?
- Did you get your money's worth?
- Was the meeting room adequate?
- Was the food adequate?
- Were the beverages adequate?
- What was the most important topic?
- What was the least important topic?
- Other comments?

TIP NUMBER 185:
Be Sure Evaluations Are Completed at the Session

The written evaluations for your first session of a new seminar are especially critical. This is the first time an audience has heard your presentation, and their reactions will provide you invaluable information. Don't lose this opportunity by forgetting to hand out the evaluations. Make sure that you leave enough time at the end of the session for the participants to complete the evaluations. Don't let them take the forms home with a promise to mail or fax them to you. The majority will promptly forget about it. The only ones who will follow up are those who really liked the program and those who want to tell you how terrible the presentation was.

TIP NUMBER 186:
Use Evaluations to Improve
Your Seminar

Make revisions to your program to deal with recurring complaints. Common approaches are to add, delete or modify material. Another is to change the delivery method. When I first started presenting my budget seminar, I dreaded the section that went into reacquainting participants to math techniques they should have learned as children, such as computing percentage increases, percentage decreases, ratios, depreciation and trends. They got bored and turned off.

Dreading this module, I subtly signaled my distaste and further exacerbated the problem. At first I added more material and explanation. When that did not work, I started deleting material and concepts. Still no improvement in audience reactions. In desperation, and not wanting to mess up an otherwise excellent seminar, I developed a quiz that was based on my *Little Budget Book*. My original thought was to give them the quiz and a copy of the book and tell them to take it home and complete it. During a break a participant happened to notice the pile of quizzes and asked when they would get a chance to take their quiz. Throwing my previous plans to the wind, I said right before lunch. The results were phenomenal. Participants loved the idea of an open-book quiz. Most wanted more time, and several worked on it during their lunch hour. They simply would not put it down until they computed an answer for every item.

TIP NUMBER 187:
Don't Overreact to Ratings and Written Comments

Remember that not everyone rates a seminar the same way. Some participants focus on concepts and will rate the seminar on the basis of an overall impression. Others are more detailed and will evaluate the seminar based on their impressions of small items. On more that one occasion, I have received a rating of three on a five-point scale, with the following written comment, "Best seminar on the topic I ever attended." Go figure!

Every evaluation form, even if it uses a Likert scale, should include a section for written comments. Pay attention to written comments that people put on your evaluation forms. They can help you refine your seminars. When they take the time to put comments on these forms, they are taking an extra step to communicate with you.

Resist the temptation to immediately change an important part of your program because of one caustic comment. Ask yourself, "Is the comment valid?" It could be that the person was having a bad day and wanted you to share their misery. Put comments into perspective.

To help keep written comments in perspective, create an analysis table that records the comments, your assessment of the validity of the comments and your proposed action, if any. The following table depicts a written comment assessment table:

Written Comment Assessment Table

COMMENT	ASSESSMENT	ACTION
Enjoyed all	Most liked the program	No action
Loved the discussion	When we had discussions, they were good	Be more relaxed and invite discussion
Less emphasis on budget padding	Sometimes people are not interested in a topic	No action; most like discussion
Read notes instead of presenting	Tried not to and was caught	Find ways to refer to notes without being obvious
Not enough time	Spent too much time on the case study	Speed up or shorten this case study
Use more examples	Good comment	Add examples
Start earlier	Time fixed	No action
More specific solutions	Can't make more specific and keep audience	Will add alternative actions
More time on case studies	Most people found timing right	No action
A little faster pace	Good suggestion	Work on pace
Spoke too loudly	First time received this comment	No action
Follow the agenda more closely	Did stray	Will make sure all topics covered
Too basic	Most people felt it was OK	No action

TIP NUMBER 188:
Check Your Learning Outcomes

Another evaluation approach is to examine your learning outcomes. Learning outcomes are the things you want your participants to be able to do as a result of attending your seminar. The supervisor's workshop discussed in Chapter 2 promised participants the following:

- Improve subordinate satisfaction and performance
- Reduce employee turnover
- Receive fewer grievances
- Lower employee absenteeism
- Receive fewer customer complaints
- Improve the supervisor's promotability

The learning outcomes or benefits listed above cannot be fairly evaluated at the end of a workshop. It will take time to determine if supervisors have acquired the skills and techniques to reduce citizen complaints and employee turnover, absences and grievances. After four to six months, a follow-up evaluation can provide critical feedback. Your evaluation questionnaires can be faxed, mailed or e-mailed. A phone interview, however, offers the best opportunity. Not only do you get participants responses, but also you can ask follow-up questions: Why do you feel that way? Did you use any of the techniques discussed in the seminar?

Although the achievement of many learning objectives cannot be evaluated immediately, you can check to make sure you adequately covered the promised topics in your presentation and handout materials. You don't want to be in the position of promising participants benefits and then short shrift them on not covering the topic at all.

TIP NUMBER 189:
Use Tests to Evaluate Results

If your seminar purpose is very specific, you can use a test at the end of the session to determine the effectiveness of the program. For example, if you are teaching an Excel workshop, you can give participants a spreadsheet problem that requires them to use all the major techniques you presented during the seminar. If you do this, make sure the test items relate to the workshop. Although this may be obvious, I have noticed that some seminar providers use test questions that have no relationship to the objectives or content of the workshop.

If you are providing seminars to companies and governments, a postseminar test can be used as a marketing tool in addition to providing you good feedback. The test can be introduced like this, for example: "All participants will have an opportunity to take a practical test to determine whether they are proficient in the use of Excel. Those who do not pass will have the opportunity for one year to attend another Excel class."

TIP NUMBER 190:
Recognize That Participants
Influence Each Other

Irvin Janus coined the word *groupthink*. Groupthink is the phenomena that occurs when a group of people become so close that they overly influence each other to the point that independent thought is lost.

People sitting at the same table can become subject to groupthink and influence each other in their seminar ratings. If one of the group leaders rates things as average, the others, even if they disagree, may wind up ranking the same way, simply to go along. You can notice this occurrence when you see the same comments showing up on evaluation forms. I once watched a whole table fall into this pattern. The informal leader quickly filled out his evaluation form and left it exposed for all to view at his table.

Recognize also that participants talk about the seminar during breaks. Again, what one person says can be picked up and parroted by others. Keep your ears tuned during breaks and lunch to pick up participant comments, moods and attitudes.

TIP NUMBER 191:
Collect Workshop By-Products

If you used flip charts to record participant input and group exercise results, collect them before you leave the seminar site. Also, gather up working papers and notes participants leave. Some of the best information I've gathered came from these sources. This information was used to improve my program and add to my books.

TIP NUMBER 192:
Be Ready to Perform Follow-Up Marketing

Participants will want to call you after the session and ask for individual advice. For seminar providers this is a great opportunity for additional business. Plan how you will handle these requests. How much free advice are you willing to provide? Decide when your consulting fee will kick in. Some participants just want to talk, whereas others will want to hire you. They know you now. They have seen you in action, and they even may have developed feelings of trust. This is an effective way to obtain new business.

You will find that people will keep your seminar advertising flyer much longer than you would have ever imagined. Some will call you and ask for an in-house seminar or consulting help. If you promise to send information to participants after the seminar, do not forget to do so. There is nothing more irritating than a promise that is not fulfilled. From the positive standpoint, it gives you another opportunity to sell your products and services. When following up, make sure that promotional material is included with the requested information.

TIP NUMBER 193:
Encourage Testimonial Letters

As discussed in Chapter 8, testimonials are important. This is your golden opportunity to collect them. When someone tells you personally that they enjoyed the seminar, let them know how much you value their comments. Then ask them to write a testimonial letter. Or suggest that you draft a letter for their review. Another approach is to ask participants if you can quote them. These letters and quotes will help with future brochures or in-house training programs.

TIP NUMBER 194:
Follow-Up with the Hotel and
Meeting Facility Management

Hotels and other meeting facilities want you to come back. If you did not receive good service, let them know about the problem. They, too, need feedback. On the other hand, if they were responsive and provided good service, send them a personalized thank you letter. Be specific about what you liked about the service. Don't forget to mention the names of people who provided the exemplary service.

If you are going to use the same facility more than once, get to know the staff members who help you. Give them modest tips, and you'll be amazed at the attention you'll get next time.

TIP NUMBER 195:
Implement a Continuous
Improvement Program

Total quality management relies on the concept of continuous improvement. The idea is to find ways to constantly improve and update your products or services. Seminar providers, to be competitive and, ultimately, successful, cannot create their program and then rest on laurels. A seminar must be continually improved or it will stagnate and ultimately die. All workshops and seminars have a life cycle. They are rolled out, honed to sharpness and ultimately abandoned. Updating and improving your workshop will increase your seminar's life span. Several ways to extend your seminar's life span include the following:

- Continue to collect information that relates to your seminar from newspapers, listservs, periodicals, Web sites and professional journals.
- Think of spin-off programs. Can you develop another program that you can successfully market?
- Identify and monitor the experts in your field. Know what they are saying and writing. Decide whether you agree or disagree with their pronouncements.
- Improve your presentation skills at Toastmasters and community service organizations. Observe public speakers. Determine what they do well and what they do not do well. How do they emphasize critical points? Do they use stories, analogies and quotations? Focus on their gestures, pace and voice modulation.
- Monitor the Internet sites that deal with your subject area.
- Keep abreast of the technological advances in presentation, equipment, software and hardware.

Tomorrow's sessions will be better if you learn to accept constructive suggestions from all your sources. If you do well and the evaluations by participants were favorable, it is still a good idea to review and revise those parts of your program that need improving or updating.

Afterword

Several years ago, an entrepreneurial friend counseled me about going into business. At the time, I was a city manager who was contemplating switching to the private sector. His advice? "If you decide to go into business, make sure you select one that has no walls." At the time I thought the comment odd—every business has walls. How do you protect resources, inventory and assets?

His sage advice floundered in my memory banks for several years, even though I did not truly grasp it—until I started giving public seminars. Only then did it start to come into focus and make sense. Unlike many businesses, seminars have no walls. You can take off in several directions, and there are no barriers or impediments to keep you from going where you want. You, rather than the walls, control:

1. the geographic locations where you conduct your business;
2. the specific places where you give your seminars;
3. the times you conduct your seminars;
4. the amount of time before and after your seminars, which is allocated for play and recreation;
5. the content you include—or do not include—in your seminars; and
6. the effort you put into spin-off business opportunities, such as consulting; counseling; developing software; recording audiotapes, videotapes and CDs; and writing articles, pamphlets and books.

Once you get into the seminar business, you'll love it. It gets into your blood and drives you to new levels of achievement. Many seminar providers say that they continue to get goose bumps just thinking about addressing an audience—even after ten or fifteen years in this business.

Good luck and happy seminars.

Appendix A

DECISION MAKING EXERCISE

Background Information

Mike Adams is a maintenance crew employee reporting to Jennifer Williams, one of several supervisors reporting to you. Mike has been a City of Secret Cove employee for ten (10) years. A good (but not outstanding) employee, Mike does tend to be fairly casual about "bending the rules".

Six months ago, Mike received an oral warning from Jennifer for borrowing a set of the City's tools over the weekend without permission. Although Jennifer has informally talked to Mike on several occasions about this casual attitude regarding City rules, Mike has not received any formal disciplinary measures other than the oral warning just described.

The Situation

Last Friday, Mike was working late. On her way home, Jennifer realized she'd left something at the office, so he turned around and drove back to the work site. As she approached, Jennifer noticed Mike's personal car beside the gasoline pumps, but by the time she pulled up to the garage, Mike had moved the car. In the brief conversation that followed, neither Mike nor Jennifer made any mention of the incident. However, upon returning to work on Monday, Jennifer obtained computerized gas pump records and discovered that Mike had pumped .7 gallons of fuel into his car on Friday. When confronted by Jennifer with the evidence, Mike said, "All I needed was a little juice in my car so I could get home from work without getting stranded on the road. I pumped less than a gallon of your gas."

As Jennifer's manager, you have been asked by your department head to make a decision regarding what action, if any, should be taken toward Mike. You have not talked to Mike and are also aware that Jennifer recommends that Mike be given an oral warning.

Instructions

Designate one member of your group to be the scribe to record group responses on the flip chart. One member should also act as spokesperson to report on the following questions.

- Given the described facts what course of action, if any, should be taken toward Mike. Assume you do not have the opportunity to do any more data collection, nor can you simply refer the matter back to Jennifer.

- Include the rationale for your decision.

Appendix B

SEMINAR COMPETITION EVALUATION
WORKSHEET

1. Company or Organization Providing Seminar

2. Seminar Name and Description

3. Seminar Locations

4. Seminar Length and Times

5. Cost

6. Siminar Leader's Credentials

7. Promised Benefits

8. Target Audience

9. Food and Beverage Provided

10. Materials Provided

11. Equipment and Visual Aids Used

12. Seminar Strong Points

13. Seminar Weak Points

14. Participant Comments

Appendix C

FREQUENTLY USED
SEMINAR LOCATIONS

Alabama
Birmingham
Huntsville
Mobile
Montgomery

Alaska
Anchorage
Fairbanks

Arizona
Flagstaff
Phoenix
Scottsdale
Tempe
Tucson

Arkansas
Fayetteville
Ft. Smith
Jonesboro
Little Rock

California
Anaheim
Bakersfield
Burbank
Carmel
Concord
Costa Mesa
Eureka
Fresno
Irvine
La Jolla
Lancaster

Long Beach
Los Angeles
Modesto
Monterey
Newport Beach
Oakland
Ontario
Oxnard
Palm Springs
Pasadena
Redding
Sacramento
San Bernardino
San Diego
San Francisco
San Jose
San Luis Obispo
Santa Barbara
Santa Rosa
San Rafael
Stockton
Sunnyvale
Torrance

Colorado
Arvada
Aurora
Boulder
Colorado Springs
Denver
Ft. Collins
Glendale

Connecticut
Danbury

Hartford
Stamford
Stratford
Trumbull
Waterbury

Delaware
Wilmington

Florida
Boca Raton
Clearwater Beach
Daytona Beach
Ft. Lauderdale
Ft. Myers
Gainseville
Jacksonville
Key West
Lakeland
Melbourne
Miami
Orlando
Ponte Vedra
Pensacola
St. Petersburg
Tallahassee
Tampa
West Palm Beach

Georgia
Athens
Atlanta
Columbus
Macon
Savannah

Warner Robins

Hawaii
Honolulu

Idaho
Boise
Idaho Falls
Lewiston
Pocatello

Illinois
Arlington Heights
Champaign
Chicago
Elk Grove Village
Elmhurst
Lisle
Peoria
Rockford
Rolling Meadows
Schaumburg
Springfield
Westmont

Indiana
Bloomington
Chesterton
Ft. Wayne
Indianapolis
South Bend

Iowa
Cedar Rapids
Davenport
Des Moines
Waterloo

Kansas
Dodge City
Manhattan
Overland Park
Wichita

Kentucky
Bowling Green
Lexington
Louisville
Owensboro

Louisiana
Baton Rouge
Lafayette
Lake Charles
New Orleans
Shreveport

Maine
Augusta
Portland

Maryland
Annapolis
Baltimore
Frederick
Gaithersburg
Hagerstown
Rockville

Massachusetts
Boston
Brockton
Brookline
Burlington
Hyannis
Pittsfield
Springfield
Woburn
Worcester

Michigan
Ann Arbor
Dearborn
Detroit
Farmington Hills
Flint
Grand Rapids

Kalamazoo
Lansing
Midland
Traverse City
Romulus
Saginaw
Southfield
Sterling Heights
Troy

Minnesota
Bloomington
Duluth
Mankato
Minneapolis
Rochester
St. Cloud

Mississippi
Biloxi
Hattiesburg
Jackson
Tupelo

Missouri
Columbia
Cape Girardeau
Kansas City
Springfield
St. Louis

Montana
Billings
Bozeman
Helena
Missoula

Nebraska
Grand Island
Lincoln
Omaha

Nevada
Lake Tahoe
Las Vegas
Reno

New Hampshire
Concord
Manchester
Portsmouth

New Jersey
Atlantic City
Cherry Hill
East Hanover
East Windsor
Edison
Freehold
Morristown
Paramus
Parsippany
Pleasantville
Princeton

New Mexico
Albuquerque
Farmington
Las Cruces
Roswell

New York
Albany
Armonk
Binghamton
Buffalo
Elmsford
Ithaca
Melville
Middletown
New York
Poughkeepsie
Rochester
Syracuse
Tarrytown

Utica
Westbury
White Plains

New Mexico
Albuquerque
Santa Fe

North Carolina
Asheville
Chapel Hill
Charlotte
Fayetteville
Greensboro
Raleigh
Wilmington

North Dakota
Bismarck
Fargo
Grand Forks
Minot

Ohio
Akron
Cincinnati
Cleveland
Columbus
Dayton
Lima
Mansfield
Toledo
Youngstown
Zanesville

Oklahoma
Oklahoma City
Tulsa

Oregon
Ashland
Bend
Eugene

Medford
Portland
Salem

Pennsylvania
Allentown
Erie
Harrisburg
Jornstown
King of Prussia
Lancaster
Philadelphia
Pittsburgh
Reading
State College
Wilkes-Barre
Williamsport
York

Rhode Island
Providence

South Carolina
Charleston
Columbia
Greenville
Hilton Head
Myrtle Beach

South Dakota
Aberdeen
Pierre
Rapid City
Sioux Falls

Tennessee
Chattanooga
Jackson
Johnson City
Knoxville
Memphis
Nashville

Texas
Amarillo
Arlington
Austin
Beaumont
College Station
Corpus Christi
Dallas
El Paso
Ft. Worth
Grand Prairie
Harlinger
Houston
Lubbock
McAllen
Midland
San Antonio
Waco

Utah
Provo
Salt Lake City

Vermont
Burlington
Rutland

Virginia
Alexandria
Arlington
Charlottesville
Fairfax
Fredericksburg
McLean
Norfolk
Reston
Richmond
Roanoke

Washington
Bellingham
Kennewick
Olympia

Pasco
Seattle
Spokane
Tacoma
Yakima

Washington, DC

West Virginia
Clarksburg
Huntington
Morgantown
Parkersburg

Wisconsin
Appleton
Eau Claire
Green Bay
La Crosse
Madison
Milwaukee
Oshkosh
Wausau

Wyoming
Casper
Cheyenne

Canada
Halifax
Montreal
Toronto
Vancouver
Victoria

Appendix D

NATIONAL HOTEL CHAINS

1. Best Western
   (800) 528-1231
   www.bestwestern.com

2. Choice Hotels
   International
   800-426-2121
   www.choicehotels.com

3. Doubletree Hotels
   (800) 222-TREE
   www.doubletreehotels.com

4. Embassy Suites
   (800) 362-2779
   www.embassysuites.com

5. Helmsley Hotels, Inc.
   (800) 221-4982
   www.helmsleyhotels.com

6. Hilton Hotels Corporation
   (800) 321-3232
   www.hilton.com

7. Holiday Inns
   (800) 633-8464
   www.holiday-inn.com

8. Howard Johnsons
   (800) 654-2000
   www.hojo.com

9. Hyatt Hotels Corporation
   (800) 882-1234
   www.interconti.com

10. Inter-Continental Hotels
    (800) 327-1177
    www.hyatt.com

11. La Quinta Motor Inns
    (800) 531-5900
    www.interconti.com

12. Loews Hotels
    (800) 563-9711
    www.loewshotels.com

13. Marriott Corporation
    (800) 831-4004
    www.marriott.com

14. Omni International
    (800) 843-6664
    www.omnihotels.com

15. Quality Inns International
    (800) 426-2121
    www.qualityinns.com

16. Radisson Hotel
    Corporation
    (800) 333-3333
    www.radisson.com

17. Ramada Inns, Inc
    (800) 228-3344
    www.ramada.com

18. Red Lion Hotels & Inns
    (800) RED-LION
    www.redlion.com

19. Registry Hotel
    Corporation
    (800) 247-9810
    www.registryhotel.com

20. Residence Inn
    (800) 331-3131
    www.residenceinn.com

21. Ritz-Carlton Hotel
    Company
    (800) 241-3333
    www.ritzcarlton.com

22. Rodeway Inns
    International
    (800) 638-2657
    www.hotelchoice.com

23. The Sheraton Corporation
    (800) 625-5144
    www.sheraton.com

24. Travelodge & Viscount
    Hotels
    (800) 525-3055
    www.travelodge.com

25. Westin Hotels & Resorts
    (800) 338-1660
    www.westin.com

Appendix E

LERN "Information That Works"

May 23, 1995

Mr. Len Wood
Len Wood & Associates
4228 Palos Verdes Drive East
Rancho Palos Verdes, CA 90275

Brochure Analysis: The Elected Official's Financial Responsibility

Dear Len:

Overall, you have a good format. It is of two sizes we recommend for seminar brochures. It takes advantage of lower postal rates for bulk mailings. The other size is the same size sheet of paper (11 X 17) folded twice into a big trifold. There is no evidence either brochure size pulls better, but both do better than other sizes.

Your seminar title is most prominent on the cover, and this is what we recommend. It is also good that you have the location and date on the cover.

Some of the more successful brochures are putting a testimonial or motivational copy on the cover. It is an option, and you certainly want to keep your copy on the cover to a minimum, but if you want more copy on the cover, this is recommended. Your screen box with examples of things the workshop will help you do (i.e.: Identify financial warning signs, etc..) is a perfect example.

For your brochure, we think a graphic design on the cover might make it a little more attractive. Look at the lines and other abstract designs. You don't need artwork or photographs. But a little graphic enhancement would make the cover sharper.

We like the color of your cover stock. You use a second color of ink on the cover, and that is good. A second color on the cover does help your image and thus registrations. A touch of second color on the inside also helps, but the first place to put that second color ink is on the cover.

Start your first inside page by repeating the title of the program. You might also consider repeating the locations and dates here at the top of the page underneath the program title.

The flow of your copy does follow in general the AIDA principle. A= attract; I= interest; D=desire; and A=action. It means that people need to go through those three steps before taking Action, or registering.

Thus, you want to attract your readers with a cover page. You want to interest them with copy about Why You Should and Who Should Attend. You want to create desire with your main copy, including Benefits, End Results, and the Agenda. And then you want to get Action by providing your registration fee, other details, and then registration information and the registration form at the end.

You might consider an introductory paragraph to generate interest in reading further. The paragraph should highlight the importance of the topic to the reader and state one or more benefits and end results from attending your program. Be sure to write in second person or "you" language.

Think about adding a section on "Why You Should Attend," "Benefits," and/or "End Results." The reader wants to know what will happen to him or her AFTER she or he attends your event, not what will happen during the event. So add copy about benefits, outcomes and end results for the participant.

Having an agenda or time schedule as you do is good. Take out the times in the morning and afternoon. That hinders your presenter and locks the presenter into keeping to a rigid time schedule. Think about adding bullets in the agenda copy. That makes the agenda seem tight, succinct, substantive and meaty. Plus they make the reading easier.

You might consider a box on this page to break up the layout. Your copy is written in second person "you" language. Keep it that way. The body copy is set in serif typestyle (little tails) and that is good. It is more readable than sanserif (no little tails).

Include a section about your organization and your USP (unique selling proposition). What is it that makes you and your organization unique and special to me as a reader and potential participant in your program? Tell me that, in clear no-uncertain-terms. Tell me about the strength of your program, not your product (the event topic). Establish your credibility and reputation with me as a reader, even though I may know about your organization or even be a frequent attendee. Tell me again why you and not the competition.

To make an impressive statement, think about including copy that underlines how your event is unique in term of benefits and results, not "features." That along with copy about how your organization is unique (from your participants' perspective, not an institutional view) will make your brochure stand out even more.

A no-cost marketing aid that would further strengthen your brochure is including some testimonials. Be sure to include the person's name. Another standard good practice is to include a sample list of past participants. To keep things current, usually providers list the companies from which participants have come. It boosts credibility another notch.

I like your emphasis on the Elected Official's Little Handbook. The opportunity to order the book if you cannot attend the seminar is excellent. It also stresses your credentials as a recognized author.

You have your registration information in the right place (at the end of the brochure), but I do have a few suggestions here. A definite way to increase activity is to offer several different ways to register. Highlight it with a nice heading like "3 Easy Ways to Register." Put "By phone," By mail, "By fax" in boldface so it is eye catching. An added plus is a little graphic drawing or icon depicting each (a phone, a stamp, a fax machine).

Boost your registrations by taking registrations by phone. It is worth it, definitely worth it. I would also strongly encourage you to accept fax registrations. Nice job with keeping the registration information clear, clean and easy to read. It is good that you offer the opportunity for multiple registrants on the same form. This has been found to increase participation. Some programs also include a toll free number. It helps boost registration and is a nice service for the few dollars involved.

Again, you have a very good brochure. We hope some of our comments will help you boost registrations and increase income. Thanks for asking.

Appendix F

CERTIFICATE OF COMPLETION TRANSMITTAL LETTER

Dear Mr. Johnson:

Mike Wilson has completed a two-day workshop titled Supervisory Skills for the Public Sector. In the workshop, we addressed the following topics:

- Leadership
- Delegation
- Coaching
- Communicating
- Budgeting
- Performance evaluation

A certificate of completion is enclosed. It will mean more to Mr. Wilson if you or another manager present it to him.

We are very interested in any reactions to the training program. If you have any subjects that we should add or modify, we would welcome your suggestions.

Thank you for trusting us with your employee's training.

Sincerely,

Len Wood
The Training Shoppe

References

Armstrong, David. 1992. *Managing by storying around.* Three Rivers, Mich.: Armstrong International.

Bianchi, Sue, Jan Butler, and David Richey. 1990. *Warmups for meeting leaders.* San Francisco: Pfeiffer & Co.

Buzan, Tony, and Barry Buzan. 1996. *The mind map book: How to use radiant thinking to maximize your brain's untapped potential.* New York: Dutton Plume Publishing.

Byers, Judy. 1997. *Words on tape.* Denver: Audio CP Publishing.

Caroselli, Marlene. 1998. *Great session openers, closers, and energizers: quick activities for warming up your audience and ending on a high note.* New York: McGraw-Hill.

Cook, Wade. Seminar: Financial Clinic, delivered in Orange County, November 1999.

Draves, William. 1995. *Energizing the learning environment.* River Falls, Wisc.: LERN Books.

Ensign, Paulette. 1998. *How to write and market booklets for cash.* San Diego: Tips Products International.

Hoff, Ron. 1990. *I can see you naked: A fearless guide to making great presentations.* Kansas City: Andrews and McMeel.

Huff, Darrell, 1993. *How to lie with statistics.* New York: W.W. Norton & Company.

Long, Mary. 1999. *The complete guide to conducting seminars at sea.* Portland, Ore.: Athina Press.

Holcomb, Jane. 1994. *Make training worth every penny.* San Diego: Pfeiffer & Company.

Jolles, Robert E. 2000. *How to run seminars and workshops: Presentation skills for consultants, trainers, and teachers.* New York: John Wiley & Sons.

Kent, Peter. 1998. *Poor Richard's Web site: Geek-free, commonsense advice on building a low-cost Web site.* Lakewood, Colo.: Top Floor Publishing.

Levinson, Jay Conrad. 1993. *Guerrilla marketing: Secrets for making big profits from your small business.* New York: Houghton Mifflin Company.

Levinson, Jay Conrad. 1999. *Mastering guerrilla marketing: 100 profit-producing insights you can take to the bank.* New York: Houghton Mifflin Company.

Lucas, Robert. 1999. *The big book of flip charts: A comprehensive guide for presenters, trainers, and facilitators.* New York: McGraw-Hill.

Otte, Miriam. 1998. *Marketing with speeches and seminars: Your key to more clients and referrals.* Seattle: Zest Press.

Pinskey, Raleigh. 1997. *101 ways to promote yourself.* New York: Avon Books.

Poynter, Dan. 2002. *The self-publishing manual: How to write, print and sell your own book.* 13th ed. Santa Barbara: Para Publishing.

Poynter, Dan, and Mindy Bingham. 1991. *Is there a book inside you?* Santa Barbara: Para Publishing.

Straker, David. 1997. *Rapid problem solving with Post-It Notes.* Tucson: Fisher Books.

Shenson, Howard L. 1990. *How to develop & promote successful seminars and workshops: The definitive guide to creating and marketing seminars, workshops, classes, and conferences.* New York: John Wiley & Sons, Inc.

Wallechinsky, David, Irving Wallace, and Amy Wallace. 1977. *The book of lists.* New York: Bantam Books.

Walters, Dottie, and Lilly Walters. 1997. *Speak and grow rich.* Paramus, N. J.: Prentice Hall.

Wycoff, Joyce. 1991. *Mindmapping: Your personal guide to exploring creativity and problem-solving.* New York: Berkley Publishing Group.

Glossary

acronyms
Words formed from the initial letters of a series of words such as RADAR - radio detecting and ranging or SWAT - Special Weapons and Tactics, as used as a police SWAT team.

ad-lib remarks
Improvised comments and statements made during a presentation.

agenda
An outline or summary of the key topics covered in a seminar.

anecdote
A short, often oral, interesting or humorous account of a real or fictitious incident, used to support or explain points made during a seminar.

attribution
Crediting the source of information, charts, stories or other data used in a seminar.

audit
Verification of financial records and internal control procedures conducted by an independent CPA or accounting firm.

A/V
Abbreviation used for audiovisual equipment, such as a slide machine, viewgraph, overhead projector, LCD projector and LCD panel.

back room projector
A projector with a long-throw lens designed to be used from the back of a meeting room.

bookmark
Electronic bookmarks are used to earmark useful Web sites. A bookmark lets you save the Web site address in a file you recall with a click of the mouse.

boot camps
In the seminar business, a boot camp is a multi-day seminar that showcases several experts.

brainstorming
A freewheeling group approach to solving a problem or focusing an issue. One person is designated as a recorder, and other group members suggest ideas that are compiled by the recorder on a flip chart or chalkboard. After all ideas are listed, the ideas are prioritized.

break-even point
The point at which revenues equal total costs (variable and fixed). At the break-even point money has not been made or lost.

breakout groups
Small groups of three to eight people organized by seminar providers to work on a case study or complete exercises. Small groups are more effective in getting people to interact.

capital assets
Assets that have an extended life and a minimum dollar value, such as computers, projectors and copiers.

case study
Real life situation or problem written up as an exercise to stimulate participant discussion and interaction.

caveat emptor
Business principle meaning: "Let the buyer beware."

clip art
Professionally created illustrations, drawings, photos and cartoons made available to seminar providers and other users through print or computer software for a fee or for free.

clipping services
Companies that identify and collect specific newspaper, Internet, magazine and other published articles for clients.

color temperature
A method of measuring the whiteness of a projector's light source. Metal halide lamps have very high temperatures compared to halogen or incandescent lights.

computer graphics
Tables, charts, slides and other visuals created with a computer.

concurrent sessions
Convention or seminar programs occurring at the same time.

conference
A meeting composed of different but related programs offered to an association or group of people with a common interest, such as dentists or publishers.

contract
An agreement between seminar partners or any two parties in which each promises to perform in some way. Contracts should always be reviewed by an attorney.

dias
The raised platform or podium in the front of the room where the speaker stands.

demonstration
Seminar technique in which a presenter shows a process, how something is put together or how something works.

drop shipment
A shipment directly from the manufacturer to the end user.

dry run
A session used to practice the delivery of a seminar, usually done with family members or colleagues.

easel
The three- or four-legged device that holds flip charts.

e-business
Term used to describe the buying and selling of goods and services over the Internet; the process of consummating a business transaction over the Internet; including negotiation, pricing and delivery.

e-mail
Message sent over the Internet.

Employer Identification Number (EIN)
An identification number obtained by a business from the IRS by filing form SS-4. For sole proprietorships, such as a beginning seminar business, a social security number can substitute for the EIN.

entrepreneur
A person who assumes the responsibility, risk and rewards of starting and operating a business.

e-zine
Electronic newsletter transmitted by e-mail.

fiscal year
Any 12-month period used by a company or government as an accounting or budgeting period. Typical fiscal years are from January 1 through December 31 and July 1 through June 30.

fixed costs
Production costs which do not vary significantly with the volume of output. For seminars, a fixed cost will be the cost of designing and marketing. (See also **variable costs**).

flame
Caustic remark or statement sent over the Internet.

flame war
A protracted, heated e-mail exchange.

flip chart
Large sized writing papers bound in a pad and used in presentations to display or record items.

foil
Term used to describe overhead transparencies.

forum
Airing of opinions in a public setting, moderated by a facilitator.

front room projector
A projector that sits close to the screen, its short throw lens projects an image size that is about the same as the distance to the screen.

handout
Supplemental training or marketing information provided to seminar participants.

hits
Commonly used to describe the number of visits to a website.

home page
The introductory or main Web page for a Web site.

honorarium
Modest payment provided to seminar and workshop speakers usually by universities, nonprofits or governments.

impromptu
Speaking or presenting without any rehearsal or preparation.

Internet
The network of computers that comprises the World Wide Web.

interview
An interactive technique used in seminars in which one person (or group) interviews another person (or group). The one being interviewed is usually an expert in the topic area.

ISP (Internet Service Provider)
A firm that provides access to the Internet for free, a service charge or other tradeoff.

key stoning
A distortion on a screen caused when the projected image is not perpendicular to the screen, making the top and bottom of the image different lengths.

laser pointer
A small pen shaped pointer, that contains a small battery powered laser, which can project a small, high intensity beam of light that is immediately very visible on the screen. Used for highlighting numbers, objects or text while explaining a point.

lavaliere
A microphone worn around the neck or attached to clothing.

lecture
Formal oral presentations characterized by one-way communication from presenters. Lectures should be kept short to avoid boring an audience.

lecturette
Short, crisp presentations designed to convey valuable information without boring participants. Lecturettes generally last from five to fifteen minutes.

lectern
A stand with a slanted top that supports a speaker's notes or books. Lecterns are confining, and most seminar presenters do not use them.

Listserv
Used to describe the most common type of e-mail list. Where people with similar interests band together as a discussion group. L-Soft International has a registered trademark on the word *Listserv*.

liquid crystal display (LCD)
A device that comes in many forms, sizes, and resolutions. Its primary purpose is to present a digital image for viewing. LCD's are used by seminar providers to project an image such as a slide on a screen.

long throw lens
A lens designed for projection from the back of a room. Long throw lenses are used in large meeting rooms, theaters and auditoriums.

markers
Large pens, approximately 4 to 6 inches long, used to record information on flip charts and white boards.

mark up
The amount added to the cost of services or goods to recover costs and produce a profit.

mind map
A diagram containing random ideas connected by a series of lines to a central concept or topic.

minimum distance
The closest position that a projector can focus an image onto a screen.

modem
Electronic device that connects a computer to a phone line, allowing access to other computers and the Internet.

multimedia
Computer-based presentation involving the use of several media, such as video, animation, sound and still images.

newsletter
A mailer, bulletin or handout composed of news, announcements, articles, tips, quotations, cartoons and advertisements and distributed to a group of subscribers.

overhead
Business expenses not directly related to particular goods or service produced. An example would be the cost of an office and general business equipment. For seminar presenters, the term *overhead* can also be used to describe an overhead transparency or overhead projector.

overhead projector (OHP)
A device designed to project images from transparencies onto a screen.

panel
A panel is the predecessor of today's projectors. Because panels lack their own light source, they are designed to sit on top of an overhead projector. The term *panel* is also used to describe a discussion group of three to six experts facilitated by a skilled moderator.

press kit
Promotional and marketing information complied for the media or seminar sponsoring groups.

print advertising
Advertising placed in magazines, periodicals and newspapers.

profit & loss (P & L) statement
A listing of income, expenses, and the resulting net profit or loss; also called an income statement.

progressive disclosure
A technique of masking an entire visual (slide or flip chart) and revealing one topic or point at a time to keep participants from jumping ahead; also known as revelation.

projector
A projector is a device that integrates a light source, optics system, electronics and displays for the purpose of projecting an image from a computer or video device onto a wall or screen for large image viewing.

public domain
Publications and materials unprotected by copyright.

Q&A (Question and Answer)
Time devoted during a seminar for questions and answers.

remote
Audiovisual control that operates projectors and other equipment at a distance, allowing presenters to move around the room.

request for proposal (RFP)
Process used to gather bids from vendors to provide a service or product. Bids are usually awarded to the lowest responsible bidder who meets the minimum specifications contained in the bid documents.

request for qualifications (RFQ)
Process used to evaluate vendors by requesting that they submit a document outlining their qualifications to provide a service or product. Bids are usually awarded to the vendor considered most capable of providing the service or product.

revelation
A technique of masking the entire visual and disclosing one topic or point at a time to keep participants from jumping ahead; also known as progressive disclosure.

role playing
Training technique used to simulate a real or contrived situation during which participants assume a character (or role) other than their own. Role playing is used to demonstrate, practice, or show different perspectives.

sales tax number
A number assigned to a business that enables the business to buy wholesale without paying sales tax on goods and products.

SCORE (The Services Corps of Retired Executives)
A volunteer management assistance program of the Small Business Administration (SBA). SCORE volunteers provide one-on-one counseling, workshops and seminars for small businesses. There are hundreds of SCORE offices throughout the United States, and they are useful for getting advice on setting up your seminar business as well as conducting seminars.

seminar
An educational session lasting from one hour to several days and presented to participants interested in a specific topic.

short throw lens
A lens designed to project the largest possible image from short distance. Most front-room projectors use a short throw lens. A typical short throw lens might produce a diagonal image size of 10 FT, from a distance of 7 to 10 FT.

sole proprietorship
The simplest (and most popular) form of business organization. The individual is personally liable for all debts of the business to the full extent of his or her property. On the other hand, the owner has complete control of the business.

spam
An unwanted commercial or other offending message, similar to junk mail, sent to Internet users.

spammed
Being sent unsolicited commercial, political or religious e-mail.

speakers' bureau
An organization that provides speakers for seminars, workshops and conferences. Presenters usually pay a fee to be listed with the speakers' bureau.

storyboard
Layout or large board used to organize slides for a presentation.

symposium
A series of lectures on a single topic, given by several different presenters.

testimonial
Verbal or written praise or recommendation provided by a seminar participant.

URL (Uniform Resource Locator)
A way of referring to an address on the World Wide Web.

variable costs
Costs that change significantly with the level of output. For seminars, variable costs include such items as participant workbooks, meals and beverages. The more participants, the higher the cost for these items.

videoconferencing
Seminar or workshop conducted at several sites simultaneously by video.

workshop
Alternate name for training session or seminar.

WWW (World Wide Web)
Has become the term for referring to the Internet.

zoom lens
A lens with a variable focal length providing the ability to adjust the size of the image on a screen by adjusting the zoom lens, instead of having to move the projector closer or further back.

Index

A

Quick Order Form

The Training Shoppe
4228 Palos Verdes Drive East
Rancho Palos Verdes, CA 90275
310-832-5652
LenWood@aol.com
www.trainingshoppe.com

Profitable Seminars: 195 Tips
for Designing, Marketing and
Delivering the Goods

	Price	Quantity	Total
Profitable Seminars	$29.95	_____	_____
Shipping & Handling	5.00		_____
CA Sales Tax (8%)			_____
Total Order			_____

Name_____

Address_____

State & Zip_____   Phone_____

Orders must be accompanied by check or money
order. Please call for multiple copy discounts.

0203061300